EARLY BUDDHIST

ROCK TEMPLES

STUDIES IN ANCIENT ART AND ARCHAEOLOGY

GENERAL EDITOR: PROFESSOR D. E. STRONG

VIDYA DEHEJIA

EARLY BUDDHIST
ROCK TEMPLES

A CHRONOLOGICAL STUDY

THAMES AND HUDSON

To my parents
who first encouraged my interest in things ancient

PRINTED IN GREAT BRITAIN BY
THE CAMELOT PRESS LTD
LONDON AND SOUTHAMPTON

ISBN 0 500 69001 4

Contents

Introduction

The long period of four hundred years between the disintegration of the Maurya Empire about 200 BC and the fall of the Satavahana Dynasty soon after 200 AD has been for almost a century, and remains, one of the most obscure and controversial in the dynastic and art history of North India and the Deccan. To some extent this is due, in North India at least, to the paucity of material evidence. There are but four major sites in North India, Bharhut, Sanchi, Mathura and Bodhgaya: three only, if the difficulties which beset Kushan chronology may be thought to exclude Mathura. The sites are distant from each other and are weakly supported by small isolated finds widely dispersed from Kathiawar to Bihar. The evidence from the Deccan is richer. There is the splendid series of rock-cut Buddhist *stūpas* and *vihāras* which are strung along the ghats leading from the neighbourhood of Bombay up to the Deccan plateau, with outliers on the east coast in the Andhrapradesh and Orissa. Complementing them are the rich groups of sculpture which decorated the many structural *stūpas* of the Andhrapradesh, of which Amaravati still remains the key site for this period. On the trade-routes linking the North-west and South-east Deccan several good stages have been discovered, at Ter, Kondapur, Sanathi and elsewhere.

It is fair to claim that if the problems of this period are to be solved, it is the Deccan rather than North India which will prove the more rewarding field in which to work. Indeed, in the Deccan a formal sequence and a relative chronology, generally acceptable but with varied emphasis on detail, have existed since the days of Burgess. The problem, in the history and the monuments, is the absolute chronology. There are those who support the long chronology for the Satavahanas, spreading out the dynasty and the monuments to cover the whole period. Others support the short chronology, concentrating everything into the first two centuries of our era. Others again, of whom Dr Dehejia is one, prefer some sort of compromise.

It is hardly necessary to say that all views, on present evidence, can be argued. What is the evidence which can be so variously manipulated? It will be clear to those who have followed the recent work of historians and geographers on the *Periplus* and Ptolemy that the western sources cannot be used to support any position. Nor are the Indian literary sources, the *Purāṇas* and so on, less dangerous. We have therefore to concentrate on the formal and stylistic analysis of architecture and sculpture, and on palaeography, epigraphy and numismatics. I should add excavation, but the excavator has been unlucky in the Deccan, as in North India, uncovering valuable new material but not solving any problems: Sewell's modest dig, admirably reported, at Amaravati in the last century remains the sole contribution to a chronology.

The full marshalling of all this evidence and the adjustment, where possible, of the results of one discipline against another, form the body of this book. Dr Dehejia devotes especial attention to palaeography and produces a more detailed analysis than any hitherto attempted. Her various sequences will, I think, find general acceptance. Of course the question must remain whether a formal sequence, both of style and palaeography, valid in the North-west Deccan runs contemporaneously with a similar sequence in the Andhrapradesh or a third in North India. A distinction has to be made, and here is the crux, between metropolitan and provincial centres, let alone between progressive and conservative craftsmen. Dr Dehejia is fully aware of this and carefully checks her palaeography against the results of her analysis of style, honestly admitting inconsistencies when they occur. The result is a clearly presented picture of the whole period, and one perfectly sound solution of its problems. Even if the reader does not accept the author's premises, he will nonetheless be forced to a careful reassessment of his own position.

DOUGLAS BARRETT

Preface

Among the most imaginative religious monuments of ancient India are an impressive series of rock-cut excavations, created initially by followers of the Buddhist faith and later by the Hindus as well. This rock architecture makes its first appearance on a small scale around 250 BC, in the days of the great Mauryan emperor Aśoka. The significant phase of rock-cutting commences some hundred and thirty years later along the west coast of India. At a varying distance of some thirty to sixty miles from the sea, a mountain chain known as the western ghats forms an almost continuous wall about four thousand feet high. Cut into the hills and valleys of this range is an extensive series of rock-cut monasteries, with chapels for congregational worship and residential halls for the monks.

In this study we shall examine the early formative phase of rock architecture in western India, which may be placed roughly between 120 BC and AD 200. This phase of activity belongs to the Hīnayāna Buddhist faith which represents the original doctrine as propounded by the Buddha. At this stage the Buddha himself had not been deified and contemporary art never represented the Buddha in human form. His presence was indicated instead by an emblem, quite often the *stūpa* or funerary mound, which was a symbol of his death and his release from this earthly life. Rock architecture belonging to the days of Mahāyāna Buddhism commenced around AD 450. During this later phase a large series of new caves containing images of the Buddha and his attendants were excavated, and at a number of sites alterations and additions were made to the earlier Hīnayāna excavations. At this later period, the Hindus and Jains also started a series of rock excavations. Here, however, we shall be concerned exclusively with the early Buddhist rock-cut monasteries executed during the days of Hīnayāna Buddhism.

The basic research for this book was carried out between 1963 and 1967 for a doctoral thesis at the University of Cambridge, England.

It incorporates various observations made during two field trips, one entirely in the area of the caves of western India, and the other including also a visit to the early excavations in Bihar, Orissa and the Krishna basin. The aim of this study is largely chronological and we have attempted to examine independently the sequences yielded by history, palaeography, architecture and sculpture. The introductory chapter contains a brief investigation of the vexed problem of Sātavāhana chronology. We have considered it proper to reject both the long and the short chronologies of Sātavāhana history that are based on purāṇic evidence, and have instead taken the evidence from inscriptions and coins as our starting point. Chapters 2 and 3 contain a detailed study of the palaeography of ancient India and of the inscriptions from the early Buddhist caves in particular. By a careful comparative analysis it is found possible to propose a coherent chronological scheme that can be applied to the otherwise undated inscriptions of the caves. In the course of our survey, several modifications are proposed in the chronological schemes of Buhler and Ahmad Hasan Dani. Chapters IV and V contain an analysis of the stylistic development of the western caves in terms of architecture, sculpture and painting. Chapter IV attempts to relate the entire range of excavations one to the other in terms of architectural and decorative elements. Chapter V considers the style of the carvings from these monuments, particularly in terms of the trend visible from the narrative reliefs on the Buddhist structural monuments at Sanchi, Bharhut and BodhGaya. Chapter VI considers various technical aspects involved in the excavation of the caves, as well as related problems such as the securing of funds and the connection between the craftsmen and the Buddhist Order. The developmental sequences yielded in the various chapters are then compared and considered together to result in our final conclusions regarding the sequence of cutting of the early Buddhist caves. The dates suggested are meant not so much to indicate a specific point in time as a general period during which the caves were probably excavated. We have attempted throughout to treat early Buddhist rock architecture as part of the general artistic activity of India during the period 200 BC to AD 200.

I must express my deep gratitude to Dr F. R. Allchin of Cambridge University, England, and to Professor J. Leroy Davidson of the University of California at Los Angeles, who supervised my doctoral research and provided me with continued guidance and inspiration. The essential method of working out the chronology of the caves in particular, is one I learned, with great profit, from Dr Allchin. To both my supervisors I owe much for help with specific problems, as also for much general help and advice. I am particularly indebted to Mr Douglas Barrett of the British Museum for the many hours he has spent in discussing various sections of my work, and for the deep interest he has taken in this project. To Dr Pratapaditya Pal of the Los Angeles County Museum of Art, I would like to express my especial appreciation for his having found the time to go through the manuscript and for his valuable suggestions and advice. I must record my gratitude to the authorities of the British Museum for facilities to examine the Mathura coin collection, and to the Illustration Department at the University of Sydney, Australia, for their careful preparation of my photographs. Finally, I must acknowledge my indebtedness to my mother and to my husband, who accompanied me on the various bullock-cart, fishing-boat and jeep trips involved in travelling to some of the less accessible caves, and who provided me with cheerful encouragement throughout my researches.

Vidya Dehejia

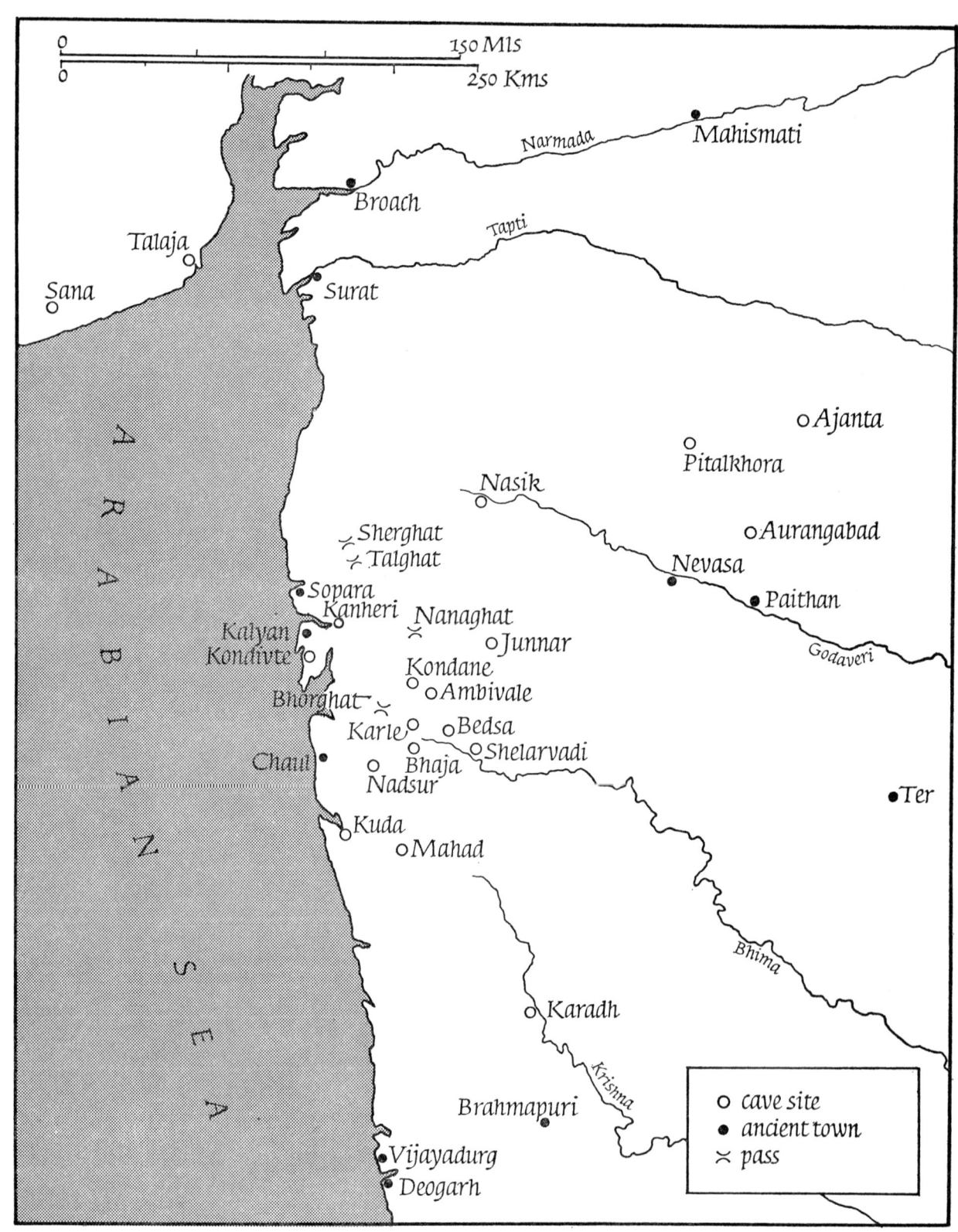

1 Map of the western Deccan

Historical and Geographical Introduction

The tradition of rock-cut architecture in India developed during the Mauryan period in and around ancient Magadha (present-day Bihar). In succeeding centuries it spread in three main directions: southwards down the eastern ghats through Orissa into the Andhra coast; in a much attenuated form with Buddhist missionaries in the extreme south of the peninsula and in Ceylon; and thirdly, throughout the Deccan and as far west as Saurashtra. It is this third group that numerically, as well as stylistically, is by far the most important, and it is this group with which we are directly concerned here.

A historical introduction to the study of these monuments is somewhat in the nature of a necessity. Several of the caves contain donative inscriptions which occasionally record the name of the king in whose reign the gift was made and also his regnal year. It will be apparent that if the dates of these rulers could be ascertained with some certainty it would greatly aid us in our chronological studies of these excavations. Our main concern, however, is not to obtain a detailed dynastic succession for western India during the period when these caves were excavated. Rather, we are interested in resolving certain crucial problems of Sātavāhana/Kshaharāta history, in so far as these affect our subject.

The entire problem of Sātavāhana chronology is a hornet's nest and controversy still continues to rage around the subject. Exponents of radically opposed theories have put forward their opinions with equal confidence. One school of thought places the beginning of the Sātavāhana dynasty at *c.* 271 BC,[1] while the other feels justified in assigning this event to *c.* 30 BC.[2] These two extreme views give some idea of how differently the same basic evidence may be interpreted. In these circumstances it is not to be expected that we can go too deeply into their various points of view, nor reconcile them with each other. The chronology we propose differs from both and is necessarily tentative.

A consideration of the sources of information for the history of the period reveals why and how such opposing views have arisen. Sātavāhana history is one of the least documented periods of Indian history. During the reigns of the early kings there is a lack of inscriptions recording political events, such as one finds in subsequent periods. On the other hand, inscriptions of the later rulers are dated in regnal years but there is no certainty about the era and hence these do not help us to obtain any absolute dates. Accounts of foreigners – the anonymous *Periplus Maris Erythraei*, Pliny's *Natural History*, Ptolemy's *Geography* – mention pertinent names and often throw interesting light on the social, economic and political conditions of the time. However, the precise dates of these works are also in dispute, which makes them unreliable as evidence for determining a chronological scheme. Coins of the Sātavāhanas and Kshaharātas have been found in fairly large hoards, but the nature of numismatic evidence is such that it can do little more than prove the existence of various rulers and arrange them in a rough sequence. It is of considerable value in supplementing historical evidence but can rarely, of itself, provide any absolute dates. Palaeography which could prove an important aid to the history of this period has, unfortunately, been neglected by most historians. Certainly the evidence it can afford has not been fully explored.

It is not surprising then that scholars have readily turned, though perhaps with undue trust, to purāṇic literature which provides dynastic lists of the Sātavāhana or Āndhra kings as well as the duration of their reigns. To use these often misleading documents as a primary source of evidence is, to say the least, unhistorical. The dynastic lists given in the different purāṇas contradict each other in several major respects and it is largely due to reliance on one account as against another that scholars disagree so radically regarding the history of the period. Thus the *Matsya-* and *Brahmāṇḍa-purāṇas* list thirty kings ruling for four hundred and sixty years, while the *Vāyu-purāṇa* names only seventeen kings ruling for three hundred years. Exponents of the longer chronology claim that the discrepancy in the purāṇic accounts arises only from the omission of certain kings of the main line from the *Vāyu-purāṇa* list. Those who prefer the shorter chronology explain the longer list as including the names of princes belonging to all branches of the Sātavāhana family, and suggest that the three hundred year stretch put forward by the *Vāyu-purāṇa* refers, in fact, to the main line. It is important to consider how far purāṇic evidence incorporates historical truth and can be considered reliable. Several discrepancies, including the corruption of names, may doubtless be traced to the process of transmission through the centuries, combined with repeated copyings of the texts. This may be partly responsible also for the inconsistency in the duration of reigns of kings, even among those purāṇas that agree in advocating a longer or a shorter chronology. Another factor to be considered is that the purāṇas were actually composed at a much later date than the events they describe, though the dynastic lists are given in the guise of a prophecy of the kings who would reign in future periods. It is then quite unjustified to state that 'the *Matsya* . . . may be accepted in preference to the other *Purāṇas*, for it is fuller in the details it furnishes as regards the princes and their names'.[3] On the other hand, the *Vāyu-purāṇa*, which gives a shorter duration to the dynasty, cannot of itself be taken as providing the correct chronological sequence. Its list[4] of the later Sātavāhana rulers omits all mention of Pulumāvi, Śivaśrī and Śivaskanda – three rulers whose historicity is proved beyond doubt by both epigraphic and numismatic evidence.

It must be made clear at this stage that one should not feel bound to accept one dynastic list as against another. Neither should one approach the history of the period with the purāṇic lists as primary evidence. It would be more proper to put together all the material we can obtain from other sources – epigraphic, numismatic, palaeographic and literary – and see how the purāṇic lists correspond with these. Approached in this manner the purāṇas can often provide valuable additional information. We need not then feel constrained to explain the conflicting statements found in these documents, and the task of unravelling the history of the period becomes considerably easier.

An outstanding example of a purāṇic contradiction concerns the rise of the Sātavāhana dynasty. If we accept the statement of the *Matsya-* and *Brahmāṇḍa-purāṇas* that the Āndhras ruled for four hundred and sixty years, the start of the dynasty has to be placed at *c.* 220 BC due to certain indubitable synchronisms of the later Sātavāhana rulers with the Western Satraps in the second century AD. If, on the other hand, we believe the *Vāyu-purāṇa*'s assertion that Simuka of the Āndhra race obtained the earth after killing the last Kāṇva ruler Suśurman, the rise of the dynasty must be assigned to the last quarter of the first century BC, the date for the termination of the

Kāṇva dynasty being *c.* 28 BC (although this date itself is entirely dependent on the purāṇas). Most historians, accepting the one statement or the other, have explained the contradiction as the work of a misinformed compiler or scribe. Candidly there is no reason why either statement should be true, while the relatively more reliable palaeographic evidence advises us against accepting either dating.[5]

It seems very likely that the total of four hundred and sixty years assigned to the dynasty was arrived at by combining the reigns of princes of both the main and the various branch lines of the Sātavāhanas. The statement that informs us that the Sātavāhanas succeeded the Kāṇvas was probably due to the compilers' sense of propriety which impelled them to make one major dynasty follow the other. It must be remembered that the modern concept of history was unknown to purāṇic writers to whom strict accuracy may well have been a secondary consideration. The last editor of the *Vishnu-purāṇa*, for instance, evidently decided to make Sātavāhana succession a strictly hereditary one as against the other purāṇas which do not always state a relationship between the rulers. Just as a father-to-son succession was considered ideal, one major dynasty following another was deemed the standard pattern. It is also possible that by the time the accounts were compiled, facts regarding the inception of the dynasty had been forgotten and false traditions had arisen. R. G. Bhandarkar acknowledged this fact as early as 1895 when he explained: 'The genesis of our Puranic literature seems to be this. Certain versified accounts of certain things purporting to be narrated by a bard to Rishis assembled together at a sacrificial session were handed down orally from generation and these were after some time committed to writing. . . . The text of the old Puranas gradually became corrupt, and the authors of the later ones were in some cases misled by their incorrect readings into putting forth statements at variance with their original account.'[6] Bhandarkar himself believed the *Vāyu-purāṇa* statement that Simuka founded the Sātavāhana dynasty after defeating the Kāṇvas. However, he regarded the hundred and twelve years assigned to the Śuṅgas to include the forty-five years of Kāṇva rule, and thus placed the establishment of the Sātavāhana dynasty at *c.* 73 BC. In view of these various interpretations, it is our contention that coins and inscriptions provide our only serious basis for this discussion.

Origin of the Sātavāhana Dynasty

Some time well after the disintegration of the Mauryan empire in 187 BC, while the Śungas were struggling to prevent rapid secessions from their territories, the western Deccan seems to have been formed into an independent kingdom under Simuka Sātavāhana. Because the Sātavāhanas are described in the purāṇas as Āndhras or Āndhra-bhritya, there has been some speculation about the original home of the dynasty and it has been suggested that they came from the Andhra country.[7] Recently, M. Rama Rao has proposed that the coin of Siri Sādavāha, found in the excavations at Kondapur, belongs to a hypothetical founder of the dynasty prior to Simuka, and from him the line must have obtained its name. He maintains that this coin indicates that the Sātavāhanas began their rule in Telengana.[8] He also lists several coins found at Kondapur and a few at Maski of a Siri Sāta whom he identifies with Sātakarni I.[9] However, the over-whelming strength of the evidence from Nanaghat and Nasik certainly points to the western Deccan as the home of the dynasty. The full-length bas-relief figures that once existed in the Nanaghat cave, identified by inscribed labels above their heads, included 'portraits' of Simuka Sātavāhana (the founder of the line), of Sātakarni I (the third ruler), and of several other members of the royal family. Moreover, a small cave at Nasik contains an inscription engraved in the reign of Kanha, the second Sātavāhana ruler. On the other hand, the earliest undisputed Sātavāhana coins to be found in the eastern region belong to Gautamīputra Sātakarni, the ruler who re-established Sātavāhana power after its temporary decline under the Kshaharāta invaders in the first century AD. The explanation of the purāṇic designation of the Sātavāhanas as Āndhra-bhrityas is presumably to be found in the fact that these documents were written at a later date when the dynasty had become established in Andhra and was remembered as a great power.

The sudden ascendancy of the Sātavāhana dynasty as a political entity was not necessarily due entirely to the aspirations, deter-mination and strength of its founder alone. Economic factors must also have contributed to their rise, as was the case with the Kushānas. A study of the geographic distribution of the various cave sites reveals, as we shall see later in some detail,[10] that these were situated along the principal trade routes that led from the ports to the market towns of the interior. Many are located at the heads of the passes through the western ghats and thus occupy positions of commanding importance. This is especially true of the cave at Nanaghat which is situated at the head of the principal pass along the route linking Kalyan and other ports to Junnar and from there to the Sātavāhana capital of Paithan. The records engraved on the side walls of the Nanaghat cave leave little doubt regarding the wealth of the Sātavāhana rulers: as many as 11,000 cows and 1000 horses were offered at a single sacrifice, and a number of sacrifices with similar donations are reported. Nanaghat of itself is an insignificant place – a small set of caves with no architectural embellishment, probably used as a rest-house at the top of the lengthy ascent, with no settlements and apparently no monastic establishments in the immediate vicinity. It acquires a position of importance only when considered from the point of view of its position along one of the main trade routes of the time. Yet it was at this spot that the early Sātavāhana rulers decided to engrave significant records and to carve out of solid rock portrait sculptures of various founder members of the royal family. The acquisition of all the major ports and passes to the interior must have played an important role in consolidating the authority of the dynasty. How significant this control was is illustrated by the fact that in later times the Kshaharātas were quick to take possession of several Sātavāhana passes and thereby interfere with their trade.[11]

The commerce of the early Sātavāhanas was probably conducted through Egyptian and Arab middlemen. The theory of Sātavāhana/Arab trade receives support from a little treatise on the Red Sea written by an Alexandrian, Agartharchides, in 110 BC. 'For no nation seems to be wealthier than the Sabaeans and Gerrhaeans [Arabs] who are the agents for everything that falls under the name of transport from Asia and Europe.'[12] Agartharchides stated that his account was based on verbal reports of eye-witnesses as well as on written reports in the royal archives at Alexandria. We hear of expeditions by sea from Egypt to India led by a certain Eudoxus of Cyzicus between 120–110 BC. Sailing to India seems to have been fairly common after this date, for between 110–51 BC, we have four dedicatory inscriptions found in Egypt that mention Ptolemaic officers 'in charge of the Red and Indian seas'.[13] The discovery by Hippalus of the art of sailing with the south-west monsoon direct from Arabia to India, which was of momentous importance for the west coast of India, was probably made early in this period.[14] Growing trade connections between India and the Mediterranean, when considered together with the importance assigned by the Sātavāhanas to Nanaghat – a strategic point on a trade route – obviously provided the solid economic foundation over which the military power of the Sātavā-hanas built an impressive political structure.

Early Sātavāhana Rulers

The remarkable Nanaghat cave inscriptions are our main source of information about the early Sātavāhana kings. The long records, engraved on the two side walls of the cave, seem to have been inscribed by the order of the widowed queen of king Sātakarni. They mention the names of various members of the royal family while listing their generosity at Brahmanical sacrifices. Against the back wall of the cave are traces of bas-relief portraits of Sātavāhana royalty identified by labels above their heads. The figures have now almost completely disappeared but the labels above them tell us that portraits once depicted Simuka Sātavāhana, queen Nayanikā and her husband Sātakarni, prince Bha . . . , general Tranakayiro, prince Hakusiri and prince Sātavāhana. The purāṇic accounts are in accord with inscriptional evidence at least regarding the names of the first three rulers of the dynasty. They inform us that Simuka (variously called Sisuka, Sipraka, Sindhuka), the founder of the dynasty, reigned for twenty-three years and was succeeded by his brother Kanha (rule of ten or eighteen years), who was in turn followed by Sātakarni I (also assigned a rule of ten or eighteen years). There is no mention of Kanha at Nanaghat but an inscription engraved during his reign may be found in a cave at Nasik. The explanation of his absence at Nanaghat quite possibly lies in the fact that being Simuka's brother, he was a usurper to the throne, the Sātakarni who followed him being the son and rightful heir. Since Sātakarni's queen was responsible for the inscription, she might have considered it proper to omit mention of the usurper.

We have earlier described the contradictory statements in the purāṇas regarding the date of the establishment of Sātavāhana rule. For this event we would rather rely on the evidence of inscriptions and coins. The palaeographic material, which we shall discuss at length in the next two chapters, indicates that the Nanaghat inscriptions were engraved around 70–60 BC.[15] Working backwards from this date and allowing roughly fifty years for the rule of the first three kings, it would seem reasonable to assign the establishment of the Sātavāhana dynasty to *c.* 120 or 110 BC.

We may point out that while we have definite historical synchronisms with other rulers to firmly date the later Sātavāhana kings,
such is not the case with the earlier rulers. Only two other inscriptions
are known which allude to a king Sātakarni: that on the south gateway of *stūpa* I at Sanchi records a gift from the foreman of the
artisans of Śri Sātakarni; and the Hathigumpha cave inscription of
Khāravela mentions a Sātakarni who ruled over the western regions.
These two Sātakarnis remain unidentified and their dates are uncertain: to ascertain this we have, in fact, to turn to palaeographic
evidence. Such evidence indicates that the Sanchi and Hathigumpha
records belong to the same phase and hence probably refer to the
same Sātakarni.[16] On palaeographic grounds this ruler appears to be
of slightly later date than the Nanaghat ruler of the same name, and
may perhaps be identified with the Sātakarni II of the purāṇas.

Coins bearing the legend *Rāno Siri Sātasa*, of uncertain pro-
venance, but attributed to the Malwa region on the basis of their
similarity with the earlier punch-marked coins of the area, have
generally been assigned to the Nanaghat Sātakarni, the third Sātavāhana ruler. The only difference between the letters on the coins and
those of the inscriptions is a definite thickening of the tops of the
verticals seen in the former. This phenomenon, as we shall see later
in detail,[17] was the result of the use of a reed pen that appears to have
been in practice in India at a much earlier date than hitherto accepted.
The pen would quite naturally have been used first on records in
which writing was of a normal size, coin moulds being part of this
category. Only after letters with thickened tops had become quite
usual would these have been imitated on monumental stone inscriptions where the letters vary from two-and-a-half to six inches in
height. It is therefore quite consistent to find this thickening of letters
on the coins of Sātakarni I and not on his inscriptions at Nanaghat.

Evidence derived from early Sātavāhana coins recovered in excavations at Nevasa would seem to run contrary to our date of
c. 120/110 BC for the establishment of the dynasty. According to the
report, these coins 'push back the origin of the Satavahanas to the
3rd/2nd century B.C.'[18] Coins bearing legends are found at Nevasa in
Period IV (Early Historic: *c.* 150–50 BC) and in Period V (Indo-
Roman: *c.* 50 BC–AD 200). The coins of the later Sātavāhana kings,
starting with Gautamīputra Sātakarni, were discovered in the layers
of Period V, but a series of five coins bearing the legend *Siri
Sātavāhana* came from earlier levels. According to the report these

coins 'help in assigning the layers of Period IV to about the 2nd century B.C.'[19] It is of course an accepted archaeological practice to date a layer from the objects found in them, but in that case the date of such objects must be beyond any doubt. In the present instance such a method is manifestly inadequate since the dates of the coins themselves are in dispute. The site has been dug in trenches and four of the five coins in question were found in the topmost layer of Period IV. Following the dating of the report itself, this level could be assigned to the period c. 80–50 BC. Only one coin was found in an earlier level, but as it is identical to the other four it does not seem possible to assign it to an earlier phase. The pitfalls of the method become apparent from the fact that Muslim coins have apparently been found in the topmost layer of the Indo-Roman period.[20] These Islamic coins have presumably filtered through, and the single Sātavāhana coin perhaps also found its way down in a similar fashion. It is unfortunate that the radiocarbon dates for the Early Historic and the Indo-Roman periods at Nevasa are inconclusive. They appear, in fact, to provide an earlier date for Period V than for Period IV.[21] The date of four of the five Nevasa coins – c. 80–50 BC – is in accord with the Nanaghat inscriptions and the Malwa fabric coins that belong to c. 70/60 BC. Thus, the coin evidence, as a whole, conforms with a date of c. 120/110 BC for the establishment of the Sātavāhana dynasty.

Lacuna

After the three early kings, Simuka, Kanha and Sātakarni I, our knowledge of Sātavāhana history is limited to the doubtful evidence of the purāṇas until we come to Gautamīputra Sātakarni, described in his inscriptions as the 'Restorer of the Glory of the Sātavāhanas'. It is indeed strange that we should know so little of the kings who ruled in the intervening period. Not a single inscription belonging to any of these rulers exists, and the evidence from coins is almost as scanty. One coin belonging to Āpīlaka has been found in Madhya Pradesh, and a coin possibly of his successor Meghasvati also exists.[22] Literary sources indicate the historicity of two other rulers – Kuntala Sātakarni, to whom reference is made in Vātsyāyana's *Kāmasūtra*, and Hāla who is assigned the authorship of the *Gathāsaptasati*.

The primary source, however, for this dark period of Sātavāhana history remains the purāṇas. The *Vāyu-purāṇa* gives us the names of ten kings to fill the gap, while the *Matsya-purāṇa* provides us with nineteen. It seems quite certain that after the rule of the early Sātavāhana kings, the dynasty split into several branches. Kuntala Sātakarni, for example, probably belonged to a branch controlling the Kuntala country comprising north Kanara, parts of Mysore, Belgaum and Dharwar.[23] The absence of inscriptions and coins is presumably due to these kings having ruled over small territories and wielded little power. During part of this period, the Sātavāhanas were ousted from the central section of their kingdom by the Kshaharātas, while various branch lines continued to rule in outlying areas. Gautamīputra Sātakarni, in defeating the Kshaharātas, restored to the Sātavāhanas all the territory taken from them and re-established one strong Sātavāhana line. The reality of the lacuna, although by no means its absolute extent, is attested by palaeography and to a lesser degree by architecture. It was, perhaps, this lacuna that led to much of the discrepancies among the various purānic accounts, which are otherwise fairly reliable for the early rulers of the dynasty, and as we shall presently see, give reasonably accurate information regarding the later kings. Curiously, at both periods there was a direct Sātavāhana line ruling as a single power. In the intervening period, when the dynasty split up into several minor branches, the various purānas give us selective information on the rulers. The *Matsya-purāna* with its list of nineteen kings presumably mentions the names of all rulers of all branch lines, thus swelling the total number of kings and greatly extending the span of time during which the dynasty was in power.

We have noted that at some time in this interval the Sātavāhanas were deprived of an important portion of their territories by the Kshaharāta Kshatrapas, probably Śakas by origin. The existence of these rulers is attested by coins and inscriptions, but their early history is as unsatisfactory as that of the Sātavāhanas. Only Nahapāna emerges as a strong personality in this list of shadowy monarchs. It appears quite certain, however, that these rulers constituted a line distinct from the Western Satrap line of Cashtana and Rudradāman.

Nahapāna and the *Periplus*

Inscriptions of Nahapāna's son-in-law Ushavadāta are to be found in the caves at Nasik and Karle, and a single record of his minister beside an excavation at Junnar. These bear the dates 41 to 46 and it has been held that they refer to the Śaka era of AD 78, thus making Nahapāna's last known year AD 124. A number of scholars subscribe to this dating, but perhaps the most persuasive and the most recent advocate of this theory is V. V. Mirashi.[24] While we do not accept this dating, we cannot agree either with scholars who assign the years 41 to 46 to the Vikrama era of 58 BC.[25] It seems most likely to us that Nahapāna's dates refer not to any known era, but to a regnal year as in the case of the later Sātavāhanas.

The identification of Nahapāna with the Mambaros or Nambanus mentioned in the *Periplus* is today generally accepted.[26] This anonymous work describes the trade conditions of its time and mentions a number of contemporary rulers. The identification of these rulers, however, remains enigmatic, while no unanimous decision on the date of the work has been reached. Recent years have seen a great deal of discussion on the *Periplus* as it affects the date of Nahapāna. The magnitude of the problems involved is perhaps best illustrated by the fact, as pointed out by Douglas Barrett that, rather than succeed in establishing Nahapāna's dates by the *Periplus*, J. A. B. Palmer has attempted to place the *Periplus* using dubious Indian evidence and assuming Nahapāna's dates to refer to the Śaka era.[27]

In attempting to date the work we may start with a premise, of which there seems little doubt, that the *Periplus* was not written as a travelogue or for a literary purpose, but specifically as a guide for intending travellers by one who had made the journey himself. We may expect the information it contains to have been collected over a certain number of years, but its purpose indicates that it must have described existing conditions. With this in mind the mention of Malichus, king of the Nabataeans, gives us a fixed point in time. There is little doubt among historians that this must be Malichus II who ruled between AD 40–71, and thus the work must have been written some time between those dates.[28] It is not possible to accept the theory that Malichus was dead when the *Periplus* was written. The book was meant for intending travellers: there were frequent caravans from Egypt to Petra and the death of the king would have been mentioned if it had occurred before the *Periplus* was written. For the same reason the theory that Nahapāna was already dead when the work was written is equally unacceptable.[29] There is no reason why a dead king should be mentioned at all.

Recently Jacqueline Pirenne has put forward the view that the *Periplus* belongs, in fact, to a period well after AD 106. We are told that the phrase 'king of the Nabataeans' is in a later corrective hand and is of value only as a conjecture. She further suggests that just because Malichus and Petra are mentioned together we should not jump to the conclusion that Malichus was king of the Nabataeans. It is suggested that the ruler referred to is a hypothetical Malichus III, dating from the period after Nabataea became part of the Roman empire.[30] While accepting Pirenne's judgement that the phrase 'king of the Nabataeans' is in a later corrective hand in the original manuscript, we feel it is quite justified to consider Malichus to be king of the Nabataeans on the basis that Malichus and Petra are mentioned together. No rulers of that name around that time are known from any other area, and it was the Nabataeans who were intimately associated with their metropolis Petra. Pirenne also bases much of her arguments for dating on the premise that the *Periplus* shows knowledge in advance of Pliny and must therefore be notably posterior to AD 70. She tells us that an examination of the historical situation seen in the *Periplus* does not allow placing it in the time of Pliny, and that it must have belonged to a phase after AD 106. As the validity of this argument is not convincing, it would be worthwhile to re-examine some basic facts.

The *Natural History*, a work in thirty-seven books, appeared in AD 77, two years before Pliny's death. No one would contest the verdict that the work shows 'some misunderstanding of authorities, overmuch reliance on others' accounts and occasional unintelligibility'.[31] A careful count of the authorities quoted apparently reveals a hundred and forty-six Roman and three hundred and twenty-seven non-Roman sources. Among those mentioned in the account of India are Alexander, Seleucus, Antiochus, Megasthenes and Dionysius. The tone of his work is vastly different from that of the *Periplus* and displays a scholarly style and a painstaking study of various earlier manuscripts. The *Periplus*, on the other hand, has rather a crisp tone and reveals a personal knowledge of the circumstances it describes, which is particularly apparent in passages such as the graphic description of the hazards of the coastal approach to Barygaza.[32] The *Periplus* no doubt *appears* to reveal knowledge in advance of Pliny, but it is equally possible that they are contemporary works. The author of the *Periplus* probably completed his work before the *Natural History*, and there was no reason for Pliny to take cognizance of a contemporary writing by an obscure sailor. Pliny was a nobleman and on intimate terms with the emperor Vespasian under whom he had served first as a procurator and later as a prefect of the Roman fleet. The author of the *Periplus*, on the other hand, was an unknown seaman. The two men obviously moved in completely different circles, whereas as a noted scholar, Pliny would naturally have consulted only the more authoritative sources. To consider the *Periplus* as such is perhaps to give it undue importance as a scholarly work of the Roman Empire.

We would then reaffirm our view that the mention of Malichus in the *Periplus* gives us a fixed point in time, and that the work may be placed some time during the reign of Malichus II, between AD 40–71. All that can be said with any certainty on the date of Nahapāna, arguing from the *Periplus*, is that the work provides us with a *terminus a quo* for the start of his reign. Nahapāna was already ruling in AD 71, but how much earlier we cannot say from the *Periplus*. For that we have to turn to a consideration of his last date which is closely linked with the dates of Gautamīputra Sātakarni.

Gautamīputra Sātakarni

Nahapāna was defeated by Gautamīputra Sātakarni who is described in the Nasik inscriptional eulogy of his mother Balaśrī as the 'Uprooter of the Kshaharātas' and the 'Restorer of the Glory of the Sātavāhanas'. The Jogalthembi hoard of Nahapāna's coins would seem to provide definite evidence that Gautamīputra himself defeated Nahapāna. Of the 13,270 coins in the hoard, 9270 have been countermarked by Gautamīputra, but not one of the coins bears the name of any king other than Nahapāna. If a ruler had intervened between Nahapāna and Gautamīputra it is reasonable to expect that his coins would have been found in the hoard. After a detailed study of the coins, H. R. Scott pointed out that the busts of Nahapāna seem to differ not only in age, but also in features, and he considered this proof that other rulers intervened between Nahapāna and Gautamīputra – rulers who retained on their coins the name of their famous ancestor.[33] This theory does not seem convincing to us, though it has recently won fresh support.[34] If this theory is to be accepted we must assume the existence of a centralized mint in those days, which is unlikely. It is also possible that the portraits of the king differed according to the capabilities of the artists concerned, and possibly some of the artists had never seen the king but produced the portrait from descriptions of the ruler. There thus seems no reason to doubt that Gautamīputra Sātakarni himself defeated Nahapāna.

A Nasik inscription dated in the year fourteen of Gautamīputra establishes the fact that the forty-sixth year of Nahapāna fell in or before the fourteenth year of Gautamīputra.[35] We know also from inscriptional evidence that Gautamīputra ruled for twenty-four years (as against the unanimous purāṇic ascription of twenty-one years). He was thus in power for about ten years after defeating Nahapāna. Arguing from the fact that the latest date for the start of Nahapāna's reign is AD 71 (on the evidence of the *Periplus*), we get AD 71 + 46 + 10 = AD 127 as the latest date for Gautamīputra's death.

At this stage it is of relevance to consider the Andhau inscriptions from Kutch[36] dated in the year 52 of what is universally accepted as the Śaka era of AD 78, and thus belonging to AD 130. These inscriptions of Cashṭana and Rudradāman as joint rulers indicate that Malwa was in their possession at this date. In fact, they must have obtained it at least five years earlier when Cashṭana's son Jayadāman ruled jointly with him, since coins of the latter have been found at Junagadh and at Pushkara near Ajmer. It thus appears that Malwa was in the possession of the Western Satraps by AD 125. If this be accepted then the theory that Nahapāna's dates refer to the Śaka era becomes untenable. According to this system of dating Gautamīputra would have defeated Nahapāna in AD 78 + 46 = AD 124. We know that he must have conquered Malwa soon after defeating Nahapāna, but Malwa was already in the control of the Western Satraps in AD 125. The powerful Gautamīputra lost none of his possessions in his lifetime, and certainly not in the very year in which he conquered them. We are thus faced with the conclusion that Nahapāna's dates cannot be referred to the Śaka era of AD 78. The Andhau inscriptions also provide a *terminus ad quem* for the death of Gautamīputra – AD 124 (taking one year before Malwa was in the hands of the Western Satraps). Working backwards from this date, his inscription of the year fourteen indicates that he must have defeated Nahapāna by AD 114. This in turn gives us a date of AD 68 (AD 114 minus 46) as the latest date for the commencement of Nahapāna's reign.

The Later Sātavāhanas

Two inscriptions, one from Girnar and the other from Kanheri, combine to provide us with significant information on the later Sātavāhana rulers. Rudradāman states in his Girnar epigraph that he twice defeated Sātakarni, Lord of the Deccan, but did not destroy him on account of their 'not-too-distant-relationship' (*sambandhāvidūratayā*). A Kanheri record mentions the queen of Vāsishtīputra Siri Sātakarni and describes her as having descended from the

Kārddamaka kings and as the daughter of *mahākshatrapa* Ru. . .
(Rudra). It is apparent that Vāsishtīputra Siri Sātakarni was the son-
in-law of Rudradāman. We are faced with the identification of two
rulers – the twice-defeated Sātakarni of the Girnar record, and the
Vāsishtīputra of Kanheri. It seems to us that the two may not be
identified with each other. The latter was Rudradāman's own
son-in-law and it is improbable that he would have described him
as not too distantly related, or indeed that he would have fought him.
It seems unlikely that Pulumāvi (Gautamīputra's successor) was the
twice-defeated ruler of the Girnar record as he never bore the name
Sātakarni. Neither could Pulumāvi have been the ruler of the
Kanheri inscription and Rudradāman's son-in-law: Ptolemy indicates
that Pulumāvi was a contemporary of Cashtana, and it would have
been impossible for him to have married the daughter of his contemporary's grandson. If the twice-defeated Sātakarni was neither
Pulumāvi nor Vāsishtīputra, then he must be identified with a
successor of the latter. As a grandson would be as close a relation as a
son-in-law, Vāsishtīputra's successor was probably not his own son,
or may have been a son through a queen other than Rudradāman's
daughter: this would explain the use of the phrase 'not-too-distantly-
related'.

At this stage it is necessary to turn to the purāṇic lists for guidance.
The *Matsya-* and *Brahmāṇḍa-purāṇas* agree in giving us the following
list of later Sātavāhana kings: Gautamīputra Sātakarni, Pulumāvi,
Śivaśrī Sātakarni, Śivaskanda Sātakarni, Yajñaśrī Sātakarni. Following the lead of several scholars, we would identify the Vāsishtīputra
of Kanheri with the Śivaśrī Sātakarni of the purāṇas and the Vāsishtīputra Śivaśrī of the coins. This would mean that the twice-defeated
Sātakarni of the Girnar inscription was probably Vāsishtīputra's
immediate successor, Śivaskanda Sātakarni.[37] There is no great disagreement among the purāṇas as to the length of the reigns of these
two kings. The *Matsya-purāṇa* assigns seven years to each ruler, and
on this basis it would be reasonable to state that the year AD 150 (the
year of the Girnar record) coincides with, say, the fifth year of
Śivaskanda (this allowing for two battles with Rudradāman).
Accordingly, the first year of Śivaskanda would be AD 145 and, in
turn, Vāsishtīputra's first year would be AD 138. Pulumāvi's reign of
twenty-eight years may be placed between AD 110–138, with
Gautamīputra Sātakarni ruling between AD 86–110. Nahapāna's
forty-six regnal years may then be bracketed between AD 54–100.[38]

It is of relevance to note an inscription of a Vāsishtīputra Chatarapāna Sātakarni, dated in the thirteenth year of the ruler, discovered at Nanaghat by Bhagvanlal Indraji.[39] Indraji assigned the inscription to Yajñaśrī Sātakarni but the latter definitely bore the metronymic Gautamīputra. Dr Gopalachari would like to identify him with the Vāsishtīputra of Kanheri, explaining *chatarapāna* as evidence of his Satrap connections.[40] However, Indraji also discovered, at Sopara, a coin of Yajñaśrī with the word *chatarapāna* on it. If indeed Vāsishtīputra Chatarapāna is the Kanheri ruler, we must adjust our dates by around seven years. This would not, however, make any fundamental difference to the chronological scheme arrived at in this chapter as no important synchronisms are affected.

Continuing with our dating, Yajñaśrī Sātakarni, to whom the *Vāyu-purāṇa* assigns a reign of twenty-nine years, must have ruled between AD 152–181. Yajñaśrī's inscriptions include one at Nasik in the sixteenth year of his reign,[41] an isolated record at Chinna in the Krishna district belonging to his twenty-seventh year, and two inscriptions in the caves at Kanheri of which one is dated in his sixteenth year. He was the last important Sātavāhana king and exerted his authority over an extensive area: his coins have been found in Gujarat, Saurashtra, north Konkan, Akola, Chanda and the Krishna and Godavari districts.[42]

In recent years a small number of silver portrait coins of the later Sātavāhana rulers have been found. These include one of Pulumāvi, one of Vāsishtīputra Sātakarni and five of Yajñaśrī Sātakarni. It has been suggested that matrimonial connections induced these rulers to take an interest in, and to copy, the Western Satrap coins which had the busts of the ruler engraved on them.[43] It is, on the other hand, possible that Gautamīputra Sātakarni himself started this practice. Although no portrait coin belonging to him has yet been discovered, a silver coin with the legend *Rāno Gotami* was probably issued by him. We have seen that when Gautamīputra defeated Nahapāna, he recalled Nahapāna's coins and had them counterstruck with his own symbols. These coins, which seem to have been in wide circulation, were all of silver and had the bust of the king with a Greek legend on the obverse, and legends in both Brāhmī and Kharoshṭi on the reverse. Gautamīputra Sātakarni perhaps received the inspiration for issuing his own silver coinage from the practice of the Kshaharāta Kshatrapas whom he had just defeated;[44] this is a situation that has precedents elsewhere in the ancient world.

The purāṇas give us the names of three rulers who followed Yajñaśrī Sātakarni – Vijaya, Candraśri and Pulumāvi. An inscription at Nagarjunakonda dated in the sixth year of Vijaya, a record from Kodavolu in the Godavari district in the second year of Candraśri, and an inscription at Myakadoni in the Bellary district in the eighth year of Pulumāvi give us an indication of the extent and importance of the southern portions of Sātavāhana territories.[45] D. C. Sircar reads Dravidian words on the reverse of the silver coin of Vāsishtī-putra Sātakarni:[46] it would appear that although Vāsishtīputra had married a Western Satrap princess, the southern dominions of the empire were already extremely important. After Yajñaśrī, the authority of the Sātavāhanas was in decline and the dynasty appears once again to have split into several branches. The Tarhala hoard of late Sātavāhana coins from the Akola district introduces us to names not to be found in any of the purāṇas: Kumbha Sātakarni, Krishna Sātakarni, and Śaka Sātakarni.[47] A single coin of a Kausikīputra Sātakarni, also unknown to the purāṇas, has been discovered.[48] These kings apparently represent late branch lines of the Sātavāhanas who ruled presumably in outlying portions of the Sātavāhana territories, while the main line continued primarily in the southern region.

Historical Summary

The Sātavāhana dynasty appears to have been established in the western Deccan around 120 BC by Simuka Sātavāhana. Simuka was followed by his brother Kanha, who was succeeded by Simuka's son and rightful heir Sātakarni I who ruled till around 60 BC. After these first three powerful rulers, whose importance is attested by epigraphic evidence, the Sātavāhana dynasty split into several branch lines, each apparently ruling over small areas and wielding little authority. During this dark period of Sātavāhana history the Kshaharāta Kshatrapas overran their territory. The most influential Kshaharāta ruler was Nahapāna who started to reign in AD 54 and remained in control of the central portions of the Sātavāhana domain for forty-six years. In AD 100, Gautamīputra Sātakarni, who had already been ruling in outlying areas for fourteen years, defeated Nahapāna and re-established a single powerful Sātavāhana line. He was succeeded in AD 110 by Pulumāvi who reigned for twenty-eight years. Pulu-māvi was followed in AD 138 by Vāsishtīputra Siri Sātakarni, who undoubtedly consolidated his position when he married the daughter of the powerful Western Satrap ruler Rudradāman. Vāsishtīputra's short reign ended in AD 145, and he was succeeded by Śivaskanda Sātakarni who twice waged war against Rudradāman and was defeated on both occasions. Yajñaśrī Sātakarni, the last of the great Sātavāhana rulers, came into power in AD 152 and reigned until AD 181. His empire extended from the western Deccan right up to the Krishna basin. After Yajñaśrī the dynasty once again split into several branches, with the main line retaining its authority in the eastern regions. By AD 200 the Sātavāhana dynasty was no longer in evidence as a power to be reckoned with.

Geographical Environment of the Early Buddhist Caves

Fig. 1

The early Buddhist caves extend from Karadh in the south to Ajanta and Pitalkhora in the north, with extensions to Saurashtra in the west. Within this area there are some twelve principal sites ranging from Bedsa with four caves to Kanheri with some hundred and twenty-eight. The total number of such excavations is around one thousand. These are cut into the hills and valleys of the western ghats, the Deccan Trap basalts with their alternation of hard and soft layers being well suited for the purpose of rock-cutting. A large number of minerals are to be found in the Trap, including agate and carnelian (some of the chief exports to the Mediterranean according to the *Periplus*). Water supplies from underground springs were abundant. This in particular must have proved extremely useful to the rock-cutters as the choice of a site was not necessarily determined by access to surface water.

The rock-cut monasteries were located along ancient trade routes, particularly along those connecting the ports to important inland towns. There are three main sets of passes through the western ghats leading to the interior, and caves are situated at the heads of all three. The Sher and Tal ghats connect Sopara with Nasik and then inland; the Nanaghat links Kalyan to Junnar and from there to Paithan; and the Bhor ghat connects Kalyan to Karle and then to Ter.[49] In addition there are smaller passes near the Bhor ghat which lead to the port of Chaul. The intimate connection between the caves and the trade routes has long been recognized. In fact, the excavations at Nadsur were discovered by the Reverend Abbott because he was convinced of the existence of caves along the route linking Chaul to the interior.[50] Some of the lesser-known trade routes of the western Deccan may actually be traced by marking the cave sites, particularly the unfinished and architecturally less significant ones. D. D. Kosambi has illustrated how this may be done: 'Thus, one feeder route went right along the foot of the Western Ghāts, and reached Junnar via Nāneghāṭ. This is marked by a line of caves such as at Hāḷ, Ambivale, Pālu-Sonāvḷe (adjacent to the foot of Nāneghāṭ), and elsewhere. Branches led up every valley. One branch might have climbed the Sāvā pass or the Kurvaṇḍā pass nearer Loṇāvaḷā, to go past Beḍsā. Another came up the valley to Khaṇḍāḷā, as is proved by the Koṇḍāṇe caves, and the much smaller caves on the opposite hillside above Central Railway tunnel No. 16, on a saddle-back over-looking both valleys. . . . Other routes besides those to the Māvaḷ [the district which includes the Karle, Bhaja and Shelarvadi caves] are also to be traced by their own line of caves, as for example from Kuḍā on Rājpurī creek, via Koḷ and Mahāḍ, past Shirvaḷ and so to the east'.[51]

A good system of communications appears to have been maintained. Nahapāna's inscriptions at Nasik describe the setting up of rest-houses at Bharukaccha, Daśapura, Govardhana, Sorpāraga; the establishment of ferries with boats on many rivers, and the construction of rest-houses with drinking water facilities on the banks of these rivers. The trade routes were of great importance to the Sātavāhanas and foreign trade was probably responsible for a considerable proportion of their dominance and prosperity.

2

Early Indian Palaeography

It may appear at first glance that a study of early Indian palaeography is of little immediate relevance to a consideration of the chronology and development of the cave architecture of western India. We propose, however, to examine all lines of evidence that may enable us to obtain this chronology, and one such method is through a palaeographical analysis of the many inscriptions contained in the caves. These cave records, if studied in isolation, reveal a distinct sequential development, but particularly in the earlier phase, they lack an undisputed historical context of the type that would enable us to place them in terms of absolute dates. In order to assign dates to them, however approximate, we must examine them in the wider context of early Indian palaeography as a whole. Our analysis of the inscriptions from the early Buddhist caves is based to an appreciable extent on the chronological scheme that emerges from the present study.

Buhler's classic work on the palaeography of India, though not acceptable now in many details, was a notable contribution to an unexplored field.[1] When studying his chronological scheme we must remember that the highly significant Besnagar inscription of Heliodorus was then unknown. One of the most valuable contributions after Buhler was Ram Prasad Chanda's monograph which considered briefly many of the inscriptions we shall be discussing.[2] Chanda, presenting his argument in a clear and logical manner, was already able to correct many of Buhler's conclusions. Recently, Ahmad Hasan Dani, in his work on Indian palaeography,[3] has put forward a chronological scheme that differs in several respects with the conclusions of both Buhler and Chanda. Of especial interest to us is the fact that he has placed in the first century of the Christian era many of the inscriptions we shall examine in this chapter, and which we would date to the first century BC. A detailed reappraisal of the records themselves suggests to us a chronology that differs from that of Buhler and also contrasts in certain important respects with the chronology presented by Dani. In particular, a great part of Dani's argument is based upon a single premise that we are unable to regard as firmly established.[4]

The method we shall follow in this study is to take certain historically dated inscriptions as fixed points and compare with these all other relevant inscriptions. The forms of letters as well as the contents of the records will be taken into account, the latter often providing us with a clue to their absolute date. It may be noted, however, that the possibility of unknown regional and local variations in script, even during this early period, rules out absolute precision in dating. Nevertheless, for reasons that will be given as we proceed, we feel justified in the approximate dates we assign to the various inscriptions. Although we have sometimes separated styles of script by a narrow margin of time, it must not be assumed that every change in character and every mutation of script indicates a chronological difference. Factors such as variations in style between two different scribes, and certainly between an older and a younger scribe, may have led to differences in script within the same period. The older scribe, writing on the same date as the younger one, would still follow the style of writing he learned in his youth, although this may no longer be in vogue. It must be stressed then, that our dates are meant to indicate a general period rather than a specific point in time. We must bear in mind that, 'Palaeography can serve history only up to a point; then it in turn must be served.'[5] As far as the fixing of absolute dates by palaeographic evidence is concerned, this is certainly true. But there is no doubt that a definite and consistent development of script through the ages can be traced without the help of any other discipline. When we wish to attach exact dates to such a chronological scheme, we must rely on historically dated epigraphs, using these as established points for comparison.

Mauryan Records

Scholars in recent years have proved that, contrary to Buhler's opinions, no regional scripts can be distinguished in Aśokan Brāhmī.[6] Royal scribes must have been responsible for the engraving of the edicts scattered all over the empire and although individual differences may often be recognized, there are no consistent regional variations. As Brāhmī was still in its infancy and as the Mauryan court was a strong centralizing factor there was little scope for the

Table 1 development of local scripts. It seems to us that particularly in the pillar edicts, and in certain major rock edicts, there was a very real attempt to achieve a monumental style. By comparison, many of the minor rock edicts show a lack of skill and precision and consequent irregularity of script (as at Sahasram, Brahmagiri, and, even more so, at Rajulamandagiri). In certain instances, such as the Sanchi pillar inscription, the script shows a decisive tendency towards the cursive. Undisputed Mauryan records include also Aśoka's inscription in the caves in the Barabar hills and those of his grandson Daśaratha in the Nagarjuni hills.

Four other records that are usually assigned to the Mauryan period are the Mahasthan plaque, the Sohgaura plate, the Piprahwa vase and the inscriptions in the Ramgarh caves. Before examining these we must consider the important Besnagar pillar record which provides us with a basis for comparison. This inscription tells of the erection of a pillar by Heliodorus, ambassador from Antialkidas to king Bhāgabhadra. It is generally agreed that Antialkidas ruled between *c.* 120–100 B C,[7] and the inscription may therefore be said to date from that period. A comparison of the letter-forms of undisputed Aśokan records with those of Besnagar proves interesting. The striking fact emerges that in a period of over a hundred years, very few changes in the forms of letters have taken place. Admittedly the form of *dha* has changed, having assumed the inverted-D form which is the accepted usage in all inscriptions from this date onwards. But apart from this factor and a slightly later form of *bha*, no changes are to be seen. The official nature of Aśokan art has been pointed out time and again: there is no doubt that this applies to the script as well. Even after the decline of the Mauryan empire the Aśokan script seems to have been taken as the standard form of writing. Judging from the Besnagar inscription the emulation of the monumental Brāhmī style continued for about a century. It will be apparent, then, that it is no easy task to date precisely the four inscriptions mentioned earlier. On the basis of the shape of the *bha* one might be inclined to place the Mahasthan and Sohgaura records later than the Piprahwa and Ramgarh inscriptions. However, the official nature of the two former inscriptions, which make provisions for the outbreak of famine, leaves little doubt that they must have issued by some centralized authority. In fact, is is difficult to escape the historical inference that they belong to the period of Mauryan government. The Piprahwa vase reveals the use of the Mauryan *dha* and is perhaps

Aśokan since it mentions a shrine for the relics of the Buddha himself. The contents of these inscriptions incline us to assign them to Mauryan times, despite the need for caution due to the slow change in letter-forms during the early post-Mauryan period.

Series A

Putting aside the Aśokan and other uncertain but probably Mauryan inscriptions, we shall now consider a more definite cluster, palaeographically speaking, that may be dated in relation to the Besnagar inscription. These include the Ghosundi record, the inscriptions on the railings of the Bharhut *stūpa*, and those on the railings of *stūpas* I and II at Sanchi. A definite *terminus a quo* of *c.* 120/110 BC is provided for the group by the Besnagar inscription we have just considered, and the records may be said to cover a period extending down to *c.* 80 BC. Here already we disagree quite radically with the chronology put forward by Dani according to which the railings of Sanchi *stūpa* I fall between 100–50 BC, while the Ghosundi record, the Bharhut railing inscriptions, and those on Sanchi *stūpa* II railings belong to the period 50–1 BC.[8]

A detailed examination of these various records shows that they undoubtedly belong together. The script of Ghosundi and Besnagar appears to be identical in every respect. Both exhibit the very angular *ga* and *ta*, and the so-called corkscrew *ra*, and in neither is there any attempt at the equalization of the verticals of any of the letters. The inscriptions on the railings of the Bharhut *stūpa*[9] and on the railings of Sanchi *stūpas* I and II follow soon after. The letter-forms are very similar to those of Besnagar and Ghosundi, differing only in having a straight *ra*. Within the group the more striking similarities are the angularity of *ga* and *ta*, the oval form of *cha* and the distinctive *kha* and *bha*. Dani somewhat arbitrarily separates the railings of *stūpas* I and II at Sanchi by a period of fifty years, but the forms of the letters refute the possibility of any such gap between them. He does not state any factual grounds for his view, and his own eye-copies seem to deny his contention (Dani: Plate VI, 2, 3). The maximum amount of time that can be postulated between the two is a decade and this is borne out by the textual evidence of the inscriptions.[10] A railing inscription on *stūpa* I reports the gift of a monk Arahaguta, an inhabitant of Sāsāda, and on *stūpa* II we find a donation of Balaka, the pupil of Arahaguta, an inhabitant of Sāsāda. Here on the two sets of railings is an obvious mention of the same person. Additional confirmation is provided by a gift from the nun Dhamasenā of Kurara, inscribed on the railings of both *stūpas*.

Series B

The next group of inscriptions starts with the Bharhut gateway record of Dhanabhūtī which provides us with a *terminus a quo* of *c.* 80 BC for this phase. This series includes the railing inscriptions at Gaya, the records (except one) on the north gateway of *stūpa* I at Sanchi, and ends with the slightly later Bhilsa pillar inscription of Bhāgavata. The Bharhut gateway inscription assigned by Dani to the first half of the first century AD[11] deserves detailed examination. The script shows some definite developments as compared with the previous group: the *ga* is rounded, the *cha* has two loops though still oval in shape, and there is a distinct tendency towards the equalization of the verticals of *pa*. One cannot afford to ignore the contents of the inscription which have been considered by most historians to provide us with an indication of its absolute date. The record starts with the words *Suganam Raje*, or 'in the reign of the Śungas'.[12] There is a general consensus among scholars that the Śunga dynasty was in power from *c.* 184–72 BC. Since the script of this record shows some notable advances as compared with the previous group it may, with some confidence, be assigned to the closing days of the Śunga dynasty, and an estimate of *c.* 80 BC would not be far out. Dani chooses to ignore the historical implications of this inscription and bases his own chronology upon the contention that this record, along with others of a group, shows that it was copied from the pen script of the Mathura Kshatrapas, even though the essential features of that script are not present in this inscription. The new features associated with the Mathura script he dates to the first half of the first century AD: such a date is contradicted by the evidence we shall be discussing.

To this phase belong also the Indragnimitra inscriptions from the railings at Gaya. A distinct angularity is to be seen in the *pa*, the *va* has a rather triangular form (more so than in the Bharhut gateway inscription where we would describe it as elongated rather than triangular), and the lower part of *ma* is optionally of a flat triangular variety. The forms of *ta* and *ga*, however, are still angular. These records belong to a slightly later date than the Bharhut gateway, but we cannot accept any appreciable difference in time between the two. The Indragnimitra of the Gaya inscriptions is described as Kausikī-

Tables 1, 2

putra and it has been suggested that he was a brother of Dhanadeva of the Ayodhya record, who was sixth in descent from Pushyamitra Śunga.[13] The historical inference would place him at *c.* 68 BC and this fits in reasonably well with our palaeographic dating.

The inscriptions on the north gateway of Sanchi *stūpa* I also belong to this phase. There can be no doubt that palaeographically the north gateway stands distinct from and earlier than the other three gateways, thus apparently contradicting the generally accepted evidence of the sculptures; and here we agree with Dani.[14] All the votive inscriptions on the north gateway are similar to the Bharhut gateway inscription, and exhibit an angular *ga* and *ta* in contrast to the records on the other three gateways. As if in confirmation of the palaeographic evidence, common link names occur between the south and west gateways and between the west and east, but none between any of these and the north. We shall discuss this problem at greater length in Appendix I (p. 186).

The Bhilsa inscription of Bhāgavata follows soon after. Both angular and rounded forms of *ga* are to be found, but the *ta* still preserves its angular nature. The feature that indicates the slightly later date of this record as compared with the previous three is the complete equalization of the verticals of *pa*. It is difficult to comprehend how it is possible for Dani to assign this inscription to the second half of the first century BC, and at the same time place the Gaya and the Bharhut gateway inscriptions in the first half of the first century AD. Here again, Dani's own charts do not seem to bear out his contention (Dani: Plate V, 9 and Plate VI, 6, 7, 8).

Series C

Series C comprises the inscriptions on the east, south and west gateways of *stūpa* I at Sanchi, and those on *stūpa* III at the same site. These possess a number of new characteristics that indicate a distinct break *Table 2* with the records we have so far considered. The group exhibits a markedly rounded *ga* and *ta*, a *cha* with two definite loops of the so-called butterfly variety, a more or less complete equalization of the verticals of *pa* and a distinctive medial *i* flourish. In addition we find here for the first time on stone a definite thickening of the tops of the verticals. This characteristic, as Dani points out, is the result of the use of a new type of pen – a reed pen – that gives a broad start to a letter and gradually narrows towards its lower half. Dani maintains that this thickening was not an intentional head to the letters (as may be found in later times) but was the natural consequence of the use of the new pen.[15] It would seem, however, to be the indubitable source from which the later fashion derived.

Dani assigns these inscriptions to the first half of the first century AD, while according to our chronology they belong to c. 50–25 BC. The explanation of Dani's dating is to be found in his premise that the thickening of the heads of letters and consequently the introduction of the reed pen, occurs for the first time in the inscriptions of the Mathura Kshatrapas in the first half of the first century AD. We shall see that this premise is a questionable one and certainly should not be the only argument used to date these inscriptions. A detailed study of these Sanchi records as compared with those of the Mathura Kshatrapas reveals sufficient differences to allow for a period of half a century between them. The Mathura script has in general a marked squareness and angularity. Advanced features, absent at Sanchi but present at Mathura, include the complete equalization of the verticals of *pa* and *ha*, an angular individual form of *la*, a triangular *va* with a very short stem, a markedly angular *ma*, a notched *bha* and a later form of *da* open to the right. All these new features certainly indicate the later date of the Mathura Kshatrapa inscriptions and we find it impossible to assign the Sanchi records to the same phase.

Series D : Mathura

As the question of the introduction of the reed pen is of crucial importance for the establishment of our chronology, and as we seem to have reached very different conclusions to those of Dani, it is necessary to digress slightly and consider the evidence relating to this stylistic innovation of the script. The inscriptions and coins from *Tables 2, 3* Mathura present us with material of paramount importance in this connection. The *Amohini* tablet of Śoḍāsa, dated in the year 72 of what scholars generally agree to be the era of 58 BC, provides us with a date of AD 15 as one during which Śoḍāsa was ruling.[16] With this as our fixed point, it is possible to work backwards in time. We know from both coins and inscriptions that Śoḍāsa was preceded by his father Rājuvala, the start of whose reign we could place around 15 BC. The numismatic evidence from Mathura reveals the names of at least three other Kshatrapa rulers who must have preceded Rājuvala. We have the coins of Śivadatta, Hagāmasha, and of Hagāmasha ruling jointly with Hagāna. It would be quite safe to assume that these rulers take us back to c. 50 BC at which date historians are agreed that the Śaka Kshatrapas conquered the Mathura area.[17] Here then we have an independent check – which Dani seems to have ignored – on the earliest date for the thickening of the tops of the verticals. The coins of these Kshatrapa rulers definitely reveal this trait which is therefore at least as early as *c.* 50 BC and need not be dated to the reign of Śoḍāsa in the first century AD.

A detailed examination of the coins of the Mathura native rulers reveals, however, that the first appearance of this characteristic may be pushed back to an even earlier date. At least thirteen local rulers are known to have preceded the Mathura Kshatrapas. We have the coins of Gomitra, Brahmamitra, Drdhamitra, Sūryamitra, Vishnumitra, Purushadatta, Utamadatta, Rāmadatta; followed by a group bearing the title *rājan*,[18] Rāmadatta, Kāmadatta, Śeśadatta, Utamadatta and Balabhūti. These coins, in the British Museum, reveal a distinct thickening of the tops of the verticals[19] in the legends of at least five of these kings – Purushadatta, Utamadatta, Rāmadatta, Kāmadatta and Balabhūti. It seems probable that this feature was present on some of the other coins as well: almost invariably the legend runs along the outer edge of the coin and in many cases the coins are so worn that only the lower half of each individual letter remains intact. In fact, all that we can say with absolute certainty is that such thickening is not to be found on the coins of Gomitra and Brahmamitra.

There is no doubt that the earliest of these kings on numismatic and palaeographic considerations is Gomitra.[20] A consideration of coin types and a comparison of his coins with the Indo-Greek coins (which this early Mathura ruler might well be expected to copy) leads to an interesting observation. The so-called 'tree-in-railing' on the reverse of Gomitra's coins bears a remarkable resemblance to the Plates 80, 81 tripod-lebes on the coins of Apollodotus I. The similarity is too striking to be regarded as mere coincidence, especially as both emblems are contained within a dotted square. In addition, while the coins of all the other Mathura rulers are round, only those of Gomitra, like the tripod-lebes coins of Apollodotus are square, thus lending further support to this theory of derivation of coin types. This striking confrontation would suggest a *terminus a quo* of *c.* 150 BC for the early Mathura coins (arguing from the approximate date of Apollodotus I),[21] and the thirteen kings known to us may be placed between *c.* 150–50 BC. It has been suggested that these native rulers belonged to two dynasties, one of mitra kings and the other of datta kings.[22] The existence of two dynasties is certainly feasible as it allocates a reign of approximately fifteen years to each ruler, as opposed to barely eight years if there were a single line.

Our study of the Mathura local coin types very definitely suggests an early date for the introduction into India of the reed pen. Scholars, however, have long been of the opinion that this thickening of the tops of the letters owes its inspiration to the square omicron, and that inscriptions in which this feature occurs are definitely later than 40 BC, and more likely belong to the first century of the Christian era. 'One fact seems beyond question', says Rapson; 'the square forms of the Greek alphabet must surely owe their introduction into India to the Parthian influence which was so strong in approximately the 1st century A.D.'[23] The evidence from Mathura, however, quite definitely points to the existence of the reed pen in India as early as *c.* 100 BC, and denies any connection between the square omicron of Parthian coinage and the appearance of the reed pen in India. Once this is admitted a large number of inscriptions fall into place as there is no longer a compulsion, felt by Dani among others, to push them forward into the first century AD merely on the basis of their use of the reed pen. In this category are the Sanchi gateway inscriptions which we have seen to exhibit letter-forms appreciably earlier than those of the Mathura Kshatrapas. These may now be assigned without hesitation to *c.* 50–25 BC.

When the reed pen was first introduced it must have been used mainly on bark and palm leaves on which writing was of a normal size. While the script on coins may be considered to be somewhat smaller than normal, it is likely that the legends were written on the dies with the usual reed pen before being incised. On monumental stone inscriptions in which individual letters varied from two to six inches in size, the practice must have been slightly different. It is generally agreed, however, that the letters of an inscription were actually written on the stone by a *lipikāra* (writer) before being incised by a stone-cutter, and it is suggested that in Aśokan inscriptions a piece of charcoal or haemetite may have been used for this purpose.[24] Judging by the size of the letters on our early stone inscriptions, the normal reed pen could not have been used for the writing. However, the letter-forms that resulted from the use of the pen were faithfully imitated on the stone. Such imitation would not have occurred until the use of the reed pen was extremely common, and the new style of writing in which it resulted had become the accepted norm. This would explain why evidence of the use of the reed pen appears at a slightly earlier date on coins as compared to stone epigraphs.[25]

We have seen that the basic element in the change of style was the introduction of a new writing instrument – a reed pen. It is perhaps of significance that the pen in question is known in Sanskrit by the name *kalama*, found first in Greece as *kalamos*. The use of the reed pen was already widespread in the Greek and Levantine world by the first century BC and is attested as early perhaps as the third century BC.[26] The probable source for the new style of script evidenced in India on the Mathura coins as early as *c.* 100 BC is likely to have been through contact with the Greek dynasties of the north-west.

Ayodhya Inscription

The Ayodhya inscription of Dhanadeva – the so-called Śunga inscription – presents us with an anomaly. On palaeographic grounds there is no doubt that it must be placed in the first century AD: in fact, the forms of the letters are even more advanced than those of *Table 2* Śodāsa. The *ya* with its hooked left arm and the *na* with a curved base are both features absent in the inscriptions of Śodāsa and argue a date some decades later for this record. The anomaly becomes apparent when we turn to the contents, which can hardly be ignored.[27] We are told that Dhanadeva the lord of Kosala, sixth in descent from the general Pushyamitra who performed two horse sacrifices, caused the erection of a shrine to the memory of his father. According to generally accepted Śunga chronology, Pushyamitra ruled from *c.* 184–148 BC, and Dhanadeva, being sixth in descent from Pushyamitra (four generations between), would have to be placed at *c.* 68 BC. But on the palaeographic grounds we have noted above we would be inclined to assign the record to a date later than AD 15.

There seems to be but one possible explanation: the inscription in its present form must be a later copy of the original record. Perhaps the inscription was defaced or mutilated in some way, or just weathered and cracked, resulting in the necessity for a fresh copy. As the slab containing the inscription is incorporated in a modern shrine, it is not possible to find definite proof of such an occurrence. Two inscriptions from Khajuraho provide us with interesting evidence of a similar situation.[28] The Pārśvanātha temple at that site appears to have been built soon after the Lakshmana temple, the latter having been constructed by king Yaśovarman while his son and successor

Dhanga was responsible for the former. The two inscriptions giving us this information were both engraved in the reign of Dhanga and bear the same date – Vikrama era 1011. We are told that there is such a marked palaeographic difference between the two that one cannot but conclude that the inscription on the Pārśvanātha was a re-engraved copy of a lost original. It appears, in fact, to have been re-engraved after the lapse of more than a century.

It would be appropriate here to mention briefly the Pabhosa inscriptions which have been grouped by Dani with the Ayodhya record. In our opinion the Pabhosa records belong to an earlier phase. The script does not exhibit all the advanced forms to be seen in the inscriptions of Śoḍāsa, but various characteristics, including the marked angularity of the letters and the curved base of the *na* point to a date later than the Sanchi gateways. These records probably belong to the end of the first century BC.

Hathigumpha Inscription of Khāravela

Several attempts have been made to date the rather controversial Hathigumpha inscription on the basis of internal evidence. K. P. Jayaswal, for instance, was quite certain of his reading of line twelve as reporting the retreat of *Yavana Rāja Dimita* and his abandoning of Mathura, which is said to have occurred in the eighth year of Khāravela. He then identified Dimita with Demetrius, whose retreat to meet the challenge of his rival Eucratides is placed by scholars of Bactrian history at *c.* 175 BC. Khāravela's reign would then have begun in *c.* 183 BC and the inscription, engraved in the thirteenth year of his reign, would belong to *c.* 170 BC.[29] However, Jayaswal's reading of Dimita has been questioned by scholars and a close examination of published facsimile copies indicates, as B. M. Barua points out, that only the letter *mi* can be read with certainty.[30] Elsewhere, Barua suggested that the reading may be Hermaios,[31] but obviously this reading is equally questionable. Claims have also been made for readings of Maurya era 165, and for 103 or 300 years after Nanda, but these readings have likewise been questioned and rejected.

The Hathigumpha script seems definitely to belong to the same period as that on the east, south and west gateways of *stūpa* I at *Table 8* Sanchi. The rounded *ga* and *ta*, the butterfly variety of *cha* and the almost complete equalization of the verticals of *pa* all point to the same conclusion. In addition a thickening of the tops of certain letters like *ta* and *va* is particularly noticeable. Existing facsimile copies of this important inscription are rather unsatisfactory, but this is understandable as the inscription itself is much weatherworn and the last eight or ten lines are carved on a sloping surface. However, a study of the record from the stone itself reveals this thickening on other letters as well. There would appear to be little doubt that the inscription belongs to the same phase as the Sanchi gateways – to *c.* 50–25 BC. It may be argued that while discussing the letter-forms of this inscription and comparing it with Sanchi or the western caves, one must remember the vast geographical distances involved. However, the Aśokan edicts at Dhauli and the hoards of punch-marked coins found at Mayurbhanja and Sonepur in Orissa indicate that this area was not isolated from the rest of the country. The mention of a Sātakarni in the Hathigumpha inscription[32] certainly indicates the close contact of the Orissa region with other parts of the country. We are of the opinion that there is no evidence of marked regional tendencies of script (if we set aside the somewhat uncertain indications of the Bhattiprolu records) until some time in the first century AD. A fairly simultaneous development of script appears to have taken place all over the country during this early phase. We would therefore adhere to our conclusion that the Hathigumpha and Sanchi gateway inscriptions belong to the same phase, which is also in accordance with Dani's conclusions.[33]

Kushāna Records

The early Kushāna records provide us with a *terminus ad quem* for our study of the early phase of the inscriptions in northern India. The unmistakable forms of *sa* and *ma* (not to be found, however, in the Sarnath inscription of the year 3 of Kanishka), the *ya* in which the left hook meets the base, the distinctive conjunct form of *ya*, and the later forms of *ha*, *la* and medial *o* all provide a definite terminus. It is interesting to note that the Kushāna script was not uniform throughout the empire: the earlier forms of *ha*, *ma* and *sa* are to be found in the Sarnath inscription of Kanishka and on the Mat image of that ruler, while all the more advanced forms are to be seen at Mathura. By the time of the Mathura inscription of Huvishka in the year 33, we find a later form of *na* and also of initial *a*, and the *va* by now has no vertical and consists only of a triangular form with a small headmark. Optionally the early forms of *ma* and *sa* are found together with the more advanced variety. The date of the Kanishkan era is a

Table 2

43

vexed problem and the exact chronological position of these Kushāna records is uncertain. We would merely state that the distinctive letter forms of these records provide us with a *terminus ad quem* sometime within the range of fifty years between AD 78 and AD 128.

Inscriptions from the Early Buddhist Caves

In the course of our brief survey of early Indian palaeography we saw that changes and advances in script took place more or less simultaneously all over the country during the early period, with regional variations beginning to appear only in the first century of the Christian era. We shall see further in the course of this review that such variations may be sharply distinguished only around the middle of the second century A.D. This was presumably linked in some way with the changing function of script and inscription. During the early phase a fairly simultaneous and parallel development of script may be expected to have taken place between the Sanchi/Bharhut area and the western Deccan. We have very definite evidence of contact and travel between these areas: merchants and traders from Nasik and Karadh in the Deccan have left records of donations at the Bharhut *stūpa*; and at Sanchi we find a donation from the foreman of the artisans of king Sātakarni.[1] It would seem therefore that no more than ten years, if that, need be postulated between similar advances in script in these regions.

In this chapter we shall examine the cave inscriptions and distinguish the various groups into which they fall palaeographically. We shall at the same time consider them in the context of early Indian palaeography as a whole, and see how they compare with and correspond to the chronological framework we have already established. The relative sequence emerging from this analysis of script will greatly aid us in defining the chronology of the early Buddhist caves, and at a later stage we shall compare with this the developmental stages resulting from an architectural and sculptural study. The exact location of some of the more important records, as well as a brief indication of their contents, may be found on Table 9. We would like to reiterate at this point that the dates suggested for various groups of inscriptions must not be upheld too rigidly, and that the period of *c.* 50–30 B C may certainly be extended by ten years either way.

Buddhist Caves: Series I (a)

The first group of inscriptions from the early Buddhist caves
Table 4 comprises the following epigraphs: Nasik 1; Bhaja 1, as well as the
recently discovered inscriptions on wood from the Bhaja *caitya*;
Pitalkhora 1, 2, and record A; the Kondane inscription; Ajanta 1 and
the two new Ajanta inscriptions. These are all short votive inscriptions merely recording the name of the donor and the town to which
he belongs. Palaeographic considerations leave little doubt that they
belong together. The records exhibit an angular *ga* and *ta*, a very early
form of *da*, and an invariably straight *ra*. There is no attempt towards
the equalization of the verticals of any of the letters (with the
exception of the cursive *ha* in the new rock inscription from Ajanta).
An examination of these inscriptions, in the context of the palaeographic sequence established in the last chapter, reveals characteristics
that would place them considerably earlier than the records on the
gateways of Sanchi *stūpa* I. They belong, in fact, to the period of the
cf. Table 1 railings of *stūpas* I and II at Sanchi, and appear to be earlier than the
Bharhut Dhanabhūtī inscription that we have assigned to *c.* 80 BC.
Later characteristics of the Bharhut inscription, as compared to these
from the Buddhist caves, include the rounded *ga* and a definite tendency towards the equalization of the verticals of *pa*. Bearing in mind
the several points we have already discussed in connection with the
dating of the Bharhut record, and our caution regarding the chronological application of such comparisons to the western caves, we
would perhaps be justified in placing this early group at *c.* 90–80 BC.

Most of the records of this Series are engraved in the *caityas* at each
site. The inscriptions on wood from Bhaja come from beams
spanning the vault of the *caitya*,[2] while Bhaja 1 comes from a *vihāra*.
The Kondane record is engraved on the façade of the *caitya*, and
inscriptions 1 and 2 from Pitalkhora are engraved on pillars within
caitya III. Pitalkhora A is inscribed on the hand of the dwarf-*yaksha*
figure discovered in recent clearance at the site. Ajanta 1 is engraved
on the façade of *caitya* X, while the new rock inscription is to be found
on the wall of the left aisle. This record was uncovered beneath a
layer of mud plaster and would seem to indicate that the murals were
not part of the original plan of the *caitya*.[3] However, the new painted
record discovered at the same time suggests that there was not much
difference in actual time between the completion of the cave and the
adding of the murals. This record, though faint and much weathered,
displays an early *pa* with no attempt at equalization of verticals, as

also an early angular form of *ta*. Nasik record 1 comes from the tiny *vihāra* XIX located beside the *caitya*. Palaeography provides us with a date of *c.* 90–80 BC for the *caityas* at Bhaja, Kondane, Pitalkhora III and Ajanta X. It is possible that some of these inscriptions were engraved before the completion of the caves. Confirmation of such a practice comes from two *caityas* at Junnar belonging to a much later phase: these have donatory inscriptions on their façades while the interiors remain unfinished.[4] We would, it seems, be justified in assuming that the period *c.* 100–70 BC would cover the construction of these early *caityas*.

This set of inscriptions is also of especial interest from the point of view of Sātavāhana chronology. Nasik 1 tells us that the cave in which it is engraved was excavated during the reign of king Kanha of the Sātavāhana family. We have seen in the course of our historical survey that this record, combined with the information provided by the Nanaghat inscriptions, gives us proof of the historicity of the purāṇic accounts regarding the first three rulers of the dynasty.[5] These records inform us that Simuka Sātavāhana, the founder, ruled for twenty-three years and was followed by his brother Kanha, who in turn was succeeded by Sātakarni I. As the Nasik inscription of the second ruler of the dynasty is to be placed at *c.* 90–80 BC, we would, on palaeographic grounds, assign the start of the Sātavāhana dynasty to the end of the second century BC – around 120/110 BC.

Buddhist Caves: Series I (b)

We have next an equally significant group comprising the inscriptions from Nanaghat; Bhaja 2–6; Nasik 2 and 3; the two known records from Nadsur; and inscriptions 2 and 14 from Ajanta. Apart from the Nanaghat inscriptions, the others are brief and record donations, giving once again the name of the donor and the town to which he belongs. We find in this group a definitely rounded *ga*, and *Table 4* a *ta* which is not quite angular but shows a tendency towards curvature. A distinct development is to be seen in the equalization of the verticals of *pa*, though only a tendency towards this is to be seen in the case of *sa*, *ha* and *la*. The form of *cha* is still that of an oval with a vertical through it, and has not yet reached the double-looped Sanchi gateway variety. These characteristics accord very well with the Bhilsa pillar inscriptions and with the records on the north gateway *cf. Table 2* at Sanchi, that we have dated to *c.* 70–60 BC. The present group of inscriptions may be assigned to the same phase.[6]

Inscriptions 2 and 3, engraved on the façade of the Nasik *caitya*, should not lead one to conclude that the cave was completed during this phase, as records belonging to a later period are engraved on pillars of the interior. These inscriptions merely provide us with a date at which work on the cave had already begun. The Ajanta painted inscription (No. 14) which belongs to this group, seems to be associated with some of the murals in *caitya* X. We shall examine the exact location of the various Ajanta inscriptions and their relation to the painted scenes in a later chapter. Ajanta 2 is engraved beside the doorway of a cell in *vihāra* XII. Bhaja 2–6 are inscribed on the series of rock-cut *stūpas* standing along the rock-face a short distance from the *caitya*.

Buddhist Caves: Series I (c)

Our third group is not separated from the previous one by any great length of time, and consists of the inscriptions in the caves at Bedsa and records 3–7 at Pitalkhora. They may, however, be assigned to a slightly later phase as they exhibit certain advanced features. A *Table 4* distinct change is to be seen in the form of *cha* which is now of the butterfly variety. The *ta* is definitely rounded and a tendency towards the later *bha* is to be seen. The *va* and the lower half of the *ma* are distinctly triangular, and complete equalization of the verticals of *ha* *cf. Table 2* has been achieved. The group compares closely with the Sanchi gateway records and may with some confidence be assigned to *c.* 50–40 BC.

Buddhist Caves: Series I (d)

We have finally the isolated Nasik inscription of Hakusiri (No. 4), which is quite definitely later than the group we have just con-*Table 4* sidered. The *ga* and *ta* are so rounded as almost to have a flat top, while the *bha* rises to a peak at the centre where its vertical is located. A tendency towards the equalization of the arms of *ya* is to be seen, and we have a unique triangular form of *va*. This inscription is engraved on two pillars within the *caitya*, and records the completion of the cave by Bhaṭapālikā, grand-daughter of Mahāhakusiri. In view of the rather unusual name, it seems likely that this Hakusiri is the same as the one mentioned in the Nanaghat record.[7] It is evident that two generations have intervened between the mention of prince Hakusiri in the Nanaghat cave and of his grand-daughter in the Nasik inscription. This length of time would also be needed to explain the

1, 2. Entrance to the Lomasa Rishi cave in the Barabar hills of Bihar. Note the sloping door jambs and the stone beam ends, which indicate its having been modelled on structural architecture in wood, thatch and bamboo. *Above*, detail of the elephant-and-*makara* panel on the façade.

3, 4 The ceiling and façade of the Guntupalli *caitya* in the Krishna basin. The ceiling (*opposite, above*) depicts curved stone ribs meeting in the apex of the circular chamber. It is possible that this ceiling itself served as a *chatra* for the *stūpa* below. Note the representation of beam ends on the façade (*opposite, below*).

5 *Below*, the inner circular chamber of the Kondivte *caitya*. The sculptural decoration on the right wall of the main chamber is a later addition.

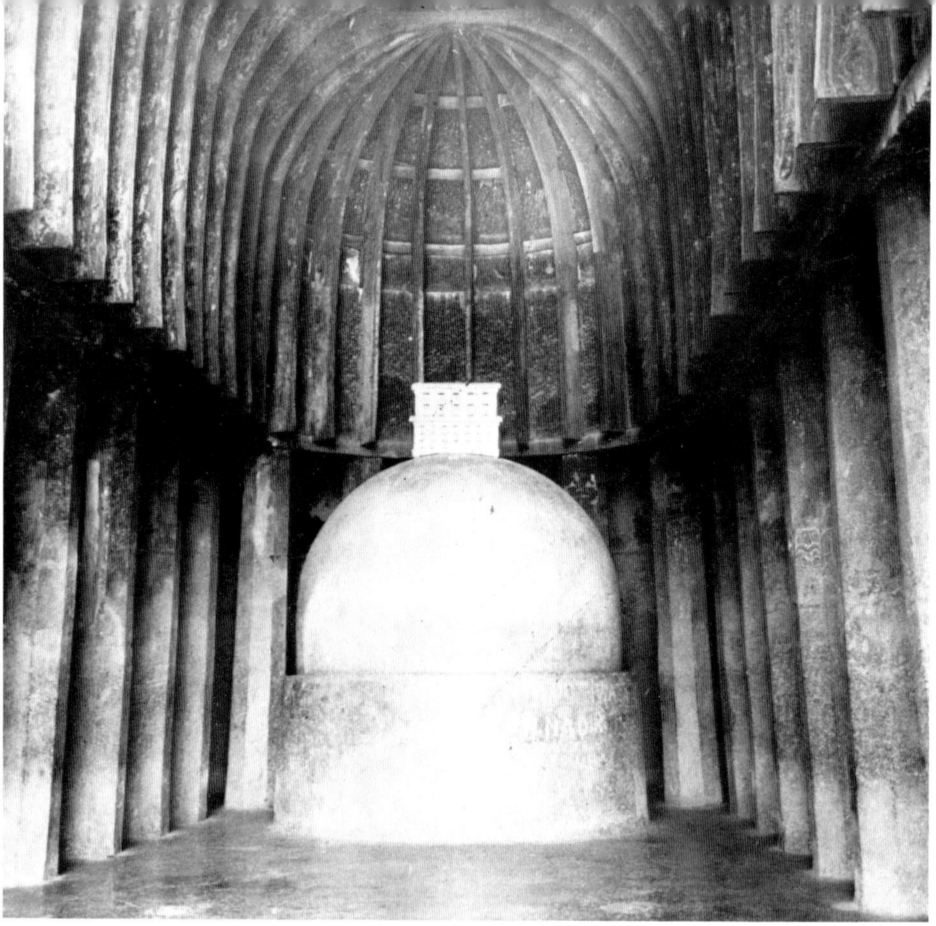
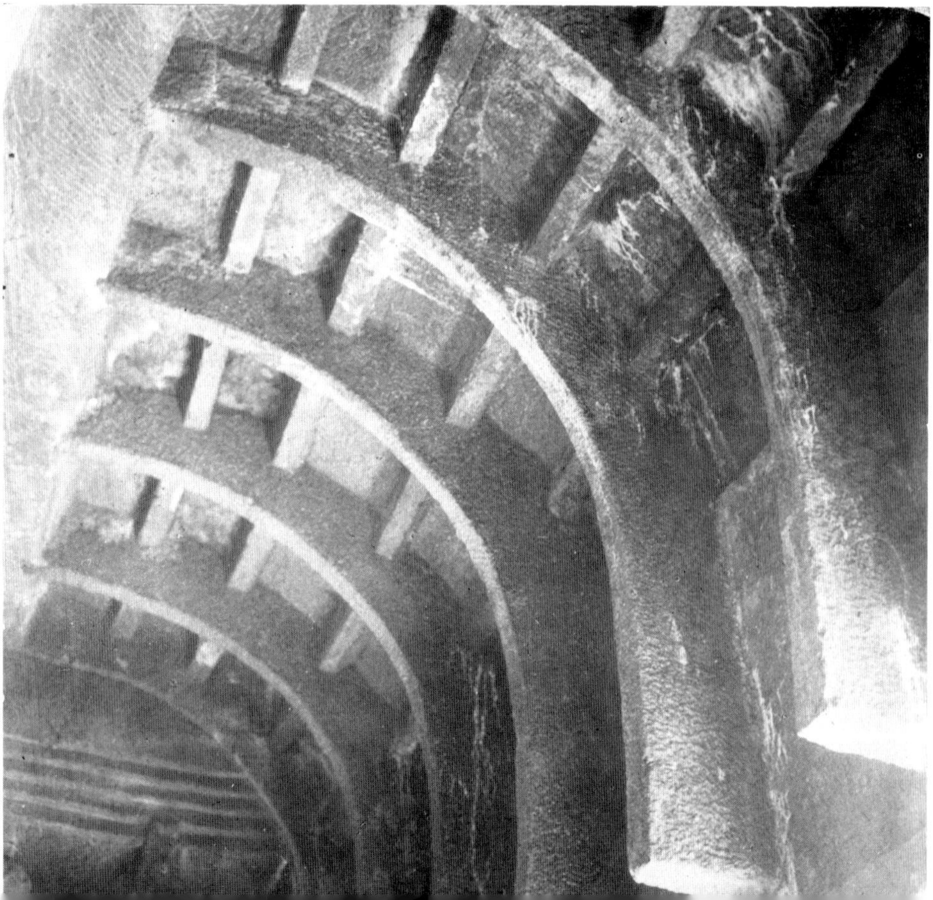

6–8 The Bhaja *caitya* and *vihāra* XIX. *Opposite, above,* interior of the Bhaja *caitya* with the *stūpa* at the far end of the nave. Note the rake of the pillars towards their upper end. *Above,* a general view. The wooden ribs in the ceiling of the nave are clearly visible. The decoration of the façade is in imitation of the frontage of a structural building. *Opposite, below,* the half-arched ceiling of the veranda of *vihāra* XIX. The stone ribs and rafters clearly indicate an imitation of wooden construction.

9–11 Guardians carved in shallow relief in the veranda of *vihāra* XIX at Bhaja. The figures are richly decorated, wear elaborate turbans and carry various weapons including the spear and bow and arrows. Note the *fleur-de-lis* armlet worn by the guardians, and the great attention paid to surface detail in the drapery of their garments, the tapestry of their head-dresses, and the details of their ornaments. The emphasis is on the frontal presentation of the human figure with both shoulders clearly visible, although the guardian of Plate 11, for example, is undoubtedly intended to be in 'profile'.

12, 13 Guardians carved in the interior of *vihāra* XIX at Bhaja. These figures are in almost complete darkness and can be seen only with the aid of a torch. Though not of the warrior category, they seem to be intended as guardians nevertheless.

14 The central horse-and-rider figure from the narrow relief panel on the left wall of the veranda of *vihāra* XIX at Bhaja. This would appear to be one of the earliest known examples in which stirrups are depicted. Note, once again, the insistence on the frontal presentation of the rider.

15 Bas-relief of a couple standing on a fish from *vihāra* XV at Nadsur. Lithograph from *A.S.W.I. XII.*

16 The centaur pilaster in the left corner of the veranda of *vihāra* XIX at Bhaja. The animal bodies are addorsed and show one male and one female figure.

17, 18 Gajalakshmī reliefs from within the arch above the cell doorways of *vihāra* VII at Nadsur. The figure of Lakshmī is rather clumsily depicted.

19 The interior of Pitalkhora *caitya* III showing the remnants of the drum of the *stūpa*. Several of the pillars are the result of restoration work done by the Archaeological Survey of India. Some of the original ones, decorated with murals, may be seen.

20 The guardian *yaksha* of *caitya* III at Pitalkhora. The piece, intact down to the knees only, measures over 5 feet, and when complete must have been well over life-size.

21, 22 *Above*, the dwarf-*yaksha* found in front of *caitya* III at Pitalkhora. *Below*, the much-damaged elephant plinth in front of *vihāra* IV. Originally a mahout stood between the forelegs of each elephant. Restoration by the Archaeological Survey of India is in progress.

23, 24 Details of the doorway to the left of the elephant plinth. Steps lead up to the level of *vihāra* IV. The guardians (*above*) wear a rather unusual fringed tunic and carry javelins. The elephants above the guardians form part of the Gajalakshmī scene *below*.

25–30 Pitalkhora. Addorsed winged animal pilasters (*above and left*) along the back wall of *vihāra* IV. The 'bell' capital resembles, in one instance, a row of reeds, and, in the other, a block draped with tapestry. The animals depicted within the ribs of the arch above the cell doorways, appear to include a *makara*. It will be seen above that the *caitya* arch is not placed centrally over the doorways. The apex coincides instead within the centre of the unique arched roof within. *Opposite, above left*, bas-relief of the scene of the Buddha leaving home. Note the absence of the human form of the Buddha, whose presence is indicated by the umbrella held over the horse. *Opposite, above right*, the Royal Couple. Note the great attention paid to the surface details – the beads of the ornaments and the tapestry of the head-dresses. *Opposite, below*, *Mithunas*, or loving couples.

31, 32 Dancing figures from the façade of the Kondane *caitya*. The panels are on a level with the springing of the *caitya* arch. Here the emphasis is on the essential planes of the body and not on surface decoration.

33 Damaged *yaksha* head from the lower part of the façade of the Kondane *caitya*. The figure, when intact, would have been more than life-size.

difference in script between them, and we would place the record around 25 BC.

The Nasik inscriptions provide us with interesting information regarding the duration of excavation of the *caitya*. Inscriptions 2 and 3 indicate that construction had begun around 70–60 BC, while the Hakusiri record mentioning its completion may be assigned to *c.* 25 BC. Although it is one of the smallest among the apsidal *caityas* in western India, it appears to be the product of half-hearted efforts. One explanation, perhaps, lies in the absence of the royal patronage that is so apparent in some of the later caves at the site.

Buddhist Caves: Series II

After this phase of intense activity evident from the many inscriptions at the various cave sites, there appears to have been a sudden lull, if one may judge from the absence of such records. For a period of seventy-five years, and perhaps slightly longer, no new inscriptions were engraved. When such epigraphs reappear they come from a site that has not been on the scene so far – Karle.

There are a number of inscriptions in the Karle *caitya*, many of which were probably engraved while the cave was still being excavated. Among these are the following three which may be taken as representative of the entire early Karle group: the inscription of the merchant Bhūtapāla from Vejayanti reporting the completion of the *selaghara*;[8] of Indradeva, mentioning the donation of the *vedikā*-band and the elephants in the veranda; and of the general Agnimitra, recounting the erection of the lion pillar outside the *caitya*. These inscriptions (Nos 1–3) possess certain common characteristics that *Table 5* distinguish them from records of previous date. There is, in general, a marked angularity of all the letters, particularly of the *pa*, *ha* and *la*, accompanied by an occasional thickening or head to the tops of the verticals. A tendency towards the notched variety of *bha*, a lengthening of the vertical of *ka*, and a complete equalization of the verticals of the *sa* are apparent. A comparison with the Nasik Hakusiri record and with the inscriptions of Nahapāna reveals that these Karle records are definitely more advanced than the Hakusiri script, but do not yet exhibit the later features of the Nahapāna records. They are, however, closer to the latter, and we would suggest a date around AD 50–70 for this group. It will be seen that, in this instance, palaeography cannot provide us with entirely satisfactory or specific evidence.

We must here pause to consider three radiocarbon dates for Karle. Calculations were made from a wooden pin,[9] and from portions of the wooden ribbing of the *caitya* ceiling,[10] and the resulting dates of 290 ± 150 BC, 230 ± 95 BC, and 125 ± 100 BC were announced. It appears to us that historical and palaeographic evidence denies the possibility of such dates, and we shall discuss the matter briefly in Appendix 2 (p. 189). We cannot agree with D. D. Kosambi that 'the foundation [of the Karle caitya] is dated by radiocarbon to a pre-Asokan epoch' and that 'the first cells of the monastery, now collapsed, must have been carved out a hundred years earlier'.[11]

Belonging also to Series II is an inscription (No. 7) from the Budh Lena *caitya* at Junnar, recording the donation of its unusual sculptured façade. The inscription is contained in the central flat surface of the half-lotus above the entrance, while the interior remains unfinished.

Buddhist Caves: Series III

Table 5

The group of inscriptions belonging to Nahapāna at Karle, Nasik and Junnar follow soon after. A detailed comparison of those from Nasik and Karle leads to an interesting observation. There seems little doubt that at Nasik we have a more developed script. The marked angularity of the letters, the notched variety of *bha*, and the *na* written in a single flourish are indicative of this. One explanation of this phenomenon may perhaps be found by assigning the single, undated inscription at Karle to an early year of Nahapāna's reign. His records at Nasik (all in *vihāra* X) mention the years 41, 42 and 45. If this possibility is rejected, then we are faced with individual differences, perhaps from monastery to monastery.

The script of the epigraphs of Gautamīputra Sātakarni at Nasik and Karle does not reveal any major variations when compared with the Nahapāna records which preceded them. This is not surprising as a period of about ten years at the most may be said to separate them. The main advance is to be seen in the base of the *na* which is invariably curved or arched, and in the common occurrence of the notched *bha*. A comparison of the Nasik and Karle inscriptions of Gautamīputra reveals, as in the case of Nahapāna, a more advanced script at Nasik. The lower ends of the verticals of *ka* and *ra* are slightly curved – a feature not to be found at Karle. Admittedly the single Karle record[12] is dated in the year 14 and is earlier than the Nasik records (all in *vihāra* III) which are dated in the years 18 to 24. But the difference in date is not enough to justify such an explanation for the variations in script.

Inscriptions 14–22 and 28–31 in the caves at Kuda appear to belong to the same phase, while the remaining records at the site are of a later date. The light curve of the lower ends of the verticals with occasional straight examples, a very simple form of *ya*, a straight-based *na* and *ṇa*, and an early form of *da* would incline us to group these records with those of Series III. This set of inscriptions has none of the flourishes characteristic of the later group at the same site.

An inscription from Lenyadri *caitya* VI at Junnar (No. 30) recounting the gift of the completed *caitya*, also belongs to Series III. The letters display a tentative curve of the lower ends of the verticals. Inscriptions 27 and 28, to be found above two cisterns in the Lenyadri caves, may be included in this group. Other records of Series III include inscription 1 at Mahad (in *caitya* VIII), and the records in certain *vihāras* of the Amba/Ambika group at Junnar.

Buddhist Caves: Series IV

Definite advances in script are to be seen with the inscriptions of *Tables 5–7* Pulumāvi. The lower ends of the verticals of *ka* and *ra* are invariably curved, and in the case of *jha* and *ña* optionally so. The left arm of *gha* sometimes curved inwards, while *dha* is no longer a strictly inverted-D shaped letter, but is often very cursively written. Equalization of the arms of *ya* is almost complete. It is perhaps the form of *ta* that is most interesting; the letter is often formed in one stroke and this results in a new hooked variety. Strangely enough, this development is not to be found at Nasik, where the elaborate flourishes of the medial *i* and *u*, to be seen at Karle, are also absent. It is at Karle that the triangular part of *kha* assumes great importance, with the hook playing a secondary role. These factors seem to indicate that during the reign of Pulumāvi, it was Karle and not Nasik that had the more advanced script, thus apparently reversing the trend observed during the previous period. It is not possible to maintain that the inscriptions at the one site are earlier than those at the other as the records at both Karle and Nasik cover a whole range of years. Neither can regional differences provide the solution as the more advanced script is not found consistently at one site. Differences from one monastery to the other, or even from scribe to scribe, seems to be indicated.

A record of the time of Pulumāvi has also been found at Amaravati. Although fragmentary, enough of it remains to show that the style is akin to that at Karle, with a marked curve of the lower ends of the verticals. Another fragmentary inscription from Amaravati, of a king Śivamaka Sada, reveals a similar script. The identification of this ruler with Śivaskanda Sātakarni, second in succession after Pulumāvi, seems convincing. In Series IV we may include also the Kanheri record of Vāsishtīputra Siri Sātakarni.

The inscription recounting the donation of Shivneri *caitya* XLVIII (No. 4), and the records in the remaining caves of the Shivneri group belong to this phase. The curved lower ends of the verticals and the distinctive *ya, ma* and *ta* leave little doubt on this score. The records in the Amba/Ambika *caitya* at Junnar (Nos 9–19) and in the rectangular flat-roofed *caitya* XV at Lenyadri (No. 29), may also be assigned to this group. An inscription at Nanaghat (No. 9) reporting the gift of a cistern, and record 2 in a *vihāra* at Mahad may be included in this same period. We have also a set of some eight inscriptions at Nasik (Nos 17–24), all recounting donations from private individuals. An isolated inscription from Bhaja (No. 7) belongs to Series IV and provides information regarding the continued occupation of the site. The two known records from Shelarvadi may also be included in this group: deciding factors include the curved lower ends of the verticals, the curved base of *na*, and the hooked variety of *ta*.

Records C, D and E from the *vihāra* at Ambivale display a definite curve of the lower ends of the verticals and a flourish of the medials, and may be assigned to Series IV. Record A has a rather tentative curve of the lower end of the vertical of *ka* and may perhaps be included in Series III, while record B may be still earlier. In view of the fact that these latter records consist of a few letters only, now much weathered, and that none of the inscriptions seem to be in the usual Pali, it is feasible that all the records are of Series IV.

An analysis of inscriptions 1–13 and 23–27 at Kuda indicates that these records probably belong towards the end of Series IV. The curved lower ends of the verticals, the *ya* with equalized arms, the notched variety of *bha*, the incurving almost notched left vertical of *pa, ha* and *ba*, and the very cursive forms of *dha* are all indicative of its late date. The flourishes given to the medial *i* and *u* in this set of inscriptions are, however, quite extraordinary: in fact, the form of medial *i* may be described as unique. But this feature may again be the result of individual idiosyncrasy. The inscriptions in the important *caitya* VI are to be assigned to this group.

Andhau and Girnar Inscriptions

In order to complete the picture we shall consider briefly the Andhau and Girnar inscriptions from Kutch and Saurashtra, which may be *Table 7* said to be roughly contemporary with Series IV. The Andhau record of Cashṭana and Rudradāman as joint rulers is dated in the year 52 of the Śaka era, and thus belongs to AD 130. In addition to a noticeable angularity of all letters, there also occurs a tentative curving of the lower ends of the verticals of *ka* and *ra*, as well as a curved base for *na* and *ṇa*. We notice that the script is not as advanced as that of Pulumāvi. Since Ptolemy tells us of the contemporaneity of Cashṭana and Pulumāvi, regional and perhaps dynastic variations of script appear to be the explanation.

The Girnar epigraph of Rudradāman of the year AD 150 is the next important inscription in this area, and furnishes us with a number of new and advanced features. The triangular base of *kha* is all-important, the hook having almost disappeared; the *bha* is always of the notched variety; the left vertical of *pa* and *ba* is often notched inwards; the *ya* is not only very angular but has its left arm curved inwards towards the base; and the lower half of *ma* is markedly triangular. An interesting feature of the letters is that the tops of the verticals have a definite head-mark which is quite independent of the use of a reed pen. In later periods, this was to develop into the horizontal from which the letter depended, but, as yet, this development is only in its initial stage.

Buddhist Caves : Series V

Our final group includes the inscriptions of Yajñaśrī Sātakarni, the record of Mādharīputra Śakasena at Kanheri, of Ābhīra Iśvarasena at Nasik, and the Myakadoni inscription of Pulumāvi, the last Sātavāhana ruler. These records reveal that the line head-mark was *Table 7* becoming important; the form of *da* is advanced; the left arm of *ya* acquired a very distinct hook; and the base of *na* is so arched as to resemble the Aśokan form of *ta* in some instances. At Myakadoni we find ornate flourishes of *ka*, *ra* and medial *i*. No startling changes in script are to be seen between Series IV and V. With the script of Pulumāvi, a standard seems to have been reached in the area of the western caves, with relatively minor changes to follow. It is in the Krishna basin that the script continued to develop with major innovations.

Regional/Dynastic Scripts

We have seen that no regional variations may be discerned in the script of Aśoka, and that it is not until the beginning of the Christian era that such differences begin to make themselves felt. During the first two centuries AD we encounter a new phenomenon which involves our considering two simultaneous aspects. While it is possible to determine overall stages of scriptual development, we are now able to discern not only wider regional variations of style, but more specifically local variations due apparently to individual hands. Such variations may be recognized, for example, between Nasik, Karle and Kuda. Our study, however, leaves us in no doubt of the broader stylistic trends that were in evidence throughout the whole province, and which, even in the absence of dynastic dated inscriptions, enables us to discuss palaeographic synchronisms.

It emerges from this study that it is necessary to recognize the development of local as well as chronological differences in the script of the second century AD. It is further probable that these regional styles were associated with the scriptoria of royal courts, and therefore the scripts may be known by the names of the dynasties with which they were connected. Thus, by about AD 150 we can clearly discern the emergence of four distinct regional or dynastic styles.

1 The northern/Kushāna script with its unique forms of *ma, sa, ha, la* and conjunct *ya*, which does not intrude into the western caves area.

2 The western/Satrap script, restricted at first to Gujarat, but slowly merging with and influencing the Deccan script.

3 The Deccan/Sātavāhana script, best exemplified by the records of the time of Pulumāvi.

4 The southern/Amaravati style. In AD 150 this area was still under Sātavāhana control, and it is only later, under Ikshvāku rule that the script severed connections with that of the Deccan. However, its flamboyant tendencies already anticipate its later development.

To realize the necessity of recognizing these regional-cum-dynastic scripts, one has but to compare the Kushāna epigraphs with contemporary Sātavāhana records. Such a comparison reveals that each script has developed along different lines with its own peculiarities. Variations in script can thus be sharply distinguished only in the second century of the Christian era. Dynastic and regional specialization implies a script in its maturity, while in the three preceding centuries this maturity had not yet been achieved.

4

Architectural Development

The early rock-cut caves of western India, excavated into the hills and valleys of the western ghats, are all Buddhist monasteries. Each site consists of one or more *caityas* – chapels for congregational worship – and several *vihāras* which were residential halls for the monks. The statement that some of these cave sites served 'also as summer retreats and places of amusement where the young rich enjoyed the dances and favours of courtesans'[1] is quite misleading. Every cave in western India was part of a monastic establishment inhabited solely by monks.

The *caitya* was the Buddhist hall of worship and its basic architectural form and character was necessarily determined by its religious functions. The earliest rock-cut *caityas* – the Sudama and Lomasa Rishi caves in the Barabar hills of Bihar – were excavated around 250 BC, during the time of the Mauryan ruler Aśoka. Buddhist ritual had already been formulated to the stage at which the basic architectural nature of the *caitya* had been decided. The Aśokan *caityas* consist of a rectangular chamber in which worshippers *Fig. 2* could congregate, and a small circular room beyond, with a domed roof. The form of the inner chamber was decided by the object of worship that it was to house – the *stūpa*. This consisted of a low circular base, the drum, surmounted by a dome known as the *aṇḍa*. Above this was a small parapet-like structure known as the *harmikā*, and from this rose an umbrella (*chatra*) on a mast (*yashṭi*). The *stūpa*, which became a symbol of the Buddha himself, was a funerary mound containing relics of the Buddha or of one of his followers. In the early days of Buddhism, before the deification of its founder, the Buddha was always represented by an emblem, most often the *stūpa*. In both the Aśokan *caityas* the inner chamber is quite empty. It is possible that the empty circular chamber itself, involving a sophisticated conception of space and emptiness, may have served the purpose. It seems more likely, however, that a structural *stūpa* of some sort occupied the chamber.

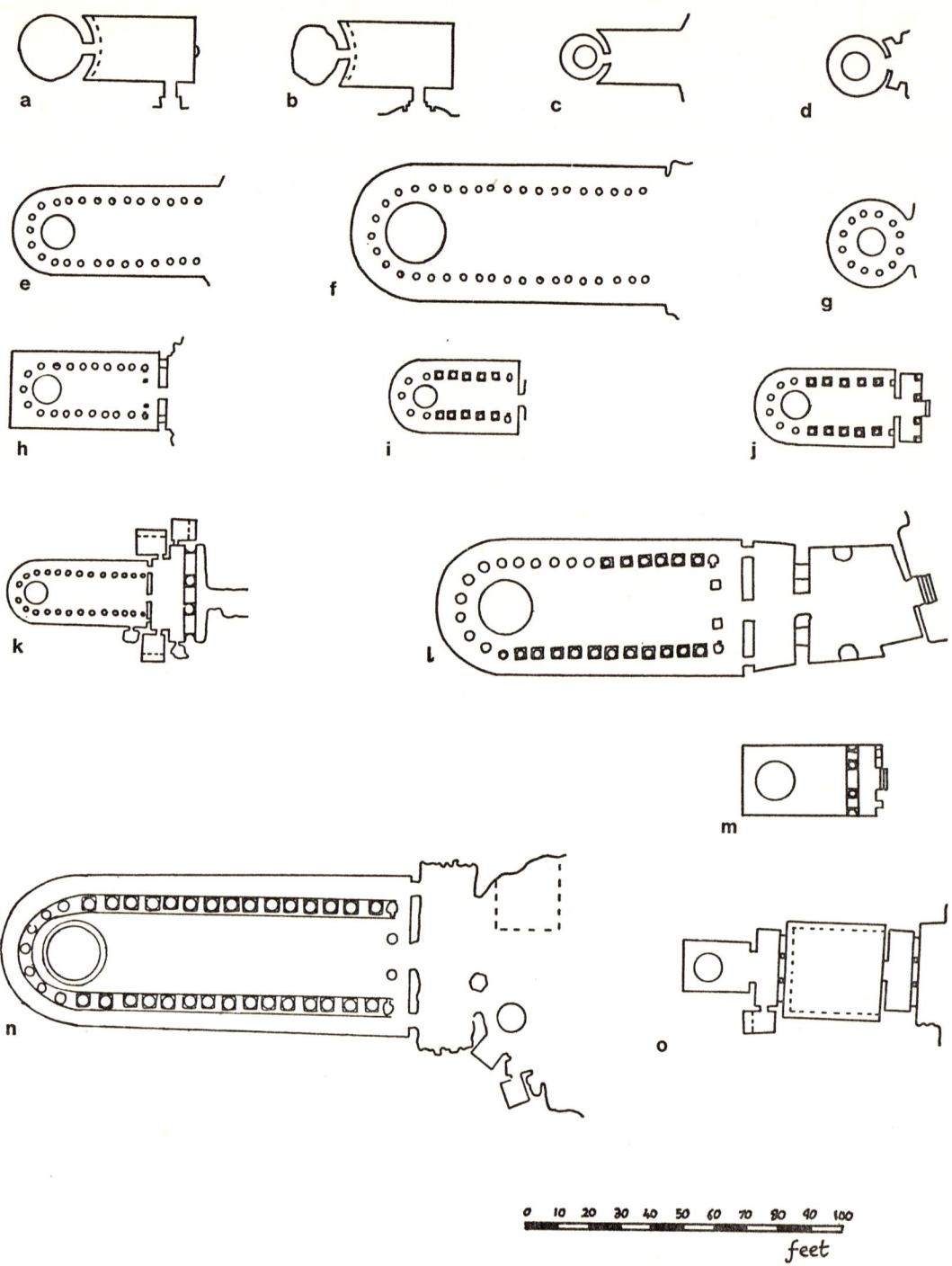

2 Caitya *floor plans:* a *Sudama;* b *Lomasa Rishi;* c *Kondivte;* d *Guntupalli;* e *Bhaja;* f *Ajanta X;* g *Tulja;* h *Ajanta IX:* i *Nasik;* j *Lenyadri;* k *Bedsa;* l *Kanheri;* m *Shivheri;* n *Karle;* o *Kuda VI*

These early *caityas* are cut parallel to the rock-face with access through the side of the rectangular chamber. While the entrance to the Sudama cave is a plain narrow doorway, the Lomasa Rishi Plates, 1, 2 entrance is dominated by a horseshoe-shaped arch around the doorway. This is undoubtedly the prototype of the *caitya* window that dominates the façade of the apsidal *caityas* of western India. Between the top of the doorway and the apex of the arch is an elegant frieze of elephants and *makaras*, and above this is a lattice-work panel.[2] These rock-cut *caityas* closely followed and modelled themselves on the technique of structural architecture in wood, thatch and bamboo. The roof of the inner chamber of the Sudama cave projects beyond its walls as in a thatched structure. Indeed, an identical practice may been seen even today in the thatched huts of the area. The faint incised lines running down the outer walls of this chamber seem to indicate an attempt to depict wooden planking. The marked slope of the door jambs was certainly in imitation of wooden construction where such an arrangement would have contributed to greater stability. In addition, the Lomasa Rishi arch terminates in a definite finial which appears to be an imitation of the pottery finial which would have topped a structural monument. The arch also reveals in stone an exact representation of the ends of beams that would have supported the roof in a wooden structure and underlines the reliance on wooden prototypes.

With the increase in architectural sophistication and in the technique of rock-cutting, it became apparent that if the *caitya* were excavated perpendicular to the rock-face, the result would be more effective. The worshipper would face the doorway of the inner chamber on entering and would get a glimpse of the *stūpa* within. Light from outside would also fall directly onto the object of worship. The introduction of the rock-cut *stūpa* and the practice of excavating directly into the mountain face led to the realization of the superfluity of the circular chamber. The architects retained its shape but removed the walls, thus arriving at an apsidal-ended structure with a fully visible rock-cut *stūpa* at the far end. With the further development of Buddhist ritual it became necessary to introduce a path for circumambulation. This led to the cutting of *caityas* with a row of pillars that followed the apsidal plan of the cave around the *stūpa*, dividing the interior into a central nave and narrow side aisles for circumambulation. This is the plan of the typical early *caitya* of western India.

It is quite evident then that we must invoke Indian rather than foreign sources for the origin of the elements of the *caitya* form. The similarity of its plan to that of the Roman basilica has been remarked upon, but the resemblance is quite fortuitous. We would completely disallow any validity to the statement that 'foreign influence alone can explain why it is that the plan of these Caitya bears such a resemblance to the early Christian church.'³ As we have seen, the *caitya* plan evolved quite naturally from the requirements of Buddhist ceremonial.

Somewhere in the course of the evolution from the Aśokan caves to the typical western *caitya*, is to be placed a rock-cut monastery at

Fig. 2 Guntupalli in the Krishna basin. The Guntupalli *caitya* consists solely of a small circular chamber containing a rock-cut *stūpa* in the centre.

Plate 3 An intriguing feature is its domed roof with curved stone ribs meeting in the apex and rather resembling an umbrella frame. Perhaps the *stūpa* was originally connected to the apex with a rock-cut *yashti*, and this strange ribbing itself served the purpose of a *chatra*.

Plate 4 The entrance doorway displays a *caitya* arch above it. While basically similar to that on the Lomasa Rishi, this arch no longer has a definite finial ornament. In further contrast to the Lomasa Rishi, the lower outer ends of the arch reveal a tendency towards an outward curve. The beam ends which would support the roof in a structural example are here again represented in stone. This last feature is one that continues throughout the development of *caitya* architecture, although, at a later stage, the beam ends are often treated as a decorative feature. The Guntupalli *caitya* may be placed at a stage distinctly earlier than the typical apsidal pillared *caitya* of western India.

The architectural form of the *vihāra* was very simple, as befitted a residential hall for monks. The basic requirement was a cell containing a raised rock-cut bed and sometimes a rock-cut pillow. A little niche in the wall near the pillow seems to have been used for a lamp. Apart from this the cell was quite bare. These cells were usually grouped around a central hall, with an open veranda in front. It has been suggested that there was an evolutionary series from single cells or rows of cells to this quadrangular form.⁴ Two ruined *vihāras* at Guntupalli seem to provide evidence of the earlier stage, as both reveal a row of cells with a miniature *caitya* arch above the narrow doorways. However, there is not much further evidence in rock architecture of such an evolutionary series, although this development could perhaps have taken place in structural building. The earliest *vihāras* in the western caves display the standard quadrangular form and a typical example consists of a narrow pillared veranda, leading into a small square hall with cells opening out from its sides.

Analysis of Architectural Elements

Since the publication of *The Cave Temples of India* in 1880, subsequent scholars have generally based their schemes on Burgess' conclusions and are agreed upon a rough sequence of excavation for the early Buddhist caves in western India. It is commonly accepted that a period of four hundred years between 200 BC and AD 200 would cover their excavation, and that the *caityas* at Bhaja, Kondane and Pitalkhora are among the earliest, while Karle and Kanheri belong to a later stage. There is, however, a considerable divergence of opinion on the matter of absolute dates. Some scholars, following Burgess, place the entire group with the exception of Kanheri in the two centuries immediately preceding the Christian era,[5] while others place the earliest of the caves around 50 BC.[6] Burgess' dating rested mainly on his opinion that Bhaja, which he considered to be the earliest of the western caves, closely resembled the Lomasa Rishi cave at Barabar. He hence placed it at *c.* 200 BC, some fifty years later than the Lomasa Rishi, and concluded that the various developments to be seen by the time of the Karle *caitya* must incorporate some two hundred years of experience. The principal writer to reinterpret Burgess' account was Percy Brown who elaborated on the grounds for such a conclusion.[7] His criteria included the extent to which wooden construction was copied, the shape of the *caitya* arch, the elongation of the *stūpa*, the elaboration of the façade, and the actual replacement of wood by stone in the construction of the caves. His admirable account has formed the basis for further writing on the subject, and though scholars may question his absolute chronology, they agree generally on his relative sequence.

There have since been two contrasting attitudes towards dating the caves on the basis of architectural details. One scholar remarks that we may well despair of obtaining a sequence based on architectural criteria.[8] Others, agreeing with Percy Brown, feel confident that the caves may be dated according to their degree of 'emancipation from wooden conventions'.[9] Although the latter point of view is more widely accepted, one sympathizes with the former attitude when trying to analyse the development of the *stūpa* form, or when examining the occurrence of stone as opposed to wooden ribs in the ceilings of *caityas*. These factors, we shall see, do not appear to have been standardized and are of doubtful chronological value. In the course of our analysis of architectural details we find ourselves faced with what Erwin Panofsky terms an 'organic situation', in which the beginning of our investigation seems to presuppose the conclusions. 'It is true that the individual monuments and documents can only be examined, interpreted and classified in the light of a general historical concept. While at the same time, this general historical concept can only be built up on individual monuments and documents.' This is not, however, a hopeless vicious circle. 'Every new discovery of an unknown historical fact, and every new interpretation of a known one, will either "fit in" with the prevalent general conception, and thereby corroborate and enrich it, or else it will entail a subtle or even fundamental change in the prevalent general conception, and thereby throw new light on all that has been known before.'[10]

An analysis of the architectural components of the *caitya* reveals that while certain features apparently occur haphazardly throughout the caves, other elements may be found together consistently. A study of Table 10 reveals a number of these 'concomitances', to borrow a word used by Phillipe Stern and Mireille Bénisti in their work on Amaravati.[11] After considering briefly factors that occur at random throughout the entire series of *caityas* and do not appear to have been standardized, we shall concentrate on the concomitant factors which form the basis of our proposed scheme of architectural development. We shall then take up the entire series of early Buddhist caves and examine briefly their probable sequence of cutting.

Form of the Stūpa

Table 10 The detailed tabulation of the various *stūpa* elements reveals that these different factors do not appear to have been standardized: the absence of concomitances does not permit our proposing a sequence. There is no consistency in the occurrence of a single as opposed to a double drum, or in the absence or presence of *vedikā*-bands separating the drum and *aṇḍa*. Neither does the appearance of an elaborate *harmikā* such as we find in Ajanta X or Pitalkhora XII appear to be of chronological value. It might be considered that the proportion of the drum to the *aṇḍa* would be of significance. In the early reliefs at Bharhut and Sanchi we find elaborate representations of *stūpas* in which the drum is always of lesser height than the *aṇḍa*. This is also the case with the Sanchi *stūpa* itself, and presumably with other early structural *stūpas*. Cunningham pointed out as early as 1854 that 'the age of almost every Tope [*stūpa*] may be obtained approximately from its shape; the most ancient being a simple hemisphere and the latest a tall tower surmounted by a dome'.[12] A consideration of the proportions of the *stūpas* within the *caityas* reveals, however, that in both the earliest and the latest caves the drum is low, while in the intervening period a tendency towards elongation appears. Thus, with regard to the early Buddhist caves, we are on rather uncertain grounds in trying to obtain a sequence on the basis of the form of the *stūpa*.[13]

Use of Wood

In accordance with the view that the caves reveal a gradual 'emancipation' from an imitation of wooden construction, it might be expected that the actual use of wood in the *caityas* would gradually decrease. We shall see that this is true in so far as the treatment of the façade is concerned, the entirely rock-cut frontage being of slightly later date than the part wooden one. There is no consistent pattern, however, in the presence or absence of wooden appendages within the *caityas*: the Karle *caitya* still has wooden ribs in the vault of the nave while the small, distinctly early *caitya* at Guntupalli has stone ribs.[14] Both early and later *caityas* appear to have wooden ribs in the side aisles and occasionally, within the same *caitya* as at Pitalkhora III and Ajanta X, we find stone ribs in the side aisles and wooden ribs in the nave. The actual use of wood within the caves is then of little chronological significance. A further indication of this is the fact that Karle has a wooden *chatra* above its *stūpa*, while earlier *chatras* are carved of stone. A consideration of the stone ribbing in the *vihāras*, which we shall examine at a later stage, only reinforces our conclusions regarding the use of wood.

It is apparent that the form of the *stūpa* and the use of wooden appendages in the caves – factors which in the past have been regarded of chronological value – do not, in fact, help us to obtain a sequence within the period of the early Buddhist caves.

Floor Plan and Façade

The earliest *caitya* in our series is a two-chamber cave excavated perpendicular to the rock-face, and consisting of a small rectangular hall and an inner circular chamber containing a rock-cut *stūpa*. We can only conjecture as to the type of façade the cave must once have had, since this is now completely broken away. Perhaps there was a doorway with a *caitya* arch around it, as we have seen on the Lomasa Rishi and Guntupalli *caityas*. This two-chamber *caitya* was followed by the simple apsidal cave, with a front now completely open, but presumably once filled in with woodwork. The size of the *caitya* soon increased and the roof rose to a considerable height. This led to the raising of the *caitya* arch above the level of the doorway, and it now became a *caitya* window through which light fell directly onto the rock-cut *stūpa*. It is possible that in some of the earliest examples the *caitya* arch itself was of wood. Below this, there must have been a wooden screen with a doorway leading to the interior. The setting up of pillars to mark a circumambulatory passage, thus dividing the interior into nave and side aisles, led to the typical *caitya* plan apparent at Bhaja. The *caitya* arch at this stage was carved out of stone, although the lower portion of the façade continued to be of wood.

On either side of the *caitya* window, the façade of Bhaja and other early *caityas* was carved in imitation of the frontage of a structural building. *Vedikā*-bands – bands carved in the form of the simple railing that surrounded structural *stūpas* and other monuments – were sculpted to represent different storeys. These bands, which often followed the line of the rock-face, resulted in various levels of balconies supported by brackets, with a superstructure above containing miniature *caitya* windows. The balconies were usually enclosed by panels of lattice-work. Occasionally, however, they were open, and human figures were carved within as if looking out on the scene below. The entire rock space around the *caitya* was covered with this type of carving, and sometimes, as at Pitalkhora, the decoration of the façade appears to have extended over an adjoining *vihāra* as well. The interior of the early *caitya* gave an impression of lofty space. This effect was primarily due to the high barrel-vaulted roof above the nave, and the wooden or stone ribs in the ceiling further emphasized this impression. The nave, with the *stūpa* at the far end, was the important part of the structure, while the narrow aisles, representing the circumambulatory passage, were of relative unimportance as far as architectural effect was concerned. The *stūpa* itself rose to an impressive height and would have dwarfed the devotee approaching it. The *caitya* window with its wooden or stone ribbing diffused the harsh sunlight of the exterior so that a mysterious half-light fell on the *stūpa*.

The next stage sees the wooden frontage of the *caitya* being replaced entirely by stone and, at this stage, the decoration of the façade becomes even more elaborate. Apart from further details being introduced into the representation of the storeyed building, the lower part of the façade now contains additional carving. Thus, at Nasik the doorway with decorated door jambs is flanked by doorkeepers. Here, a row of beam ends below the *caitya* window has been treated as a decorative item and every alternate one has been carved to represent a human head. The simple apsidal plan was next elaborated through the addition of a veranda, the nature of which varied considerably. At some sites, it was a small, neat structure, less in width than the interior, with no sculptural decoration at all. At other sites, it was broad and wider than the interior and lavishly decorated with figural sculpture. The two side walls of the veranda of the Karle *caitya*, for example, are carved to represent a five-storeyed building resting on the shoulders and backs of life-size elephants. The upper part of the main wall of the veranda continues the depiction of a storeyed monument, while the lower section contains carvings of couples (*mithunas*). The large *caitya* window which still retains some of its original wooden ribbing, dominates the front of the veranda. There are now three doorways leading into the *caitya*, the two side ones opening directly into the circumambulatory paths and the central one into the nave.

The appearance of the 'blind' *caitya* window on the façade of some caves is of interest. Three such windows are known and all three occur among the many caves at the site of Junnar. The Budh Lena façade displays a decorative treatment of the *caitya* window, which has not been cut through but is of solid stone. The central semi-circular space within the arch has been carved to represent a half-lotus with seven petals. The figures sculpted within the petals represent an unusual version of the Gajalakshmī theme. The Leny-adri and the Bhima Shankar *caityas* both have small verandas, and the *caitya* window is carved in shallow relief on the rock-face above the outer wall of the veranda. The surface within the arch has been smoothed and this rules out the possibility of their representing unfinished work. In any case, to serve a functional purpose and throw light on the *stūpa* in the interior, it would have been necessary to cut through an excessive thickness of rock – the entire width of the veranda and more. These are no longer true *caitya* windows. However, the traditional association of the *caitya* window with the apsidal *caitya* seems to have resulted in the retention of the classic shape of the arch in shallow relief on the façade. The 'blind' *caitya* windows appear to be a regional variation of uncertain chronological significance.

The final stage of evolution saw the addition of a wall screening the veranda of the *caitya* and an open courtyard with a low balustrade in front. Apart from the veranda, the courtyard balustrade also lent itself to further decorative treatment. We see then that the *Fig. 2* development of the apsidal *caitya* represents basically a progression from simple to elaborate as an evolutionary sequence. Since we have a fairly large body of material to substantiate this, we can state with some confidence that the elaboration of the *caitya* plan has also a chronological significance.[15]

At some stage in the course of this development of the apsidal *caitya*, we come across the introduction of a new *caitya* plan. The shrine is now rectangular, often with a hall in front and a veranda. Sometimes, as at Kuda VI, such a hall has one or two cells opening out from it. These caves no longer have the *caitya* window decorating the façade. The chronological position of such an innovation is not immediately apparent on a consideration of plan and façade alone. We shall see that other architectural features, notably the form of the pillars, indicates that these rectangular *caityas* first appear at a relatively advanced stage of development. We have also in the Tulja Lena caves at Junnar a single example of a circular *caitya* with a *stūpa* surrounded by a ring of pillars. While the cave displays affinities with the circular *caitya* at Guntupalli in the Krishna basin, the occurrence of pillars defining a circumambulatory path suggests a date not earlier than Bhaja. We can say very little about the completion of the façade since the rock is sharply undercut and no longer retains its original surface. The cave appears, however, to constitute an early variation on the apsidal plan.[16]

Ceilings

The apsidal-ended *caityas* have barrel-vaulted ceilings above the nave, but the roof of the side aisles varies, being either half-arched or flat. This factor seems to be of some significance and a study of Table 10 suggests that half-arched side aisles are generally indicative of an early date, with flat ceilings replacing them at a later stage. An examination of the Bharhut gateway sculptures would appear to confirm this: in the three undoubted *caitya* representations, the side aisles are depicted as half-arched.[17] Table 10 reveals the popularity of these half-arched ceilings which, at an intermediary stage, apparently persisted side by side with flat examples.[18] All the rectangular *caityas* have low, flat roofs above the *stūpa* with the *chatta* commonly engraved on the ceiling itself.

Pillars

The earliest form of column, as may be expected, is the plain octagon with neither base nor capital. It will be seen that this column usually has an inward slant towards the top. This rake has long been accepted as evidence of an early date and as an indication of the extent to which wooden construction was being copied. In wooden buildings, sloping door jambs would presumably counter the pull of the bent wood arches, but in solid rock such a representation would be structurally meaningless although craft convention may well have led to its retention. In the Buddhist caves we find that at a certain stage the pillars become perpendicular. It has hitherto been generally agreed that the rock-cutters realized that such strict imitation of wooden structures was unnecessary and perhaps ungainly. But there may well be other reasons for the introduction of perpendicular pillars. It may imply that the very technique of wooden architecture had so progressed as to altogether dispense with the sloping columns in actual wooden buildings. A study of the reliefs at Bharhut, BodhGaya and Sanchi provides us with an interesting clue in this context. It is on the Sanchi gateway reliefs that we first come across representations of the *caitya* arch with the tie-rod. This comparatively minor detail *Fig. 4* is so clearly and emphatically depicted in the reliefs that we may conclude that it was a recent innovation, which is why it is given such prominence.[19] With the introduction of the tie-rod, there would no longer be any need to have slanting columns as the tie-rod would support the roof and thereby counter the outward thrust. It would thus seem that the architects who straightened the pillars in the caves were still closely following the wooden techniques. The first caves in which entirely perpendicular columns appear may then be considered to be roughly contemporary with the Sanchi gateways, or to follow soon after. It is interesting to note that in the depiction of the *Indra Śāla Guha* on the north gateway (east pillar, upper panel, west face), the cave is semi-artificial with a representation of the *caitya* arch embodying the tie-rod.

The early slanting octagonal column was followed by the straight octagon, which then acquired a base consisting of a waterpot (*ghata*) on a stepped platform, and a rudimentary capital in the form of a rectangular block as at Nasik. The fully developed pillar in the *caityas* was achieved when an elaborate capital was added consisting of a 'bell', an enclosed *āmalaka*,[20] a stepped abacus and crowning animals. The chronological development of these stages is apparent. A number of variations may, however, be seen among the fully developed columns, and a detailed analysis reveals four significant categories based on changes in the representation of the 'bell' capital.

1   In the first phase the 'bell' is noticeably incurving, almost 'waisted', and has distinctly depicted petals. The Bedsa capital is of this type and seems to follow the earlier Aśokan tradition which may also be seen at Sanchi *stūpa* II and at Bharhut.

2   In the next phase the petals are no longer clearly indicated but are marked as ridges on the 'bell'. This phase is evident on the interior pillars at Karle. It is interesting to note that the lion pillar standing outside the Karle *caitya* has a 'bell' with petals more akin to the Bedsa variety, but this may well be because the lion pillar was designed presumably in emulation of the Aśokan prototype.[21]

3   The third phase sees the disappearance of the petal markings though the slightly elongated 'bell' shape is retained. Due to the absence of petal markings, the form is now described as an inverted waterpot (*ghaṭa*). This phase is evident at Nasik *vihāra* X.

4   The final phase sees the inverted *ghaṭa* losing all hint of its original 'bell' form and acquiring a distinctly rounded shape with the 'neck' of the *ghaṭa* very clearly depicted. It is as if the *ghaṭa* at the base were exactly reduplicated at the top of the column, but inverted. Pillars with this type of capital may be seen in Nasik *vihāra* III.

It will be evident that the presence of 'bell' capitals of the same category in different caves does not necessarily indicate the exact contemporaneity of the excavations. It only suggests that the caves belong fairly closely together in time. Undoubtedly there must have been some degree of overlap between the different phases.[22] However, Table 10 shows that a meaningful sequence may be obtained from a study of these changes in the form of the 'bell' capital.

Brackets and Stepped Merlons
These two decorative details have not been included in Table 10 because their presence or absence in the caves becomes more

meaningful only when their occurrence in both *caitya* and *vihāra* are considered together. Decorative elements such as these were not restricted to the one form or the other. Brackets are to be found on the Bhaja *caitya*, Kondane *caitya*, Ajanta *caitya* IX, Ajanta *vihāra* XII, and among the *vihāras* at Nadsur, Tulja and Pitalkhora. Stepped merlons appear in a Kondivte *vihāra*, the Bhaja *caitya* and *vihāra*, Kondane *caitya*, Ajanta *caitya* IX, Aurangabad *caitya* IV, Ajanta *vihāras* XII and XXX, the Pitalkhora and Nadsur *vihāras*. Merlons may also be seen in abundance at Bharhut, BodhGaya, Sanchi and the Orissan caves, and the brackets only at the two latter sites. It may generally be observed that these two decorative elements occur in monuments of an early date, being noticeably absent in the later caves of our period.

Sequence of Excavation of the Early Buddhist Caves

The Caitya

The sequence of *caitya* architecture in western India begins with the *Fig. 2* two-chamber cave at Kondivte which is roughly 30 ft deep including the inner room, and 17 ft wide. A single doorway and two latticed windows open into the circular chamber containing the rock-cut Plate 5 *stūpa*. The roof above the *stūpa* is domed but is rough and unfinished, and the floor too does not appear to have been levelled. Following Kondivte are the apsidal pillarless *caityas* at Nadsur and Pitalkhora XII. Both caves are very small, Nadsur measuring roughly 24 × 16 ft, and Pitalkhora XII being even smaller. Both have vaulted roofs and that of Pitalkhora XII contains rock-cut ribs and rafters. The *stūpa* in the latter has an elaborate *harmikā* containing depictions of human figures. However, the early architectural character of the *caitya* seems in little doubt and it is apparent that the extent of embellishment of the *stūpa* is no gauge of its date.

The next stage of development is exemplified by the Bhaja *caitya* which is a simple apsidal cave, approximately 59 × 27 ft, divided into nave and side aisles by a row of pillars which follows the apsidal plan around the *stūpa*. Below the *caitya* arch, which is carved of stone, the Plate 8 façade is now completely open. This would originally have been filled in with a wooden screen containing a doorway leading to the interior. The numerous pinholes in the fronton of the arch itself indicate further wooden additions of some nature. The vaulted ceiling of the nave still retains its original wooden ribbing and the side aisle ceilings are half-arched. The pillars are plain octagonal columns exhibiting a marked inward slope of five inches towards their upper end. This clue to the early date of the structure reveals a close imitation of a method of wooden construction before the invention of the tie-rod. Brackets, stepped merlons, miniature arches and *vedikā*-bands may been seen in the decoration of the façade. The *stūpa* within consists of a simple drum and *aṇḍa*. Similar *stūpas* may be seen among the row standing along the rock-face a short distance from the *caitya*, as well as those with a *vedikā*-band separating drum and *aṇḍa*. This goes to show that the occurrence of such a band is of no chronological significance.

Plate 6

Roughly contemporary with Bhaja are four other *caityas* – Kondane, Pitalkhora III and XIII and Ajanta X. The Kondane *caitya* measuring roughly 66 × 27 ft, is quite similar to Bhaja in its plan, pillars, ceilings and in the treatment of its façade. The actual curve of the *caitya* arch is here stronger and more definite. Pitalkhora III is a somewhat larger cave, the façade of which has completely broken away and even the *caitya* arch is non-existent. While the ceiling of the nave has wooden ribs, the half-arched side aisles have stone ones – an indication that the occurrence of stone as opposed to wooden ribs is of no sequential significance. Recent clearance has revealed a flight of rock-cut steps in front of the *caitya* leading down to the stream. Its simple apsidal plan, obviously part wooden façade, and its plain octagonal columns with a distinct inward rake, place this *caitya* in the same category as Bhaja and Kondane. Pitalkhora XIII is a small cave, only 28 × 15 ft, that belongs to this same group. The vaulted roof of the nave contains rock-cut ribs and rafters, with the side aisles displaying plain half-arched ceilings. *Caitya* X at Ajanta is the largest cave of this early group. It measures 95 × 41 ft, and is quite similar in plan and treatment of pillars to those we have just considered. It is interesting to note that the façade on either side of the *caitya* arch has been left quite plain and was not carved in imitation of a structural building. The ceiling of the cave is similar to that of Pitalkhora III, with wooden ribbing in the nave and stone ribs in the half-arched side aisles.

Plate 19

Plate 36

Two other caves, Pitalkhora X and the Tulja circular *caitya*, appear to belong fairly closely in date with this group we have just considered. Both constitute variations on the basic theme. It is rather difficult to assign Pitalkhora X to a specific chronological position and its placing with regard to the Bhaja *caitya* remains somewhat uncertain. The cave is a tiny pillarless apsidal excavation, approximately 17 × 8 ft, with a plain vaulted roof. The absence of pillars to mark a path for circumambulation would seem to indicate its priority to the plan achieved at Bhaja. Its façade, however, is completely of stone, and contains a narrow doorway with a rectangular window above this. The completely stone façade is usually an indication of the later date of a *caitya*. The replacement of the usual *caitya* window of the façade by a plain undecorated rectangular opening, is also somewhat unusual. Combining earlier and later elements, the exact architectural position of Pitalkhora X is problematic. The Tulja *caitya* at Junnar is a circular cave, about 30 ft in diameter, with twelve Plate 54 octagonal columns surrounding the *stūpa*. The circumambulatory path at Tulja marked out by the ring of pillars, suggests a phase as advanced as Bhaja. It is unfortunate that the façade is so completely broken away as to give no clues to its original decoration. The domed roof over the *stūpa* is accompanied by a half-arched roof over the circumambulatory path. The simple octagonal columns appear to have a slight inward slant and suggest contemporaneity with Bhaja, and with a phase of wooden building prior to the invention of the tie-rod.

The next significant stage in the development of the *caitya* form is illustrated by two caves which appear to be roughly contemporary – Ajanta *caitya* IX and Nasik. Ajanta IX is a square-ended cave approximately 45 × 23 ft, but the pillars follow the apsidal plan and the square end of the cave does not appear to be of any especial consequence. The front is now entirely of stone, and, below the *caitya* window, one doorway and two windows open into the cave. Plate 34 The façade is elaborately carved with miniature arches, *vedikā*-bands and rows of stepped merlons. Another feature indicative of the advanced date of this cave is the flat ceiling over the side aisles. The pillars, however, are still plain octagonal columns which slope inwards some two inches. The Nasik *caitya* is a small apsidal cave, some 39 × 22 ft, divided by a row of pillars into nave and side aisles. Its façade is again entirely of stone with a single doorway opening into the cave. The side aisles here retain their half-arched ceilings. A distinct advance on Ajanta IX is to be seen in the pillars which are no longer plain slanting octagonal columns, but have acquired a base consisting of a *ghaṭa* standing on a stepped platform. Those along Plate 49 the left aisle have no capital, while those on the right have a rudimentary one in the form of a narrow rectangular block. This lack of uniformity would seem to imply two stages in the excavation of this cave. Ajanta IX and Nasik, both with stone façades, appear to be roughly contemporary,[23] but reveal two interesting differences. Ajanta IX has a flat ceiling over the side aisles, while that at Nasik remains half-arched. On the other hand, Ajanta IX has the earlier variety of column, while the Nasik pillars have a base as well as a rudimentary capital.

Belonging to this same phase are the Budh Lena *caitya* at Junnar and Aurangabad cave IV. The unfinished Budh Lena *caitya* appears to have had a façade entirely carved of stone, although much of this has now broken away. While the interior is incomplete, it reveals the typical pillared apsidal plan, and the right aisle ceiling, which has taken definite shape, is half-arched. The pillars have only been roughly blocked out, and we have no indication of how they were to have been treated. The cave is about 30 ft deep with a partially hewn *stūpa* at the far end. A bad stratum of rock, combined with extensive leakage of water, seems to have resulted in cutting being abandoned. The façade contains a 'blind' *caitya* window which has not been cut through and the central portion contains a sculptured semi-circle. Aurangabad cave IV is a small *caitya*, 38 × 22 ft, with a square end. However, as at Ajanta IX, the plain octagonal pillars follow an apsidal plan, and the square end does not appear to be of especial significance. The façade is completely destroyed but was probably of stone. The vaulted roof of the nave contains stone ribs, while the side aisles reveal flat ceilings. A unique feature of this cave is the row of miniature arches sculpted above the pillars of the nave and below the ribbing of the vault.

The next decisive phase is exemplified by the Bedsa *caitya* which reveals a notable advance in floor plan. The apsidal cave, measuring 45 × 21 ft, has been elaborated by the addition of a veranda wider than the interior of the cave, and containing two full and two engaged columns. A single doorway and two lattice windows open into the *caitya*. A rather unusual feature is the cells opening out from the veranda, there being two at either end, one of which has been left incomplete. The side aisles still have half-arched ceilings – an early feature that appears to survive for a long time. The pillars of the *caitya* reveal a major advance. Those of the interior are plain octagons with neither base nor capital, but those in the veranda are of the fully developed variety. The tall, elegant shafts, reaching a height of 25 ft, entirely perpendicular, rise out of a *ghaṭa* standing on a stepped

Plate 55

Plate 56

Plate 37

Plate 39

platform, and terminate in an elaborate capital. Above an elegant 'bell' is an enclosed *āmalaka* surmounted by a stepped abacus support-ing animal-and-rider figures. The animals include horses, elephants Plates 40, 41 and bulls and there is one rider on each. The petals of the 'bell' are very clearly marked out and belong to the earliest stage of the 'bell' capital. The near perpendicularity of the interior columns[24] would lead us to assign the *caitya* to a phase roughly contemporary with the Sanchi gateways. The mass of rock in front of the *caitya* has not been cut away to give a view of the magnificent façade: only a narrow passage has been hewn through it. This remains inexplicable, par-ticularly as it must also have added to the problems of those who did the preliminary cutting.

At Karle we see the elaboration of the plan of the Bedsa *caitya*, and a stone screen is added to enclose the veranda, with a free-standing lion pillar (perhaps originally two) beyond this. The cave itself is the largest in our series, measuring roughly 124 × 45 ft. The vaulted roof rises to a height of 46 ft above the nave of the *caitya* and still retains its original wooden ribbing. The ceilings of the side aisles are now flat, while the pillars of the interior are of the fully developed variety. The 'bell' no longer has its petals as distinctly depicted as at Bedsa, but merely as a series of ridges, and thus belongs to the second phase in the development of the 'bell' capital. A further elaboration is that each animal above the stepped abacus now has two riders – a man and a woman – rather than the single rider of Bedsa. The *āmalaka* is not so clearly contained within the frame as at Bedsa, nor is the 'bell' so incurving. It is interesting to note that the lion pillar 'bell' by contrast has petals closer to the Bedsa example, though not so clearly distinguished. As we have suggested earlier, this may well be in emulation of the Aśokan prototype.

On architectural grounds the exact chronological position of Lenyadri cave VI is not quite clear: it could be regarded as contem-porary with Karle, or as belonging somewhat later. This apsidal-ended *caitya* has a veranda narrower than the interior, as distinct from the practice at Bedsa and Karle, with a single doorway leading into the cave. The façade above the outer wall of the veranda has a 'blind' Plate 64 *caitya* window with a *vedikā*-band engraved below it. The arch has here lost its functional purpose and become a mere traditional motif. The side aisles have half-arched ceilings, suggesting that the *caitya* may be earlier than Karle which reveals a flat roof over the aisles. However, the pillars both of the veranda and the interior suggest a Plates 62, 64 date in advance of Karle, as they have a distinctly bell-shaped inverted *ghaṭa* belonging to the third phase in the development of the 'bell' capital. There are no riders on the animals surmounting the pillars either within the cave or in the veranda.

A large number of *caityas* belong quite distinctly to the period after Karle, but on architectural grounds alone it is not possible to define their exact sequential position in relation to the *caityas* of Karle and Kanheri. We shall consider some of these *caityas* very briefly. The Amba/Ambika *caitya* on the Manmodi hill at Junnar is of the typical apsidal plan and has a small veranda in front narrower than the

Plate 61 interior. The two full and two engaged columns are of the fully developed variety and terminate in a rounded inverted *ghaṭa* which belongs to the final phase in the development of the 'bell' capital. Above the inverted *ghaṭa* is the stepped abacus and then a small rectangular block. The *caitya* window is located on the inner wall of the veranda and is a true functional one. The actual opening itself is

Plate 60 in the form of a narrow horseshoe rather than the usual semi-circle. The interior is incomplete with a roughly hewn *stūpa* at the far end. The pillars have not yet been commenced, and the ceiling, meant to be vaulted, is incomplete. The cave measures 26 ft to the commencement of the *stūpa*, and some 13 ft across. A large natural fault in the rock is doubtless responsible for its unfinished condition.

The Bhima Shankar *caitya*, also on the Manmodi hill at Junnar, reveals veranda pillars treated in a manner exactly similar to that of

Plate 59 the Amba/Ambika *caitya*. The *caitya* façade displays a 'blind' arch located high up on the exterior wall of the veranda. Here even the classic shape of the arch has been abandoned and it consists of a simple semi-circle, with a horseshoe excavated within it in fairly deep relief. Although the interior of this cave too remains incomplete, enough has been hewn to reveal that it was not meant to be an apsidal vaulted structure such as its treatment of façade and veranda might lead one to expect. The *caitya* was meant to be a narrow rectangular cave with a flat roof. Burgess informs us that there were traces of plaster on the ceiling – traces no longer in existence. The *stūpa* has been left at the far end as an enormous mass of rock, and this has been carved recently to represent a seated image worshipped locally as Bhima Shankar. The occurrence of a well of water just beside the *stūpa*, presumably a natural underground reservoir, seems to provide the reason for excavation having been abandoned. The Bhima Shankar cave is the only *caitya* that reveals an association of a *caitya* window, although a 'blind' one, with a rectangular flat-roofed interior. The remaining series of *caityas* with this plan abandon the traditional *caitya* arch motif.

Typical of the rectangular flat-roofed *caitya* is Shivneri cave XLVIII at Junnar. The cave measures 31 × 20 ft, and consists of a vestibule separated from the main hall by two full and two engaged columns. Towards the back of the hall is the *stūpa* with its *chatra* engraved on Plate 67 the flat ceiling that rises to a height of 18 ft. One door and two windows open into the vestibule of the cave. The pillars are of the fully developed variety and terminate in a rounded inverted *ghaṭa* that belongs to the final phase in the development of the 'bell' capital. Above the inverted *ghaṭa* is a stepped abacus with a rectangular block connecting it to the roof. On the basis of the departure from the normal apsidal plan and the absence of any *caitya* arch motif, it could be argued that the cave belonged to an early phase before the *caitya* plan was well established. The pillars suggest instead that this cave, and others of the rectangular flat-roofed variety, belong to an advanced phase, when rock-cutting was well enough established for the cutters to depart from the norm.

Kuda caves VI and IX are other typical examples of this new plan. Kuda VI consists of a veranda opening into a large empty hall roughly 29 ft square, beyond which a vestibule leads into the main shrine. This is a rectangular chamber approximately 20 × 15 ft, containing a *stūpa* with its *chatra* engraved on the flat roof above. A single cell opens out from the vestibule. The roof outside the veranda projects some eight feet and was held up at either end by a standing elephant: now only the one at the western end remains. *Caityas* I and IV at Kuda, though much smaller, are similar in plan to cave VI. *Caitya* IX is also a rectangular cave but is simpler in plan. It consists of a veranda with two full and two engaged columns, opening directly onto a flat-roofed shrine, 8½ ft deep, containing the *stūpa*. The pillars are of the fully developed variety and display a 'bell' capital with ridges, similar to those in the Karle *caitya*, and Plate 72 belonging to the second phase of development. Here, however, there are no crowning animals. Lenyadri *caitya* XV at Junnar is very similar in plan to Kuda cave IX. Unfortunately the pillars at Lenyadri have been destroyed and only the stepped platform of the base and the stepped abacus of the capital remain. Cave XVII at Nasik, intended according to an inscription to be a *caitya*, appears to belong to the same category as Kuda VI. A veranda with two full and two engaged columns leads into a rectangular chamber 32 × 23 ft, with cells in its sides. An antechamber at the rear is separated from the hall by two unfinished columns, and the shrine has just been commenced. The pillars reveal a bell-shaped inverted *ghaṭa* that belongs to the third stage of the 'bell' capital.

The *caitya* at Shelarvadi appears to have consisted of a hall with cells opening out from its sides, and leading into a long rectangular flat-roofed shrine at the rear, approximately 25 ft long × 15 ft. The *stūpa* has recently been hewn away to make room for a Śiva *linga* but the *chatra* may still be seen engraved on the ceiling. Mahad *caitya* VIII is almost exactly similar in plan to Shelarvadi. Here too the *stūpa* has been hewn away while its *chatra* is still visible on the flat ceiling. At Karadh, there are three rectangular flat-roofed *caityas* of which cave XLVIII is of especial interest. This consists of a veranda with square pillars and pilasters, and what appears to be five cells opening out from its back wall. The central one, however, is a shrine about 27 ft deep × 11 ft wide, containing an intact *stūpa* with its *chatra* engraved on the flat ceiling above. On the right wall of the *caitya*, some distance in front of the *stūpa*, are traces of relief sculpture depicting two figures. The surface of the stone is badly damaged, and unfortunately only the outlines of the figures remain. It is, however, unusual to find sculptured decoration within a *caitya*. *Caitya* V at Karadh calls for especial attention as it combines early and late elements and is somewhat problematic. This small apsidal but pillarless cave, some 35 ft deep and 13 ft wide, has a stone front with a single doorway and a square window above. Although the roof is slightly arched, it is different in conception to that of other apsidal *caityas* as the *chatra* of the *stūpa* is engraved on the low ceiling. On either side of the doorway is an engaged column of which the lower portion is damaged. The upper part consists of a roughly sculpted inverted *ghaṭa* belonging to the third phase in the development of the 'bell' capital. Above this is an *āmalaka* and stepped abacus, surmounted by a lion on one side and a wheel on the other. Despite its apparently early floor plan, the cave appears to represent a late variation on the rectangular flat-roofed *caitya*. We must also mention briefly the *caityas* at Sana and Talaja in Saurashtra. The caves at Talaja include a single rectangular flat-roofed *caitya* with the *chatra* of the *stūpa* engraved on the ceiling. The cave is of the same type as some of the Kuda and Karadh *caityas*. At Sana we find an apsidal pillarless *caitya* roughly 31 × 18 ft, with a flat roof. This appears to be similar to Karadh V, although at Sana there seems to have been a narrow veranda in front. These rectangular flat-roofed *caityas* all belong to the period after Karle. However, on architectural grounds alone their exact position may not be defined precisely.

The final stage in the development of the apsidal *caitya* is to be seen in the Kanheri *caitya* which further elaborates on the plan of Karle. Beyond the stone screen of the veranda is an entire courtyard, Plate 75 enclosed in front by a low wall with guardians at the entrance. The courtyard contains within it two lion columns, not free-standing as at Karle, but engaged. The front wall of the cave appears incomplete and even the fronton of the *caitya* arch has not been marked out. Three doorways lead to the interior which measures roughly 86 ft × 40 ft. As at Karle, the side aisles have flat ceilings. The pillar bases have a thin flat *āmalaka* between the stepped platform and the *ghaṭa*. The shaft terminates in a rounded inverted *ghaṭa* belonging to the final phase of the 'bell' capital, a thin *āmalaka*, and a stepped abacus sup- Plate 77 porting a sculptured block. This is usually carved with representations of elephants and human beings worshipping a *stūpa* or other emblem of the Buddha, but occasionally the animal-and-rider theme is to be seen. We find that only six interior pillars on either side have been cut in this fashion. On the left side the next five pillars have a fully carved capital such as we have just seen, but have no base, while the corresponding five on the right side are completely plain with Plate 76 neither capital nor base. There appear to have been two phases in the excavation of this *caitya*. For some unknown reason cutting seems to have been abandoned after the first six pillars on either side had been carved, and the next five on the left had their capitals sculpted. When the cave was later completed the original sculptural plan was not adhered to. It is possible that the later donation to continue excavation of the *caitya* was not sufficient to employ sculptors. The cave may have been completed by stone masons alone and this would presumably account for the situation described above. The inscription engraved on the right doorpost of the *caitya* throws some light on the matter and would doubtless have furnished the entire explanation, but the stone has flaked away in portions and the record is fragmentary. The evidence, as it may be pieced together, reveals that excavation was started by two merchants, brothers Gajasena and Gajamitra. Apparently left unfinished, the record states that it was completed (*samāpitā*) by a number of monks with the help of the merchant Aparenuka, together with stone masons and polishers.

The Vihāra

Fig. 3 The standard *vihāra* of the early Buddhist caves is of the simple quadrangular variety. A typical example is the tiny *vihāra* XIX at Nasik which consists of a hall approximately 14 ft square, with two cells in each of three sides. A miniature *caitya* arch may be seen above the doorway of each cell, and these arches are connected by a band in imitation of a structural railing – a *vedikā*-band. Two lattice windows and a doorway open onto a narrow veranda in front, with slender chamfered columns. A group of caves from various other sites belongs to this same category and we shall briefly consider some of the more important ones. Bhaja *vihāra* XIX consists of a hall roughly 17 ft square, with two cells in two sides. An additional cell opens out from the right wall of the narrow pillared veranda in front. As at Nasik XIX, the cell doorways have a small *caitya* arch above them with a *vedikā*-band connecting the arches. The area between the arches is carved with further miniature arches resting on miniature *vedikā*-bands. This type of decoration represented, as in the case of the *caitya* façade, an imitation of the frontage of a structural building. It became the standard decoration of *vihāra* cells and it is doubtful if the degree of elaboration of this embellishment is of much chronological significance. An interesting pilaster in the

Plate 16 Bhaja *vihāra* consists of a striated 'bell' capital, a stepped abacus and crowning figures. This 'bell' capital does not appear to belong to any of our categories since it has neither petals nor ridges marked on it, but appears rather as if a row of reeds had been put together. This *vihāra* at Bhaja is of especial importance because of the amount of relief sculpture it contains and which we shall consider in a later chapter. *Vihāras* XII and XXX at Ajanta are of the simple quadrangular form and belong to this same early phase.

The *vihāra* at Kondane immediately adjoining the *caitya* is also of quadrangular form, but differs from the norm in that it is pillared. Only the stumps now remain of the 15 pillars that extended along three sides of the cave, some 3½ ft from the walls containing the cell doorways. The flat roof of the *vihāra* is panelled in obvious imitation of woodwork: large beams span the ceiling and the spaces between are divided by smaller rafters. This pillared *vihāra* appears to provide an early variation on the quadrangular plan. Pitalkhora *vihāra* IV belongs to this same category. While in a much ruined condition today, it is possible to see that it once contained rows of pillars. Here too the entire ceiling is carved in imitation of woodwork with flat thin stone rafters. A rather unusual feature of the cells of this *vihāra* is that the ceilings are arched and contain curved stone girders overlaid with rafters. This is a unique feature since all other *vihāra* cells among the early Buddhist caves have flat roofs. It is interesting to note that the *caitya* arches are not placed centrally over the cell door- Plate 25 ways, but appear to correspond to the centre of the arched roof within. Between the arches are pilasters. The shafts are surmounted by ungainly 'bells' and the stepped abacus supports various winged animals including the lion, goat and sphinx. There appear to be two varieties of 'bells'. One is of the striated variety, comparable to that in Bhaja *vihāra* XIX, and appears as if a bunch of reeds or strips of Plate 26 bamboo had been tied together. The other variety gives the impression of tapestry of some sort draped over a block with a band of Plate 25 the same material tied around it. In fact, the design is closely akin to that on head-dresses represented on sculptures at the site. Recent clearance of the frontage of the cave has brought to light a plinth supported on the backs of a row of majestic life-size elephants. To the left of this plinth is an ornamented doorway flanked by guardians, Plates 22, 23 and a flight of steps leads down to this from the higher level of the *vihāra*. Traces of the usual decoration in imitation of a storeyed building, seen on the façade of *caityas*, may here be seen high up on the rock-face above the *vihāra*. It would appear that at Pitalkhora this decoration was carved over both the *caitya* and the adjoining *vihāra*.

We find among the western caves a certain number of departures from this usual quadrangular plan. One of the most interesting variations is displayed by the *vihāra* at Bedsa immediately adjoining the *caitya*. This reveals a unique apsidal plan and has eleven cells opening out from its walls. It measures about 32 ft deep and 18 ft across, and the ceiling consists of a complete barrel-vault such as may be seen above the nave of some of the early pillarless apsidal *caityas*. The front of this *vihāra* has completely fallen away and we have no indication of how it was completed. The meaning of the plan is extremely uncertain and it is of doubtful chronological significance.

The general trend is for the quadrangular *vihāras* to become larger and, at some sites, double-storeyed. A significant development, however, is to be seen with *vihāras* X and III at Nasik, which contain bas-relief representations of *stūpas* flanked by worshippers engraved Plate 50 on the back wall of the cave. This could perhaps be interpreted as a step towards the later development of the *vihāra* (of Mahāyāna

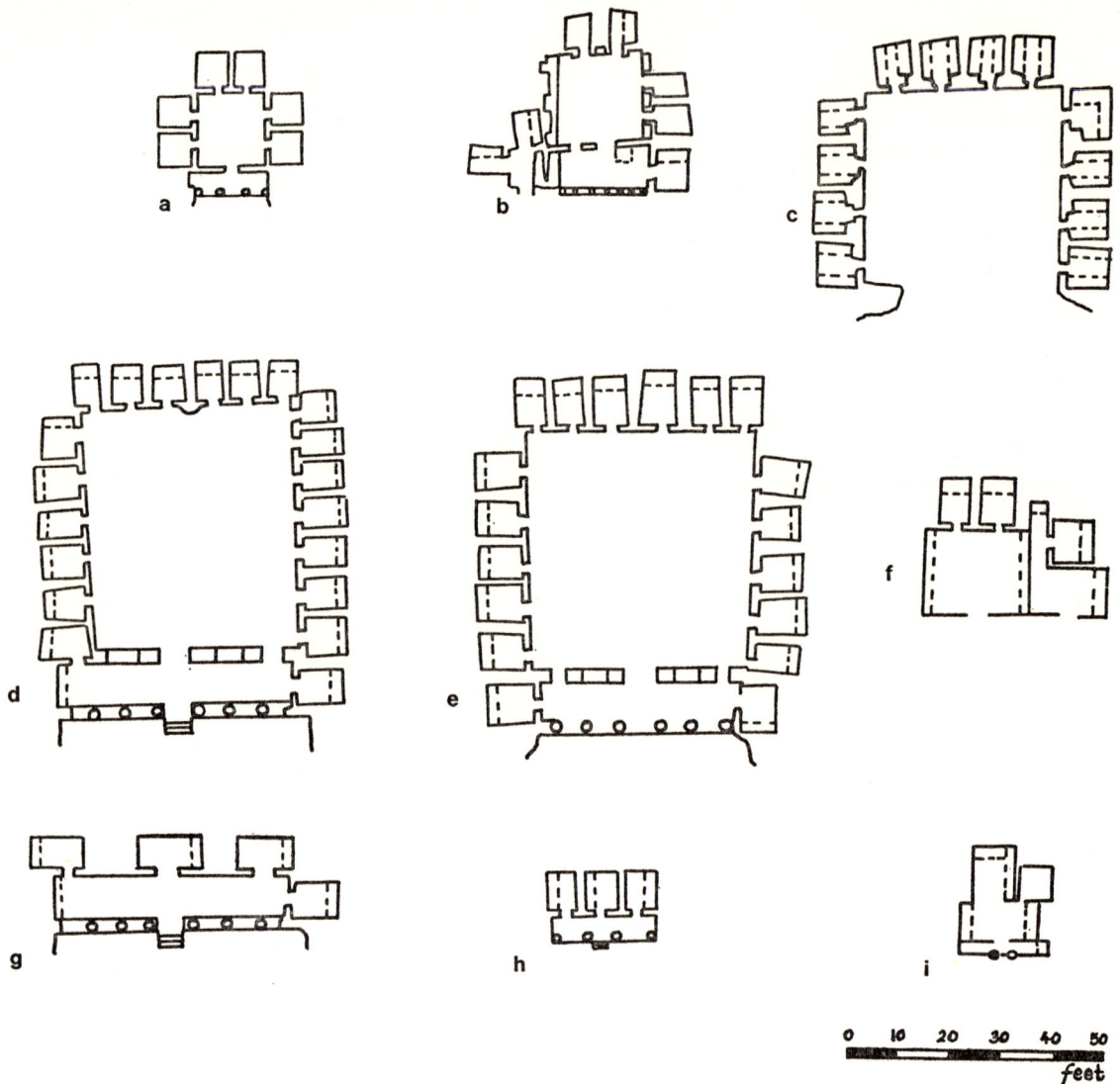

3 Vihāra floor plans: a Nasik XIX; b Bhaja XIX; c Ajanta XII; d Nasik III; e Nasik X;
f Lenyadri; g Nasik III (conjectural original); h Bhima Shankar; i Lenyadri

times) in which a shrine is excavated into the back wall. Both *vihāras*
are of the quadrangular plan and consist of wide pillared verandas
leading into a large hall with cells opening out from three sides. The
hall of *vihāra* X measures 43 × 46 ft and that of *vihāra* III is of similar
dimensions. In cave X a recent image of Bhairava has been imposed
over the relief *stūpa* on the back wall, but portions of the original
representation may still be recognized. The pillars of both *vihāras*
Plate 47 *ghaṭa* belong to the fully developed variety. In *vihāra* X the inverted
is elongated and bell-shaped and belongs to the third phase we

94

outlined. The crowning animals include lions, elephants, bulls and a sphinx, and the number of riders on each animal varies from one to three. In *vihāra* III the veranda pillars have no base and rest on the balustrade running along the veranda. They have a rounded inverted *ghaṭa* of the final phase, and the *āmalaka* is enclosed between two slabs with a tiny *yaksha* figure at each corner. Stone beams as well as the beam ends have been carved along the entablature of both *vihāras*.

Plate 48

A detailed study of the plan of *vihāra* III as well as of the inscriptions it contains has resulted in a number of theories concerning the enlarging or re-cutting of the cave. It will be seen by comparison with the plan of *vihāra* X that one cell opens out from the left end of the veranda and cannot be entered from the main hall. The *vihāra* appears to have three doors and two windows opening into the hall as in *vihāra* X, but here the third door actually leads into the cell: only two doors open into the main hall. In addition the evidence from inscriptions appears contradictory. The records of Gautamīputra Sātakarni (AD 100–110) on the west wall of the veranda refer to 'the cave that is our meritorious gift', while that of Balaśrī engraved on the main wall of the veranda in the nineteenth year of Pulumāvi (AD 129) is definitely of a dedicatory nature.[25] According to one theory, the cave as it stands today was started by Gautamīputra but left unfinished. When completed in the reign of Pulumāvi, the dedicatory inscription of Balaśrī was engraved.[26] The main objection to this is the strange positioning of the veranda cell. If the cave were the result of one original plan, then the cell would surely have opened into the main hall, and the third doorway would have led into the hall and not into an isolated cell. It is also doubtful if Gautamīputra would refer to the cave that was 'his meritorious gift' if it had been incomplete. Another theory maintains that the cell, which now opens into the veranda, originally formed part of a small hall. There was a veranda in front which was demolished when the cave was renovated in the reign of Pulumāvi to reach its present form.[27] The projection in front of the present veranda is put forward in support of this theory, and the cave is certainly set back enough from the rock-face to admit such a possibility. However, we find two main objections to this theory. Firstly the inscription of Gautamīputra would then have been engraved inside the main hall in a dark area. If there had been a veranda in front, surely that was a more appropriate place to engrave the record. Secondly, the pillars and frontage of the present veranda would then have had to be carved

Fig. 3

out of the wall separating the main chamber from the veranda. This wall would have had to be of amazing thickness to admit such an occurrence, when one considers the width across the pillars at the top of the capital. In addition, the balustrade along the present veranda would imply that the original narrow main hall had a bench along one side only, and this appears unlikely.

We suggest that the original cave consisted of a veranda (the present one) opening directly onto four cells – a plan somewhat similar to that of the Bhima Shankar *vihāra* at Junnar which we shall consider shortly. The cave was cut under the orders of Gautamī-putra Sātakarni who then had an inscription engraved on the west wall of the veranda recording his grant of a field to the monks who lived in the cave that was his gift. In the reign of Pulumāvi, Gautamī-putra's mother, Balaśrī, had the cave enlarged to reach its present form. She left Gautamīputra's inscriptions on the west wall and inscribed her own on the main one. Balaśrī's record consists largely of a lyrical eulogy of Gautamīputra, and details his exploits and his character and ends by describing him as one who prepared a cave on the hill. The Great Queen then proceeded to donate the cave and a village to the Bhadāyanīya monks. A continuation of this record a few years later indicates that the cave was now known as the Queen's cave. This interpretation of the two stages in the cutting of the *vihāra* seems to pose less difficulties than those hitherto advanced.

Plate 65

The Gaṇeśa Lena *vihāra* on the Lenyadri hill at Junnar is very similar to Nasik *vihāras* III and X. The veranda has six full and two engaged columns with pillar capitals displaying an inverted *ghaṭa* of the third phase. The pillars have no bases and rest on the balustrade of the veranda. The hall measures roughly 50 × 56 ft, and has 19 cells opening out from its walls. The Ambivale *vihāra* also follows this quadrangular pattern. It consists of a large hall with twelve cells opening out from its sides. Two doors lead from the pillared veranda into the hall. The pillars rise from a balustrade and terminate in

Plate 74

a rounded inverted *ghaṭa* of the final phase, an *āmalaka*, and a stepped abacus supporting the roof. Two of the shafts are octagonal and two are sixteen-sided. This *vihāra* has an open raised courtyard in front with two sets of steps leading up to this level. Shivneri *vihāra* XXVI at Junnar is a typical example of the two-storeyed quadrangular *vihāra*. The lower storey consists of an open veranda with one door and two windows leading into the hall which has ten cells. Stairs at the right front corner lead to the upper story which is here an empty

34   The entirely stone façade of *caitya* IX at Ajanta. The Buddha figures sculpted at the sides
are later additions.

35 The interior of *caitya* IX at Ajanta. Note the inward rake of the pillars. The murals on the columns are of later date.

36 The interior of *caitya* X at Ajanta. The *stūpa* at the far end has a double drum. The inward rake of the pillars is quite noticeable. As in *caitya* IX, the paintings on the columns belong to a later phase.

37 The interior of *caitya* IV at > Aurangabad. An unusual feature is the row of miniature *caitya* arches sculpted just below the stone ribbing of the ceiling.

38   The Bedsa *caitya*. The mass of stone in front of the cave merely has a passage cut through it. It is strange that it was not hewn away entirely to reveal the impressive façade of the cave.

39 The interior of the Bedsa *caitya* with a double-drum *stūpa* and a small stone *chatra* above it.

40, 41 Capitals of the columns in the veranda of the Bedsa *caitya*. The elegant 'bell' is surmounted by an enclosed *āmalaka*, a stepped abacus and powerfully modelled animal-and-rider figures.

42, 43 Two *mithuna* couples from Karle: *Above*, posed so that they are accommodated comfortably within the springing of the *caitya* arch; *above, right*, in the veranda of the Karle *caitya* facing the *caitya* doorways. The inferior workmanship of this couple is quite noticeable and it would appear that the master craftsman carved the main *mithunas*, leaving these and others in secondary positions to his apprentices.

44 The guardian standing beside the doorway of the Nasik *caitya*.

47, 48 Nasik. *Above*, the façade of *vihāra* X, also known as the Nahapāna *vihāra* because of the many inscriptions of that ruler found in the cave. Note the representation of beam ends along the entablature. *Below*, the façade of *vihāra* III. *Yaksha*-like figures supporting various architectural members was a popular motif in ancient Indian art. In this case the entire cave is seemingly supported by such figures who carry beams on their shoulders. Note also the beam ends depicted along the entablature.

45, 46 Guardians on either side of the doorway leading into *vihāra* III at Nasik.

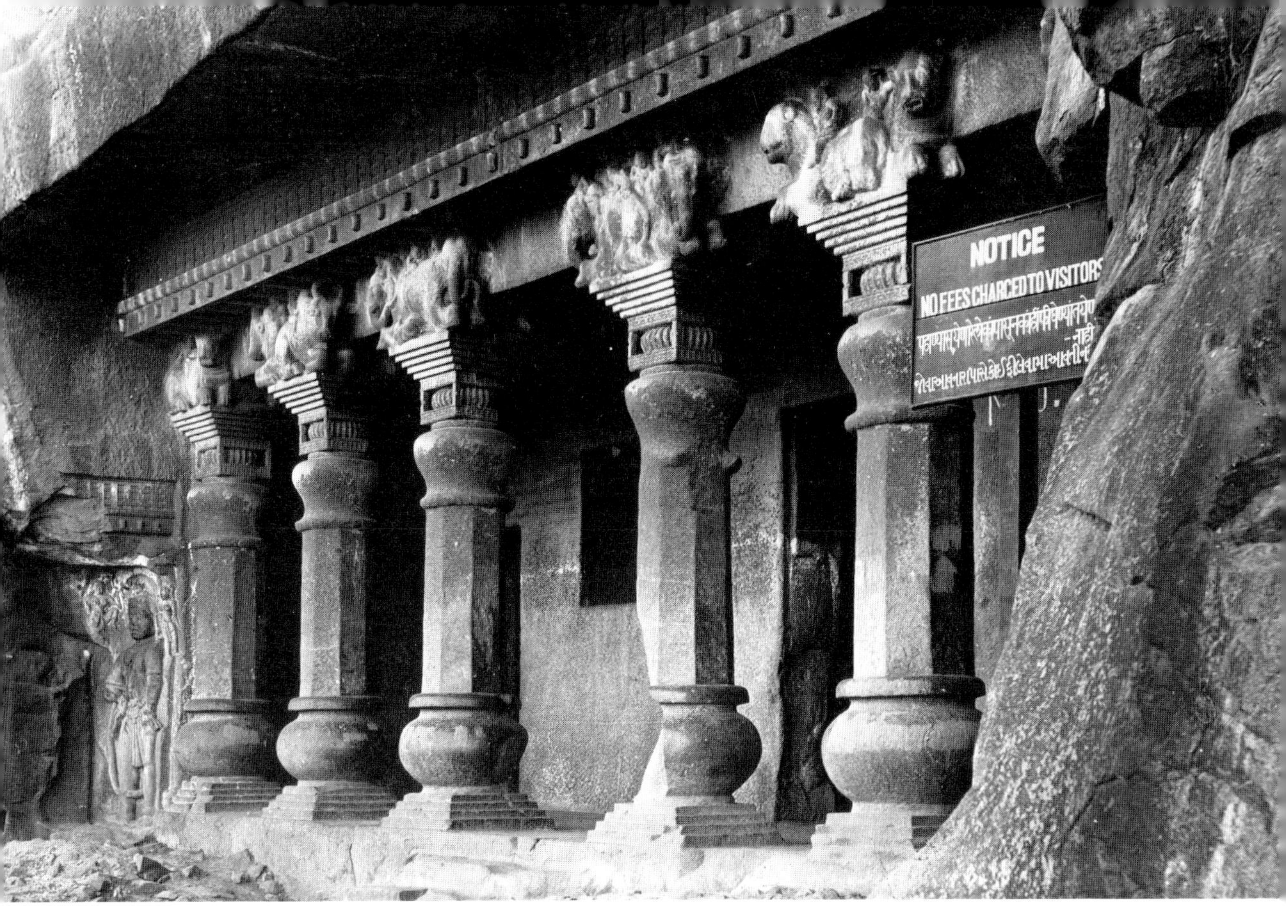
NOTICE
NO FEES CHARGED TO VISITORS

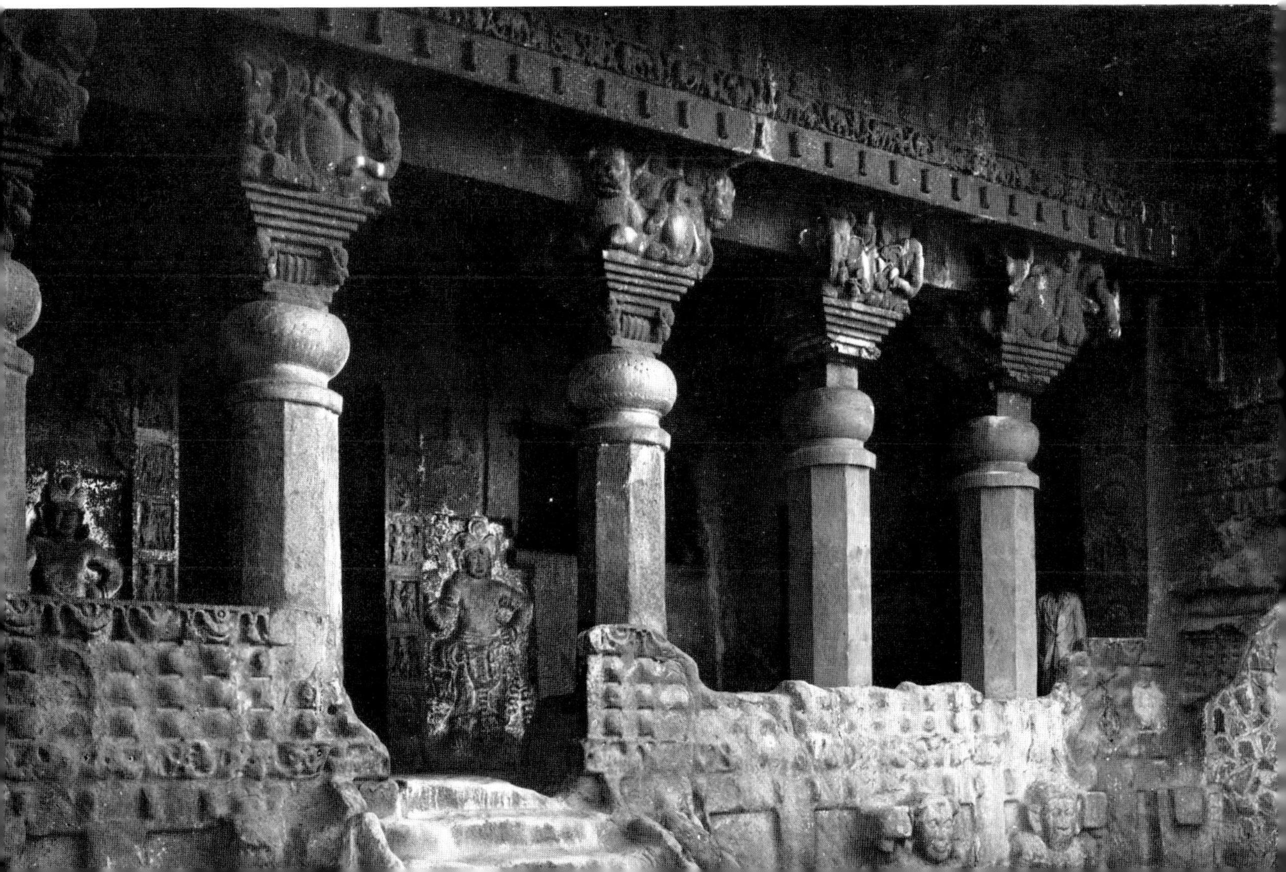

49 The interior of the Nasik *caitya* prior to restoration by the Archaeological Survey of India. The pillars of the right aisle have a rudimentary capital in the form of a rectangular block. This is missing in the left aisle pillars and would indicate two stages in the completion of the cave. Note the inscription engraved lengthwise along two of the pillars.

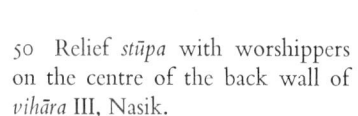

50 Relief *stūpa* with worshippers on the centre of the back wall of *vihāra* III, Nasik.

51, 52 Inscribed labels above now non-existent portrait relief in the Nanaghat cave. The epigraphs read *Rāyā Simuka Sāta-vāhano Sirimāto* (*above*) and *Kumāro Sātavāhano* (*below*).

53 Part of the inscription of Queen Nayanikā (*below*) along the left wall of the Nanaghat cave.

54 The circular *caitya* in the Tulja hills at Junnar.

55 The façade of the unfinished Budh Lena *caitya* in the Manmodi hills at Junnar. The >
caitya arch is here a 'blind' one.

56　Detail of the Gajalakshmī theme sculpted in the seven petals of the half lotus carved within the 'blind' arch of the Budh Lena *caitya*. The figures in the two lower petals on either side appear to depict a dancing *yaksha* and *yakshi*.

57　The façade of the *vihāra* adjoining the Bhima Shankar *caitya* in the Manmodi hills at ＞ Junnar.

58　The decoration above the cell doorways of one of the *vihāras* of the Budh Lena group.

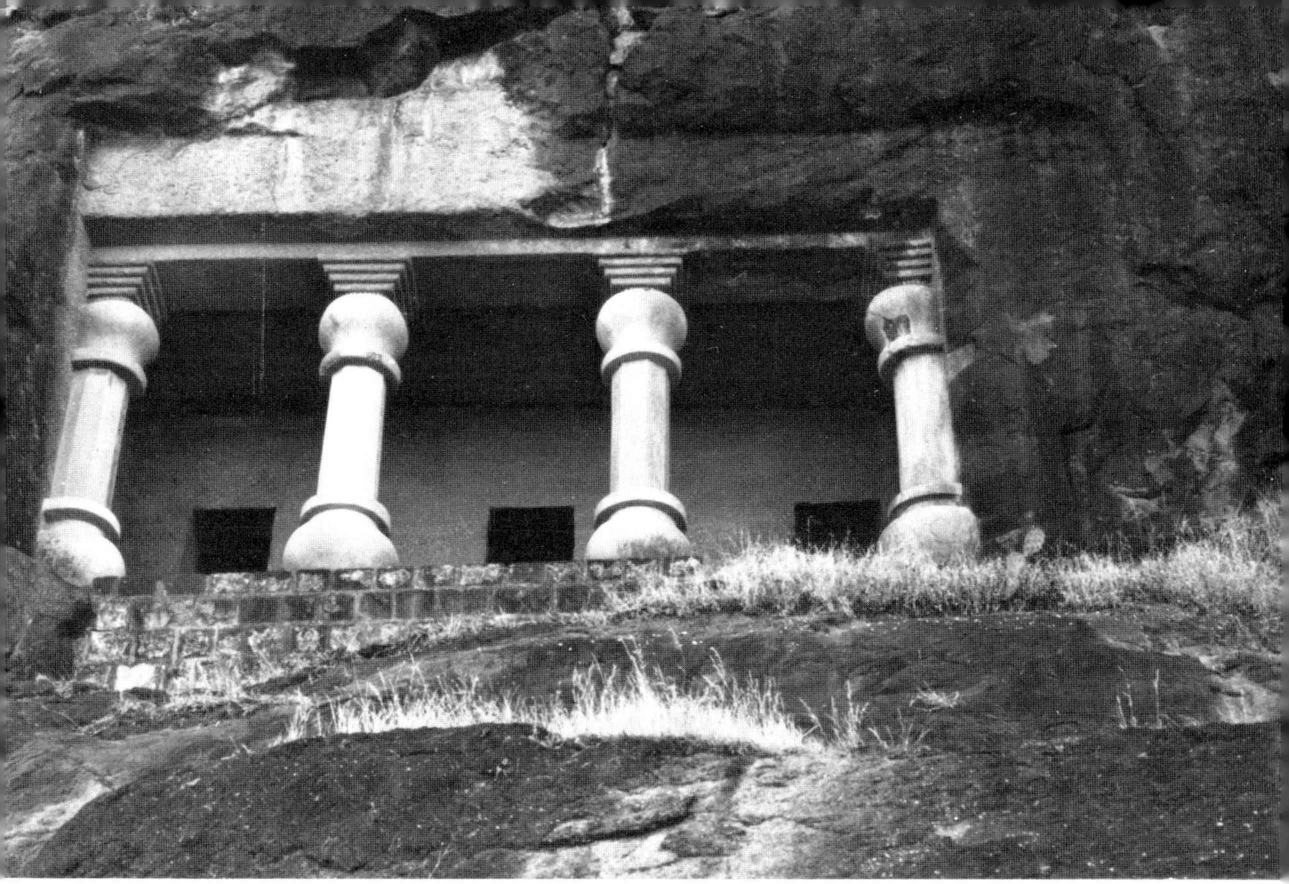

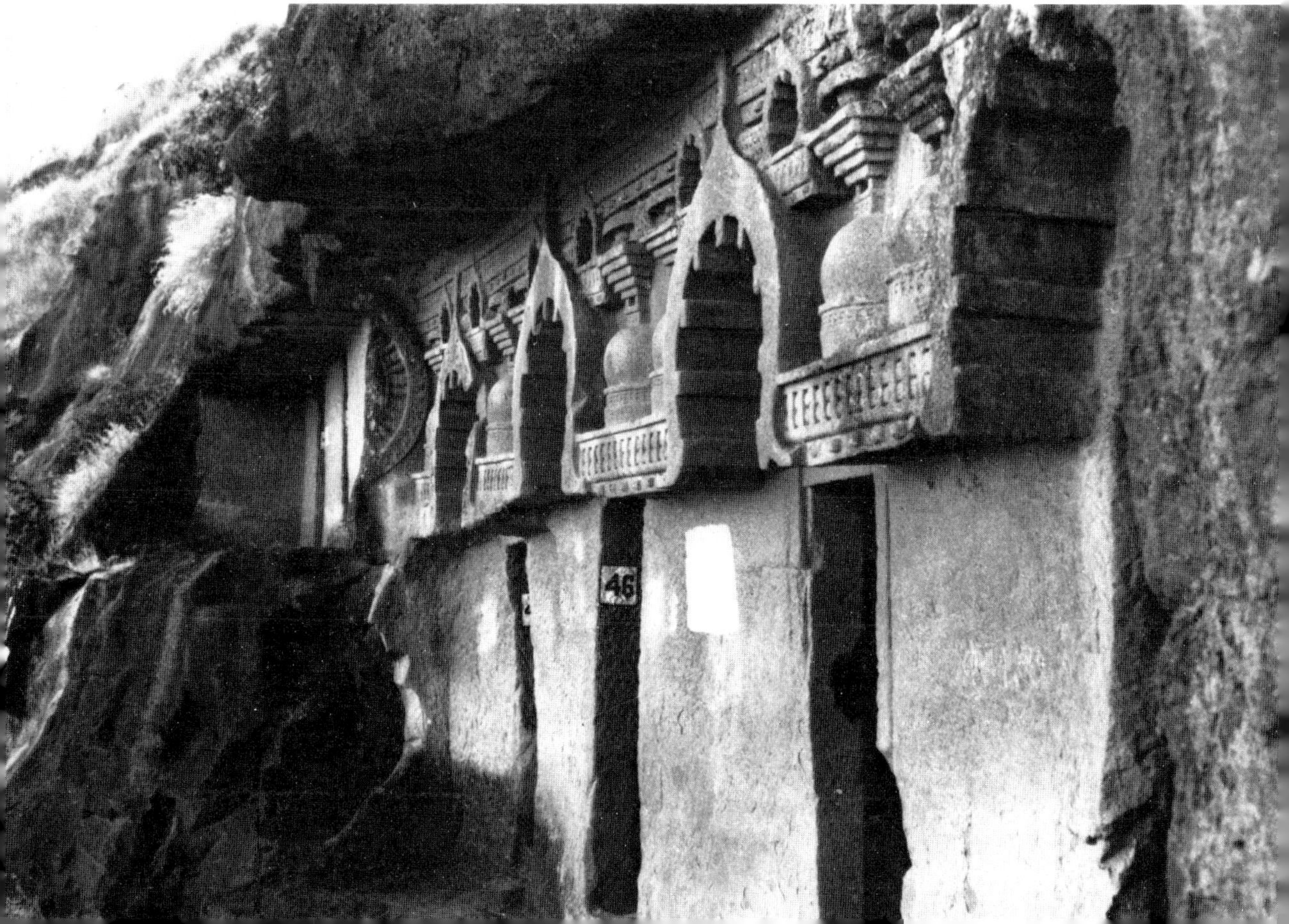
46

59   The façade of the unfinished Bhima Shankar *caitya* in the Manmodi hills at Junnar.
Once again we find a 'blind' *caitya* window, but here, even the classic shape of the arch is
not adhered to.

hall, intended, according to an inscription, to be used as a reception room.

We seem to have a number of departures from the quadrangular plan that all appear to belong to a relatively advanced date. Thus, on the Lenyadri hill at Junnar, we find several *vihāras* that consist entirely of strings of interconnected cells. Some of these could almost be described as dormitories as they merely comprise row upon row of cells. The Bhima Shankar *vihāra* on the Manmodi hill at Junnar has a rather unusual plan that combines two features not often found together. A veranda with two full and two engaged columns leads, not into a hall as one might expect, but directly through three doorways into three cells placed side by side. This is the plan we have suggested for the original *vihāra* III at Nasik. Here the pillars have an inverted *ghaṭa* of the final phase, above which is the stepped abacus Plate 57 and a rectangular block. The Shelarvadi *vihāra* is somewhat akin to this in plan and consists of an open veranda leading into four cells placed side by side. Between the doorways are pilasters rising out of *ghaṭas* on stepped platforms, and terminating in 'bell' capitals with crowning animals. The 'bells' have ridges marked on them and belong to the second phase of the 'bell' capital.

In conclusion then, we find that an analysis of architectural components reveals distinct sequential stages in the development of the apsidal *caitya*. The rectangular flat-roofed *caitya* belongs generally to an advanced stage of development later than Karle. The exact position of these caves with relation to the apsidal *caityas* of Karle and Kanheri cannot be ascertained with categorical certainty. It is only possible to surmise that they belong somewhere in the period between the two. With the *vihāra* form it is not possible to trace a consistent development such as may be done with the apsidal *caitya*. The basic *vihāra* plan was of the quadrangular variety and this generally increased in size and occasionally became two-storeyed. There were, however, a number of variations from the standard plan, and while most of these seem to belong to an advanced date, such variations were not completely unknown at an earlier stage either.

5

Sculpture and Painting

Among the various caves of the early Buddhist rock-cut monasteries are to be found a series of bas-reliefs and a few painted murals that illustrate the gradual development and sophistication of the artists' craft. A discussion of the stylistic development of this sculpture and painting suffers, to some extent, from the fact that the total amount of such decoration is rather limited. While it is both possible and valuable to study this material in isolation, with regard to the earliest phase a comparison with the relatively abundant sculptures from Bharhut, BodhGaya and Sanchi proves instructive. The stylistic development evident from the relief carvings on these monuments provides us with a trend against which to examine the bas-reliefs and paintings from the caves. Considerable geographical distances separate these sites and in making this comparative study we do not claim the exact contemporaneity of similar pieces of sculpture in these areas. However, it is known that traders and craftsmen from the Deccan visited the *stūpas* at Bharhut and Sanchi, leaving inscribed records of their donations to these monuments, and *yavanas* from northern areas, in turn, visited the western Deccan, making gifts of caves and cisterns to the monastic establishments.[1] It may be assumed with some confidence that the artists' craft in these areas did not develop in complete isolation. Rather, along with the migration or travel of pilgrims, merchants and artisans, styles also spread from one region to another. During this early phase of art in India, coming after the primarily centralized and imperial sculpture of Aśokan times, stylistic development would seem to have followed roughly similar lines throughout the country. Distinct regional styles appear at a somewhat later date – towards the end of the period of the early Buddhist caves – with the increasing skill and maturity in the craft of the sculptor and painter.

Bhaja *Vihāra*

Some of the earliest sculptural materials from the western caves come from *vihāra* XIX at Bhaja. Prominent among the carvings are the two large narrative bas-reliefs, one starting on the extreme end of the back wall of the veranda and continuing onto the right wall, and the other beyond the cell doorway on the right wall. These were originally identified as representations of Sūrya destroying the demons of the night, and of Indra riding his elephant Airāvata over the landscape of the earth. Opinion has since largely swung over in favour of a *jātaka* identification, although there is no agreement on the scenes depicted. Some scholars feel that they are episodes from the story of Māndhātā, while others consider them to be scenes from the *Samyuttanikaya*, one representing Sakra fighting the *asuras*, and the other depicting Māra in the form of a gigantic elephant attempting to frighten the Buddha.[2] Yet others have re-affirmed the Sūrya and Indra identifications, one scholar raising the question of whether this *vihāra* belonged at all to the Buddhists.[3]

To us it seems probable that these reliefs represent an unidentified *jātaka* story. The right hand panel, which we shall label the Elephant panel, appears to include a narrative in several stages, in which the principal scene depicts an elephant and two riders. The first rider is heavily bejewelled and has one hand raised holding a goad. Behind him is an attendant with a banner, wearing a rather curious fringed skirt and an unusual head-dress. The elephant holds in its upraised trunk, a tree from which a series of human beings appear to be falling out. Below this is a further representation of a tree surrounded by a railing, with human beings apparently hanging from its branches. Beneath the elephant is a third stage of the narrative showing in the centre a similar tree hung with garlands and crowned with an umbrella. To the left is a royal personage seated on a throne under an umbrella with female attendants, musicians and dancers. To the right are several grotesque animal heads as well as animal-headed human figures. It seems likely that the three scenes are related. The panel to the left of the doorway and continuing onto the main wall – the Chariot panel – is a simpler one. The upper part is dominated by a chariot drawn by four horses, bearing a royal personage with two female attendants, and accompanied by two horse riders. Beneath the chariot are four grotesque sub-human beings, and also a representation of a deer and a bird-like creature.

The frontal treatment of the human figure is evident in both panels. The chariot in the one and the elephant in the other are depicted in profile, but the figures in the chariot and on the elephant are portrayed frontally. The strange female demons of the Chariot relief have their feet turned upwards in a most unnatural way. These sculptures appear at first sight to display affinities with the reliefs on *stūpa* II at Sanchi: there is the same frontal depiction of the human figure, the awkward treatment of the feet and the shallowness of the carving. At neither site is there any attempt at polishing of the stone. These similarities are not, however, significant enough to assign Bhaja to the phase of Sanchi II. The frontal treatment of the human figure is a characteristic to be seen also at Bharhut and occasionally as late as the Sanchi gateways. The awkward treatment of the feet may be seen in some medallions at Bharhut and the same may be said regarding the shallow carving. Bhaja reveals, in fact, some notable differences as compared with Sanchi II. At the latter the composition is very simple with a basically symmetrical scheme, while at Bhaja there is little attempt at symmetrical arrangement and the Chariot panel disregards even the corner of the cave wall as it sweeps across it. A striking example is provided by the deer whose head is depicted on the right wall, while its body may be seen above the lower demons on the main wall. There is considerable overlapping of figures and the sculptors have dropped their insistence, evident at Sanchi II, on depicting both shoulders completely. In the Elephant panel one shoulder of either figure is in the shadow and left to the imagination. The same is the case with the attendants and the accompanying riders in the Chariot panel. This indicates a distinct advance on Sanchi II where such an effect was never sought after. It is more akin in style to some panels at Bharhut, such as the dancing scenes on the Prasenajit pillar, in which a number of women are depicted sideways without an insistence on the portrayal of both arms and shoulders. A consideration of motifs also inclines us to suggest the rough contemporaneity of Bhaja with Bharhut. The decorative plume on the heads of the horses, the fly-whisk and umbrella are similar to those on the Prasenajit pillar at Bharhut. The attendant on the Elephant panel carrying a banner with a *triratna* emblem, is reminiscent of the Indra/Indrāni medallion at Bharhut, where we see two riders on a similar though more sedate elephant also holding a tree in its trunk.

Plates 9–13   Apart from these two narrative panels, five full-length standing figures, three in the veranda and two in the interior, also embellish this *vihāra*. They are apparently guardians and carry various weapons including the sword, spear, bow and arrows and club. The three in the veranda are elaborately dressed and wear the *fleur de lis* armlet, an ornament which appears only in the early sculptural phase. The two in the interior are very simply clothed and, though of the non-warrior class, are guardians nevertheless. They are all carved in low flat relief and are frontally represented with both shoulders clearly visible, but with feet turned sideways in the same direction. The guardian to the extreme right in the veranda is undoubtedly meant to Plate 11 be in profile. Great attention is paid to surface decoration: every bead that makes up the bracelets and necklets, every fold in the garments, and the detailed design of the head-dress tapestry have been painstakingly depicted.

The narrow relief panel on the eastern wall of the veranda includes the representation of a winged horse, two figures with upraised arms as if supporting the balustrade, a central horse-and-rider figure, and Plate 14 two fighting bulls with apparently a prostrate figure between them. Here again we see an insistence on the frontal depiction of the human figure, while the animals are carved entirely in profile. It is apparent that the composition in this relief centred around the schematically conceived frontal human figure. The comparatively naturalistic delineation of animals must surely have had something to do with the fact that they were, perhaps, considered of secondary importance, and no rigid schema had been evolved for their depiction. As soon as an animal body is crowned with a human head, as for example, in the centaur medallion at Sanchi II, the upper part of the body once Plate 88 again becomes strictly frontal. Along the wall above this panel were two pilasters with centaur couples crowning the 'bell' capital. Today only one remains, the other being known solely from Burgess' Plate 16 accounts.[4] It is rather difficult to distinguish the male from the female except by the beaded waist band and the more slender waist of the female compared with the knotted cloth band of the male. Centaurs are to be seen on *stūpa* II at Sanchi and at BodhGaya, and a female centaur with a male rider makes an appearance in a medallion at Sanchi II.

There is little doubt that the Bhaja guardian figures may not be compared with some of the advanced Bharhut carvings such as the pillar *yakshis* and *yakshas*. However, the narrative reliefs definitely display an advance on the depictions of *stūpa* II at Sanchi. Stylistic considerations, as a whole, incline us to place the Bhaja *vihāra* sculptures somewhat in advance of Sanchi II and perhaps roughly contemporary with the Bharhut carvings.

Nadsur

The small series of caves at Nadsur, unknown to Burgess and Fergusson when they wrote their classic *Cave Temples of India*, were later briefly described by Cousens.[5] These caves contain a few examples of decorative sculpture that appear to belong to a very early phase. *Vihāra* XV at Nadsur contains a bas-relief depiction of a

Plate 15   man and woman standing on a large fish, of which unfortunately there appears to be no photographic record. Cousens' drawing reveals that although the man is portrayed frontally, his feet are shown awkwardly turned in the same direction. The decoration of *vihāra*

Plates 17, 18   VII includes two Gajalakshmī representations contained within the arch above the cell doorways. The two sets of elephants standing on half-lotuses, with water-pots in their trunks, have rich trappings on their backs. Such decoration is consistently absent in Gajalakshmī reliefs at Bharhut and Sanchi. In both Nadsur examples Lakshmī holds the stalks of the lotus in her hands and wears a long skirt and an elaborate head-dress. It seems clear that both reliefs display greater

Plate 87   affinities with the Sanchi II representation than with that on the Bhar-

Plate 89   hut medallion where the style is more assured and crisp. The sculptural decoration at Nadsur appears to belong to the period of Sanchi II and is slightly earlier than or perhaps roughly contemporary with the Bhaja *vihāra* reliefs.

Pitalkhora

The transition from the shallow stiff style of Bharhut to the more free and easy rendering of the human body evident at BodhGaya and to a fuller extent in the sculptures of *stūpa* I at Sanchi, is achieved in the Deccan at Pitalkhora. Recent clearance at the site has yielded a large number of carvings among which, however, a diversity of style is apparent. Some of the sculptures are more advanced and are presumably of slightly later date than others. The most impressive of the

Plate 22   discoveries is a high plinth in front of *vihāra* IV, seemingly supported on the backs of a majestic row of life-size elephants. Originally a mahout stood between the forelegs of each, and the fragments recovered reveal that these tall, rather stiff figures had great dignity. To the right of the row of elephants is a badly damaged relief of a horse and attendants. To the extreme left of the elephants is a

Plate 23   decorated doorway leading up to *vihāra* IV. The guardians on either side of the doorway contrast with the flattened Bharhut figures and are closer to BodhGaya in the rounded treatment of the planes of the body. They appear, however, to belong to a different tradition with their unusual costume consisting of a fringed tunic worn over a *dhoti*, and they carry a shield and javelin unlike the guardians at the Nasik *caitya* and on the Sanchi gateways who merely carry flowers. The Gajalakshmī panel that fits over the doorway resembles the Bharhut medallion representations in the depiction of the lotus flower and in the way the elephants' legs are placed on the lotus. However, the execution of the motif is much more accomplished than at Bharhut, although not yet comparable to depictions on the Sanchi gateways. An uncommon feature that we have seen also at Nadsur, but which does not appear at Bharhut or Sanchi, is the decorated cloth on the backs of the elephants.

Plate 24
cf. Plate 89

The more than life-size guardian belonging to *caitya* III is an unusual figure. The completely flat treatment of the planes of the body is comparable to the style at Bharhut and contrasts strangely with the rounded modelling of the head. It is almost as though two sculptors had worked on the piece. The firm outline of the eyes reminds us strongly of a similar treatment of the eyes on the Bharhut figures and there is also a comparable fine polish. The figure wears the *fleur de lis* armlet, and carries a staff and sword, and is undoubtedly one of the earlier pieces carved at Pitalkhora.

Plate 20

The striking dwarf-*yaksha* apparently found in front of *caitya* III, has been described eloquently as 'exulting as though possessed of some unholy secret'.[6] The figure, intact down to the knees only, measures about $3\frac{1}{2}$ ft, and represents a powerful squat dwarf wearing a *dhoti* with necklaces, ear-rings, armlets and bracelets. The human amulet threaded on his necklet is worthy of notice. At Bharhut a number of *yakshas* and *yakshis* have inverted *triratnas* on their necklaces. The similarity of these two forms is so close that there seems little doubt that it is this *triratna* that has been elaborated into a human amulet. The figure wears the *fleur de lis* armlet – an ornament that makes its last appearance on the Sanchi gateways and is not repeated in sculptures belonging to any later phase. His hair is twisted into a series of rolls and he has a wide grin on his face. His arms are uplifted and support a shallow bowl on the top of his head. A clear inscription engraved on the outer side of his right palm states that the figure was made (*katā*) by a goldsmith named Kanhadāsa. It is an accomplished work and though the firm outline of the eyes is certainly reminiscent of the treatment at Bharhut, we would consider the figure to belong to a slightly later phase. The goldsmith who carved

Plate 21

Fig. 4

4 *Some significant motifs: a-f Lotus-and-stem motif; a Bharhut; b Pitalkhora vihāra; c Nasik caitya; d Sanchi stūpa I, north gateway; e Sanchi stūpa I, north gateway; f Sanchi stupa III; g Bharhut, necklace with inverted tri-ratnas; h Pitalkhora, necklace with 'human amulets'; i Sanchi tie-rod*

the figure was apparently quite adept at the art of stone carving too. The figure reminds one quite strongly of the dwarf-like *yakshas* who with their upraised arms, support the architraves of the west gateway of the Sanchi *stūpa*. These dwarfs have a similar gleeful and almost wicked grin on their faces. M. N. Deshpande suggests that the Pitalkhora figure actually provided a model for the Sanchi examples.[7] However, the motif of dwarf-like figures holding up various architectural members is a popular one, and is already to be seen at Bharhut where blocks of the railing are shown supported by such figures. It is not necessary to derive the Sanchi gateway figures from this Pitalkhora example. The grinning dwarf figures holding up the balustrade of the stairs in front of *caitya* III appear to belong to this same category of dwarf-*yaksha*.

A theme that seems to have been rather popular at Pitalkhora is that of the *mithuna* or the couple. This was a favourite subject with the Indian sculptor and is found on the ring-stones of Mauryan times, at Bharhut, BodhGaya and Sanchi, and in several of the early Buddhist cave sites. The couples very rarely betray any erotic suggestion such as is sometimes seen in the art of later periods. It has been suggested that these figures represent donor couples, but several sculptures depict dancing couples, and it would seem that the term *mithuna* is more applicable. The carvings depict broad-shouldered, athletic men, and curvaceous female forms, and illustrate the inseparability of religious and secular themes in Indian art. It was not considered incongruous to find such figures carved on a religious monument. Most of the reliefs depicting *mithunas* at Pitalkhora are in a fragmentary condition. Among them one piece, on which only part of the male figure is intact, is of interest because of the joyous   Plate 29 expression portrayed on the face of the man. Another striking fragment depicts a man holding a woman by the hand, as if persuading   Plate 30 her to follow him or join him in dance. It has been pointed out that . 'the sculpture reminds one of the panels on the façade of the *chaitya-*cave at Kondane'.[8] A comparison is indeed possible and serves to emphasize the highly advanced carving at Kondane. Although the *cf.* Plates 31, 32 Pitalkhora figures are imbued with a sense of movement, the Kondane dancers by comparison are more spirited and ebullient. At Pitalkhora importance is still attached to the detailed depiction of the folds of the garments and the beads of the necklaces, while at Kondane the emphasis is entirely on the planes of the body.

The Great Departure panel depicting a horse with an umbrella   Plate 27 held over it and a gateway in the background, is an advanced piece as compared to the carving at Bhaja. The handling of the figures in relation to the background space seems to set it apart from Bharhut and closer to Sanchi I. The gateway closely resembles those depicted in the early paintings in *caityas* X and IX at Ajanta. The Royal Couple panel displays a rounded treatment of the planes of the body quite Plate 28 unlike anything to be seen at Bharhut. There is a fair amount of overlapping of figures and the arm of one of the attendant maids disappears into the shadow. The sculpture is in several planes and, with its graceful flowing style, is sophisticated in treatment; it is one of the latest and certainly one of the most advanced pieces to be seen at Pitalkhora. Remnants of the female figure to the extreme right of the elephant plinth would seem to display a similar style, and the graceful posturing of the legs makes us regret very much the loss of the rest of the panel.

Fig. 4 One of the more significant motifs at Pitalkhora is a repeated lotus-and-stem design that appears on the jambs of the doorway leading up to *vihāra* IV. A similar motif is to be seen on the doorway of the Nasik *caitya* and also on the pillars of the north gateway at Sanchi. At Nasik, on every alternate lotus-and-stem unit, the curved stem-like portion has been replaced by a tiny human figure. On the north gateway at Sanchi both varieties are to be seen: the entirely floral design on the east face of the left pillar, and the human figures combined with the floral motif on the west face of the right pillar. At Pitalkhora and Nasik the lotus flower is given prominence, while at Sanchi emphasis is on the stem, the flower having shrunk in size or being completely absent. A much enlarged version of the same motif is also to be found on the inner face of the gateway of *stūpa* III at Sanchi. The decoration is at its simplest and apparently its earliest at Pitalkhora.

The pilasters on the back wall of *vihāra* IV have representations of various winged animals, both real and mythical – types found com-
Plates 25, 26 monly from Sanchi *stūpa* II onwards. A closer look at the *caitya* arches above the cell doorways reveals an interesting detail. The arch contains the usual representations of wooden ribs, but between these are tiny figures of animals, including lions, horses and elephants. Odette Viennot suggests that the animal at the corner of each panel is,
cf. Plate 1 in fact, a *makara*, accommodated in a manner similar to its position on the Lomasa Rishi façade. This appears to be the case. She suggests further that the *makara* is to be found in a similar position on the Nasik *caitya* and in the Budh Lena *vihāras* at Junnar.⁹

The sculptures at Pitalkhora illustrate the various stages in the transition from the flat static depictions reminiscent of Bharhut to the free easy style seen on the Sanchi gateways. Among the earliest carvings is the guardian *yaksha* of *caitya* III – a piece that compares well with some of the advanced work at Bharhut. The next stage is represented by the majestic elephant plinth and the doorway with the Gajalakshmī panel above and the doorkeepers on either side – all obviously part of a single plan. The feeling here is one of a slight advance on Bharhut and of greater affinities with the style of Bodh-Gaya. Towards the lower end of the transitional period is the Great Departure panel where the handling of the figure sets it apart from Bharhut and closer to Sanchi. Finally, there are fragments such as the Royal Couple where the treatment of the planes of the body indicates definitely that this was one of the latest pieces carved at the site. M. N. Deshpande indicates that the purpose of the various detached, as opposed to rock-engraved, sculptures was to cover up the worn out surfaces of the rather poor quality rock at Pitalkhora.[10] Such a theory explains the variations in sculptural style seen at the site, since the detached pieces were obviously carved at a later date than the caves themselves.

Nasik *Caitya*

Clad in a *dhoti* and adorned with characteristic knotted head-dress and heavy ear-rings, the guardian standing beside the doorway of the Nasik *caitya* holds the ends of his *dhoti* in one hand and a flower in the other. In the treatment of the planes of the body the closest parallels are the Indra figure at BodhGaya and the Sanchi gateway guardians. However, the weakly rounded shoulders and the somewhat cramped depiction of the left arm of the Nasik figure indicate a lesser craftsmanship that was unable to achieve the grace and vigour of the Sanchi guardians. The balustrade beside the figure has one full and two half roundels with buds depicted at the angles, and it runs upwards at an incline similar to that of the balustrade leading to the upper circumambulatory path of *stūpa* I at Sanchi.

    The door-jambs of the *caitya* are decorated with an elaborate lotus-and-stem design similar to that found at Pitalkhora *vihāra* IV. We have seen that the pattern at Nasik, with its tiny human figures on every alternate unit, is an elaboration of the simpler design at Pitalkhora. The arch above the doorway, as in Pitalkhora *vihāra* IV, contains a representation of wooden ribs with horses, elephants and bulls depicted in the spaces between. Here, however, the ribs have been combined into an intricate knotted pattern with a *triratna* in the centre. The row of beam ends depicted all along the façade above the level of the doorway is noteworthy as every alternate beam end has been carved into a human head. The façade is elaborately carved: *stūpas* with miniature arches above them are sculpted between pillars with addorsed animal capitals, and trellis work is abundant. The carvings on the Nasik *caitya* would seem to be roughly contemporary with some of the more advanced work at Pitalkhora,[11] and are earlier than the sculptures on the gateways of *stūpa* I at Sanchi.

Plate 44

cf. Plate 90

Kondane

The principal sculptural decoration now remaining at the Kondane caves consists of a panel of dancing figures on either side of the springing of the *caitya* arch. The carving of these panels of dancing or dallying men and women is of unsurpassed elegance. The artist's ease in handling the animated, graceful and lively figures certainly reveals his mastery over his craft. The men, who are possibly warriors, are shown holding a club in one panel, bow and arrow in another, and a shield in a third. The sculptor has imparted to their faces a touch of whimsy as he has given them smiling countenances. No longer is there the stiffness that we see in the Bharhut dancing scenes: the poses are graceful and easy and the relief is much deeper. The angles at which the body is posed display a mastery not to be found at Bharhut or even BodhGaya, and in the rounded planes of the body the treatment of the figures is akin to the style of the Sanchi gateway sculptures.[12] We have here moved well away from the preoccupation with surface decoration evident in the portrayal of the guardians in the Bhaja *vihāra*. There is no detailed depiction of the tapestry of the head-dress or of the beads of the necklets and bracelets: the emphasis is on the essential planes of the body.

Plate 33 A single, damaged head, more than life-size, may be seen lower down on the façade of the *caitya*. The figure when intact must have been of impressive proportions. The pattern in the tapestry of the head-dress has been depicted with painstaking care: this attention to surface detail would seem to contradict the evidence of the dancing figures just considered. The Kondane carvings are apparently representative of a transitional phase in stylistic development, during which the earlier emphasis on surface decoration was occasionally still to be found.

Ajanta *Caityas* X and IX

There is a complete absence of sculptures belonging to an early date in *caityas* X and IX at Ajanta, but both caves contain early paintings (as well as later examples). An examination of available reproductions of these fragments inclines us to assign the paintings to two phases, one slightly more advanced than the other. In terms of actual time, however, the difference may well be negligible.

The exact location of the various paintings in *caitya* X is best seen from Fig. 5. The three scenes on the left wall of the *caitya* appear to be part of the same painting, but large sections having peeled off in

Plates 31, 32 (margin note)

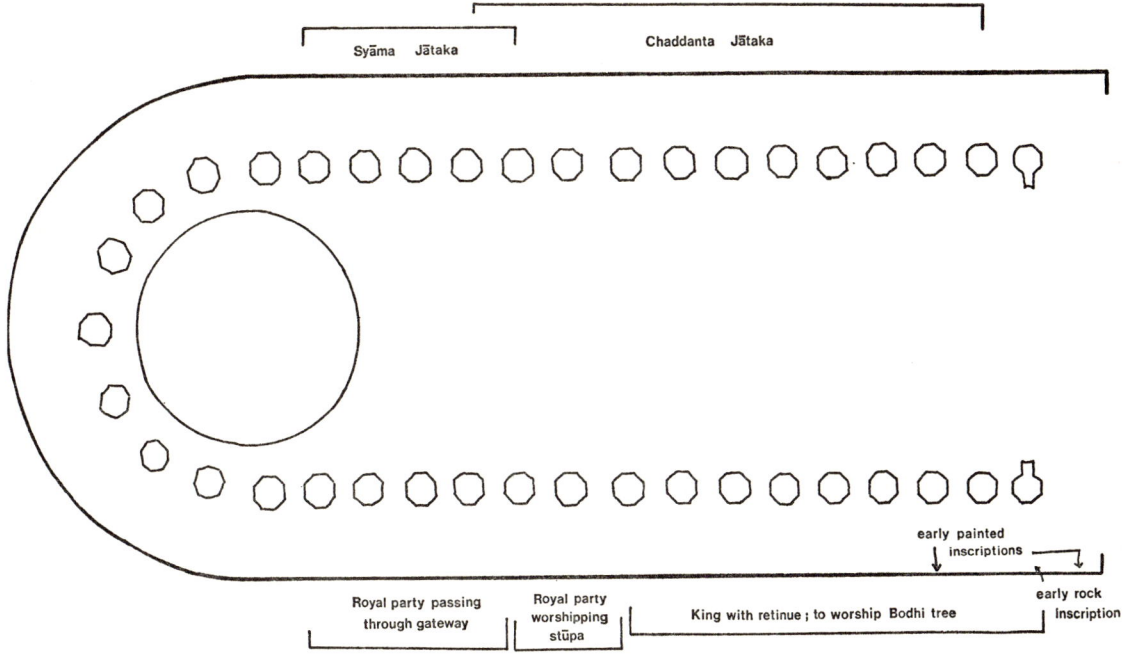

Syāma Jātaka

Chaddanta Jātaka

early painted
inscriptions

Royal party passing
through gateway

Royal party
worshipping
stūpa

King with retinue ; to worship Bodhi tree

early rock
inscription

5   Ajanta Caitya X: Location of early paintings

between, the three have been separately labelled. We see a king with
his retinue first worshipping a *bodhi* tree, then a *stūpa*, and finally
passing under a gateway. The free and easy poses of the women
suggest a phase akin to some of the advanced work at Pitalkhora,
and the gateway is similar to that depicted in the Great Departure
relief from the same site. It is interesting to note that the king is
depicted wearing a *fleur de lis* armlet. There are three inscriptions
in *caitya* X that are of relevance from the point of view of the murals
themselves. The fragmentary painted inscription No. 14, which we
have assigned palaeographically to Series I (b), is on the wall of the
left aisle, and would appear to be associated quite definitely with the
scene of the king and his retinue. The two newly discovered inscriptions both seem to belong to a slightly earlier palaeographic
phase. The rock inscription is to be found on the wall of the left
aisle, occupying the space just beneath the first and third ribs. This
record, donating the wall of the cave, was uncovered beneath a

layer of mud plaster, and would seem to indicate that the painted decoration was not part of the original conception of the *caitya*. However, the new painted inscription, belonging apparently to the same palaeographic phase, indicates that the idea of the addition of the murals arose very soon after the completion of the excavation. This record is painted in white on the third rafter of the left aisle and, while much weathered, it is still possible to decipher its donatory nature.

The *Syāma jātaka* painting on the right wall of cave X depicts rows of hunters, somewhat similar in conception to the more hieratic figures at Bharhut, and also to be seen on a few panels at Sanchi. The elegant conception of the *Chaddanta jākata* scenes, also on the right wall of *caitya* X, seems to be the counterpart of the advanced sculptures on the Sanchi gateways. The assured handling of complex groups, the distinct effect of depth, the easy manner of depicting the human body in various positions, the mobility of the figures – all these characteristics are reminiscent of the carvings on the gateways of Sanchi *stūpa* I.

Caitya IX contains two sets of early paintings. The animal-and-herdsmen frieze is located immediately above the first few pillars on the left side facing the nave. The free, graceful movement of the herdsmen seems to recall the panels of dancing figures at Kondane. The group of *Nāga* votaries approaching a *stūpa* commences on the inner wall and continues along almost the entire length of the *caitya*'s left wall. The figures are conceived in a manner similar to those of the king and his retinue composition in cave X. Thus, in general, the murals in *caityas* X and IX at Ajanta seem to be the painted versions of the sculptures at BodhGaya, the latest reliefs at Pitalkhora, and the panels of dancing figures from Kondane. The *Chaddanta jātaka* painting appears to be more advanced than the other fragments and may, perhaps, be considered to belong to a phase contemporary with work on the Sanchi gateways.

cf. Plates 27, 28,
31, 32

Tulja Lena *Caitya* (Junnar)

Traces of painting may be seen on the pillars of the circular Tulja *caitya* at Junnar, and one relatively well preserved fragment depicts a standing woman.[13] The elegance and grace of the pose is reminiscent of the *Chaddanta jātaka* scenes at Ajanta, but on the basis of a single fragment it would be very unwise indeed to express any positive judgement.

Bedsa

The only carving to be found in the small set of caves at Bedsa is in the form of the animal-and-rider capitals crowning the tall, slender columns in the *caitya* veranda. The conception of these figures is similar to that of the riders depicted on the gateways at Sanchi, and in both we find a single rider on each animal. The grace and ease with which the Bedsa figures are portrayed reveals a technical accomplishment certainly equal to and perhaps somewhat in advance of the carvings on the Sanchi gateways. The side walls of the veranda are carved with row upon row of miniature arches resting on *vedikā*-bands. As with the façades of the *caityas* at Bhaja, Kondane and Nasik, this was in imitation of the front of a structural building.

Budh Lena (Junnar)

The Budh Lena *caitya* has a unique façade consisting of a 'blind' Plate 55 *caitya* arch and, within it, a half-lotus with seven sculptured petals. The theme portrayed appears to be that of Gajalakshmī, the standing figure in the central petal with one hand placed on her hip being Lakshmī. The elephants in the petals on either side stand on half-lotuses and hold water-pots in their raised trunks. The remaining two petals on either side contain the dancing figures of a *yaksha* and *yakshi*, with one leg flexed and hands joined together above their heads. The conception of the theme is rather unusual as most other representations depict only Lakshmī and the elephants. The assurance with which the artist has handled his space, as well as the essential relationship between the figures and their background, would imply a date well in advance of the sculptures on the Sanchi gateways.[14] The figures, in fact, are strongly reminiscent of the *mithunas* in the Karle *caitya*, and perhaps more so of the couples placed within the *cf.* Plate 42 springing of the Karle *caitya* arch. The two male figures at the top of the Budh Lena arch, the one winged and the other with *Nāga* hoods raised above him, are also similar in conception to those seen at Karle.

Karle

The Karle *mithuna* couples, large, calm and dignified, engage one's attention as soon as one enters the veranda of the *caitya*. The figures are cut in deep relief and the planes of the body are rounded and flowing. It would be no exaggeration to say that these figures constitute our finest examples of sculpture from the early Buddhist caves. A striking feature is the great difference in workmanship displayed by these couples. One may compare, for example, the two splendid *mithunas* to the right of the main doorway with the couples at the corners of the outer screen, facing the *caitya*. Or, again, we may contrast the superior sculpting of the couple immediately to the left of the main doorway with those further to the left. One assumes that the master craftsman carved the main couples, leaving the others to his assistants who were unable to capture the indefinable quality and skill of their master. There is little doubt too that some of the figures are partly incomplete – the polishing and the finishing touches are lacking. Two elegant *mithunas* on a smaller scale may be seen above the elephants on the side walls of the veranda, and two more beside the main *caitya* arch. Great skill is shown in the way these two latter dancing couples are comfortably accommodated within the curve formed by the springing of the *caitya* arch. There is some disagreement as to whether these figures are best described as donor couples or as *mithunas*. One scholar describes them as 'Mithuna couples, wrongly identified as donors',[15] while others feel that they should not be called *mithunas* as there is only a hint of eroticism about the figures.[16] If indeed they were intended to represent specific donors, it is not unreasonable to expect epigraphic evidence to this effect, particularly in view of the large number of donative inscriptions in the *caitya*. The theme is one we are familiar with in early Indian art, and we would be inclined to describe the figures as *mithunas*. The side walls of the veranda, seemingly supported on the backs of three life-size elephants, are carved in imitation of the façade of a five-storeyed building. We have seen that this type of decoration was the normal practice on *caitya* façades.

The capitals of the columns within the *caitya* are crowned with animal-and-rider figures carved almost in the round, and as one looks up, the figures appear to 'merge themselves into a kind of sculptured frieze',[17] the effect of which is quite overwhelming. Facing the nave we find two seated elephants with two riders on each, usually one man and one woman, but occasionally two women. In the aisles, horses with single riders are to be seen, and in two instances the horse is replaced by a sphinx. On one of these capitals a *mithuna* couple is to be seen instead of the more usual seated riders. In general, the riders display the same formal properties as the veranda *mithunas*. Outside the *caitya*, to the left, stands an impressive lion pillar, although in their plastic quality the lions are not among the

Plate 43

Plate 42

best works at Karle. However, the extremely abraded surface of the rock may be partly responsible for this impression. Originally there was probably a corresponding pillar on the right side, but the place where it must have stood is now occupied by a Śaiva temple painted in bright colours.

Nasik *Vihāras* X and III

The capitals in *vihāras* X and III at Nasik are also of the animal-and-rider variety, as seen at Karle, but are quite differently conceived. At Karle, the riders, carved almost entirely in the round, are given as much importance, if not more, as the animals. At Nasik, the riders are not only depicted in shallow relief but are so diminutive as to be completely overshadowed by the animals. The number of riders on each animal varies from one to three. Although the roof rises forward above these capitals and rather draws attention away from the riders, it is possible to see that these tiny figures are depicted with great ease and freedom. These capitals, while different in conception, would appear to belong to a date at least as advanced as Karle.

Plates 47, 48

Some half a dozen steps lead up to *vihāra* III that is seemingly supported by *yaksha*-like figures emerging from the ground waist upwards. The *yakshas* hold in their hands or carry on their shoulders the ends of the large beams that would have supported a structural building. We have seen that this type of motif was a popular one in early Indian art. At Bharhut and BodhGaya we find *yaksha* figures supporting entire blocks of railing, at Pitalkhora dwarf-like figures hold up the balustrade of the stairs in front of *caitya* III, at Sanchi dwarf-*yakshas* support the gateway architraves, and similar figures may also be seen at Amaravati. The low front wall of the veranda of *vihāra* III at Nasik is carved in imitation of a railing and is decorated with three full lotuses. The coping stone above and below is carved with the meandering lotus stalk motif. The entablature is decorated in a similar manner but with animal figures and a herdsman added within the undulating lotus stems.

Plate 48

The central doorway of the *vihāra* is carved in low relief in imitation of a structural gateway. On either side of the doorway are a series of sculptured panels depicting *mithunas* and, placed one above the other, they form a pillar that terminates in two architraves supported by brackets. The lower one is supported by a rampant lion, while the upper has a plain rod-like bracket. Human figures, *stūpas* and pillars separate the two architraves. Also on either side of the

Plates 45, 46   doorway is a guardian in shallow relief with one hand on hip and the other holding up a bunch of flowers. The figures are short and stocky with broad shoulders, and the carving of the hands and feet is awkward. There is a noticeably flat treatment of the planes of the Plate 50   body. On the back wall of the *vihāra* is a relief representation of a *stūpa* with female worshippers. Although the women are iconographically of the same type as at Karle, and even the poses are similar, their masterly rendering at Karle contrasts ostensibly with the inferior workmanship at Nasik. A *stūpa* adored by worshippers is a familiar motif at Amaravati, and recently a relief portraying the same theme has also been found at Ter.[18]

Lenyadri (Junnar)

Sculpture at Lenyadri consists solely of animal figures crowning the capitals of the apsidal *caitya* VI and the adjoining Gaṇeśa Lena *vihāra*. These are somewhat similar in conception to the capitals of Nasik *vihāras* X and III, although the absence of riders and the general paucity of material makes it difficult to make a detailed comparison.

Kuda *Caitya* VI

Plates 68, 70, 71   The *mithuna* couples placed against the back wall of the main chamber of Kuda *caitya* VI display some differences as compared to those at Karle, and appear to belong to a slightly later date. The carving has less depth but the poses are more free and easy. One of the women is depicted as standing somewhat behind the man and her hand is hidden by the man. The other woman rests her left hand on the head of a seated boy attendant, who also holds her bent left foot in his hands. The head-dress of the women is more elaborate than any we have come across so far. Both men rest one hand on their hips in a relaxed pose and have the other raised. Below each of these couples Plate 69   is a narrow animal-and-herdsmen frieze with running animals and little dwarf-like figures. The theme is strikingly similar to portions of the Amaravati coping[19] and to the painted frieze in *caitya* IX at Ajanta. It is also to be seen in the Khandagiri caves in Orissa and on a brass vessel found at Brahmapuri. It was thus a popular theme in early Indian art. The roof outside the veranda of Kuda *caitya* VI projects some eight feet and was held up at either end by a standing Plate 73   elephant: now only the one at the left remains. As at Pitalkhora and Karle, the head and two front feet alone are carved out of the rock.

Brahmapuri

The important Kundangar hoard discovered in a simple Sātavāhana house in the course of excavations at the site of Brahmapuri seems to have comprised a trader's stock. The hoard contained several interesting objects of Roman origin including a statuette of Poseidon which the trader no doubt acquired from the foreign merchants who visited the coastal towns.[20] Among the number of objects of local origin is a tiny bronze seated elephant with riders. This remarkable   Plate 83 piece, only 2½ inches long and 2 inches high, reflects without doubt considerable experience in metal casting. The motif is familiar to us: we have seen it at Sanchi, Bedsa, Karle and Nasik. Here, however, there are four riders, a number not met with elsewhere. At Sanchi and Bedsa we find one rider on each animal; at Karle, two; and at Nasik, from one to three. The four riders at Brahmapuri include, beside the lady and her lord, a female attendant and a page boy. Their dress is familiar to us and the man wears the characteristic *dhoti*, turban and ornaments. Considering the popularity of the theme it has been suggested that on occasions such as visits to shrines, men and women of nobility moved around on elephants.[21] Such an   *cf.* Plate 82 explanation could not, of course, be extended to the many depictions of riders on lions, goats, griffins and sphinxes. This little bronze elephant was obviously fashioned for a decorative purpose as the stump of a broken peg still remains under its stomach.

Brief mention may be made of a few other significant objects. A brass vessel engraved with a frieze of running animals and a single herdsman[22] would seem to be of the same category as the panels at Kuda, Ajanta IX, Amaravati and Khandagiri. Fabulous animals are to be seen in the hoard in the form of a plaque shaped as a griffin, and a metal ring with four animal heads including that of a griffin and a sphinx.[23] Worthy of note is the ornamental hook of a hanging lamp,   Plate 84 exquisitely carved in the form of an elephant's head. It has been pointed out that similar heads are to be seen in the Amaravati throne carvings.[24] The objects from the Brahmapuri hoard undoubtedly belong to the period after the Karle sculptures and in date are somewhere in the second century AD.

Ter

Surface finds from the banks of the river Tirna at Ter include several bone, soapstone and terracotta figures, besides a notable ivory female   Plate 85 figurine. This figure, over six inches high, contains a vertical aperture

Plate 86
in its head reaching down to the navel, to a depth of almost 2½ inches. A similar aperture exists in the head of the Pompeii ivory where it reaches down to the loins. This unique characteristic certainly seems to establish a relationship between the two: it appears probable that the Pompeii ivory is of Sātavāhana workmanship. The Pompeii figure has a horn-like protrusion on its head and there also seems to be the fragmentary remains of one on the Ter ivory. Both figures have one arm raised, seemingly touching their ear-rings. Douglas Barrett comments on the 'dry' treatment of the Ter figure and considers it to be closer in style to the art of Sanchi and the western caves,[25] while Moti Chandra sees greater affinities with Amaravati.[26] A comparison with terracottas found locally suggests that the ivory was made at Ter itself and M. N. Deshpande concludes that, as Ter was situated midway on a trade route, influences from both areas may reasonably be expected.[27] Recently discovered fragments of drum slabs at Ter indicate the existence of an early *stūpa* at the site. Douglas Barrett points out that one piece is strikingly similar to the bas-relief in *vihāra* III at Nasik, while the other is akin to depictions at Amaravati. This would indeed suggest that Ter received influences from both the western Deccan and the Krishna basin. These examples of sculpture from Ter belong, in general, to the period after the Karle *caitya*, and are perhaps roughly contemporary with *vihāras* X and III at Nasik.

Kanheri

Plates 78, 79
By comparison with Karle and Kuda, the *mithuna* couples in the Kanheri *caitya* appear flat, static and lifeless. They have a vacuous expression and there is little variety in their poses: the vitality to be seen at Karle is absent here. The Kanheri capitals are quite different in conception to those at Karle. The rounded inverted *ghaṭas* are crowned by a block of relief sculpture with scenes such as those of elephants and human worshippers paying homage to a *stūpa* or other emblems of the Buddha. Occasionally an elephant-and-rider theme is to be seen, but this again is quite differently conceived: a man seated on an elephant bends down to help up the woman, while other figures are shown around them. The Karle effect of animals

Plate 77
and riders almost in the round is here replaced by a block of relief sculpture.

Plate 75
The low wall enclosing the courtyard is decorated with a railing in a manner somewhat similar to Nasik *vihāra* III, and depicts three

lotuses on the uprights and a coping with an undulating lotus stem. The space below is divided into panels containing lotuses and tiny *yaksha* figures. On either side of the courtyard entrance is a guardian with one hand raised and the other on his hip. The treatment is similar to that of the guardian in *vihāra* III at Nasik. At the far right is a figure with a *Nāga* hood, similarly conceived, carved in low relief and in a much weathered condition. Engaged lion columns may be seen in the courtyard. One shaft is interrupted halfway up its height by a large inverted *ghaṭa*, and while one abacus supports seated lions, the other apparently supported dwarf-like figures. The entire rock is in a much ruined condition.

Concluding Remarks

The general trend visible during the period of the early Buddhist caves is a development from shallow relief sculpture with an emphasis on surface decoration to a truly sculptural style of deeper relief with simplified details. At Bhaja and Nadsur, as at Sanchi *stūpa* II and Bharhut, what we may perhaps term the ivory-workers' technique is evident: every detail of the tapestry of the head-dresses and every bead in a necklace is depicted. This early sculpture centred around the schematically conceived frontal human figure, a basically symmetrical composition and shallow carving. Every figure had to be shown with both shoulders and legs clearly visible, and the profile was avoided. Soon this attitude began to change and by the time of the Pitalkhora and Kondane sculptures, the artists had learned to handle the human figure in various positions and to organize their space better. An equally striking development is to be seen from the Nasik *caitya* guardian to the Karle *mithunas*. At Karle emphasis is no longer on the flat masses of the body as at Nasik, and arms and legs are no longer separate entities but are organically joined to the body in a naturalistic fashion. There is also a much more detailed knowledge of anatomy that is evident in the representation of stomach muscles. The flowing planes of the body and not the details of turban decoration are now emphasized, and the relief is so deep the figures seem to stand by themselves. These later figures have a power and vitality about them altogether lacking in the shallow reliefs at Bhaja with their preoccupation with fussy surface details. Gradually then the artist modified his schema, both due to observations from life and to the increase in the sophistication of the craft,

13

and part of this 'long road through schema and correction'[28] is apparent in the period of the early Buddhist caves.

Several common motifs are to be found throughout these centuries and among them is the dress and ornaments of both men and women. The men are clad in *dhotis*, with elaborate head-dresses, bangles, necklets and heavy ear-rings. The women have a beaded band around their hips and wear a skirt that is indicated merely by a line along the ankles. Their head-dress is not as elaborate as that of the men, but they wear similar bangles, necklaces and ear-rings. Armlets too are common, and the variety described as *fleur de lis* is of especial interest as it is restricted in occurrence to the beginning of our period. It may be seen at Sanchi *stūpa* II, Bharhut, Bhaja, Pitalkhora, in the paintings in *caitya* X at Ajanta, and on a few figures on the Sanchi gateways, where it is by no means common.[29] It is intriguing to notice its occurrence at Begram on a pottery vase shaped in the form of a sphinx.[30] Winged animals, griffins, centaurs and sphinxes are to be found throughout the western caves, and also at Sanchi II, Bharhut, BodhGaya, the Sanchi gateways, Amaravati and the Orissan caves. It does not seem necessary to seek to derive the Karle sphinx (sculpted on a pillar capital facing the aisle) and the Bhaja centaur from an imported statuette.[31] The animal-and-herdsmen frieze seems to have been a popular one and we find it sculpted at Amaravati, Khandagiri in Orissa, Kuda, Brahmapuri and Ajanta IX (paintings). Another favoured motif is that of the dwarf-*yakshas* holding up various architectural members – blocks of railing at Bharhut and Amaravati, the architraves of the west gateway at Sanchi, the balustrade of the steps at Pitalkhora and the entire cave at Nasik III. Yet another popular theme is the *mithuna* which is depicted throughout our period.

A consideration of style and motifs suggests that during the earlier part of our period, it is justified to regard all this art – on the structural monuments at Bharhut, BodhGaya and Sanchi, as in the caves at Bhaja, Nadsur, Pitalkhora, the Nasik *caitya*, Kondane, Ajanta X and IX, Tulja Lena and Bedsa – as part of one homogenous tradition. With the further increase in the sophistication of the craft, however, it becomes easier to discern regional styles, as for example between the western Deccan and Amaravati, although at the same time parallel developments may be traced in these regions.

6

Social, Economic and Craft Organization

The entire modern conception of art and artists must be set aside to arrive at an understanding of ancient Indian art. The distinction between artists and workmen was then unknown, and the man, whom we regard today as an artist, belonged together with the stone mason, potter and blacksmith, to a class of craftsmen or artisans. These were not people who turned to art because they had a 'leaning' towards it: to them it was a hereditary vocation.[1] Art was part of the social order and it is in this context that the almost complete anonymity of Indian art may best be understood.

It is probable that the initial conception of any cave, as of other monuments, was the work of a single master craftsman. Since his ideas were executed by many hands, one of his main tasks must have been to organize his craftsmen accordingly. Excavating a cave such as Karle would appear to present several problems and the workmen must have had a detailed plan before them. Those who did the preliminary stone cutting knew the exact number of large blocks to be left standing for later conversion into pillars. They knew the number of blocks to be left on an apsidal plan, and the exact height and width of the roof. An accurate system of measurement must have been employed to have resulted in the alignment of the columns. It could have been no easy task to excavate into a mountainside, keeping the row of pillars in line, maintaining them of the same height, and seeing that the pillars in the two aisles corresponded exactly with each other. At Bedsa, for example, there was first the cutting of a passage which was then expanded into a veranda with columns, and only then could excavation of the cave itself commence. The exact location of the site would probably depend on the choice of a suitable mass of rock with no visible or probable faults, and on the existence of a large natural ledge in front of the rock-face to be worked. Presumably it was the master craftsman who chose the precise location and he must have been prepared to make an extensive search before choosing. At most cave sites this must have involved considerable climbing.

The *navakarmika*[2] – the monk in charge of new works – could hardly have been an expert in such technical matters. Presumably he was just a supervisor who left the actual architectural details to a professional craftsman. However, he must have been the one to formulate the specifically religious requirements of the monuments. A Sanchi inscription refers to the *āvesanin*[3] – the foreman of the artisans. We would seem to be justified in assuming that this is our master craftsman. If we are to believe that the *navakarmika* was in charge of the actual building, we must conclude that he was an architect by profession, probably a lay follower, who was taken into the Order to fill the post of *navakarmika*, and this is indeed possible. A Kanheri inscription referring to *selavaḍhakins* (stone masons) and *miṭhikas* (polishers) among other unidentified craftsmen,[4] confirms that there were several classes of stone workers. The sculpture and painting would have been in the hands of different persons, the *rūpakāra* of Bharhut[5] and the *lūpadakhe* of Ramgarh[6] being sculptors. Carpenters (*vaḍhakis*) too were employed to help, no doubt, with the various wooden additions to the early *caityas*. It has been remarked upon that no architect today can get his masons to carve a rich capital without a model of it.[7] Unfortunately we know far too little about the use of artists' copybooks and patterns at this time in ancient India. Later indeed there is evidence that such aids were in use.

The unfinished caves at various sites give us a fairly good idea of the actual process of excavation. Presumably an outline of some sort was first marked out on the rock. The cutting seems, in general, to have started from the ceiling moving downwards, thus minimising the necessity for scaffolding in the preliminary stage. Cave V at Ajanta clearly reveals this process: the interior roof has been smoothed and the blocking out of pillars commenced, but the floor was never reached. It is evident from this and other examples that after the pillars had been blocked out, scaffolding of some sort was necessary for the sculptors to work on the capitals. There are definite indications that the rough cutting, sculpting and polishing were undertaken simultaneously. While the interior was still in the process of being cut, the sculptors were putting finishing touches to the exterior.[8] The *caityas* on the Manmodi hill at Junnar certainly suggest that this was the general procedure. The pillared verandas of the Bhima

Shankar and the Amba/Ambika caves are complete, while the interiors remain unfinished due to a bad stratum of rock combined with extensive leakage of water. In the case of the Budh Lena *caitya* the decorative carving of the façade is complete, while the interior has been roughly blocked out and abandoned, due again to the poor quality of the rock.

It would be reasonable to assume that at any cave site, one or more of the *vihāras* was excavated before the *caitya*. If on the other hand, work on several caves was commenced together, then obviously the much smaller and architecturally less adventurous *vihāra* would be completed before the *caitya*. At the three Manmodi hill sites at Junnar, the Amba/Ambika, Bhima Shankar and Budh Lena, work on the *caityas* has been abandoned, while the *vihāras* appear complete. Either excavation of the *caitya* and *vihāras* started simultaneously; or the *caitya* was commenced after completion of the *vihāras*. Certainly work on the *vihāras* would not continue after excavation of the *caitya* was abandoned. All the *vihāras* at a site, however, were by no means cut before the *caitya*, several being added with the growth of the monk community. An example of such a later addition is the double-storeyed *vihāra* at Karle which contains an inscription recording the gift of the cave in the reign of Pulumāvi, while we know that the *caitya* was completed much earlier.

We can only conjecture as to the amount of time it must have taken craftsmen to complete work on any one *caitya*. Scholarly opinion on the matter is divergent: for Karle, it ranges from an estimate of sixty years[9] to 'just a few years',[10] with no definite evidence one way or the other. The estimate of sixty years rests largely on the basis that the much smaller *vihāra* III at Nasik took about twenty years to complete. As we have seen, Nasik III is the result of two periods of cutting,[11] and the basis for the estimate of sixty years is hence invalid. Another scholar, advocating a similar span, remarked, 'the formidable undertaking, chipped by patient hand labour out of the most refractory of stone (which even now turns the points of pneumatic drills) must have taken several generations'.[12] Certainly it was an enormous undertaking, particularly when one considers the free-standing lion pillar at Karle and the vast quantity of stone to be chipped away all around it just to reach the rock-face from which the main cave was to be commenced. A period of sixty years, however, seems to us to be excessive, although on the other hand a few years may be inadequate. The *caitya* was the plan of a single master craftsman and to extend work to more than his life span is questionable. A period of ten to fifteen years would seem to be more acceptable.[13]

There is a complete lack of evidence regarding the amount of time involved in excavation and the number of workers at any cave site in India. The early Chinese caves, however, provide some interesting information on the subject. The Buddhist caves at Lung-Men in China are described in some detail by Seiichi Mizuno, with a number of photographs illustrating his text. One excavation in particular, the Feng Hsien Ssu, is of great interest to us. This enormous cave, with a completely open front, is entirely sculptural: the back wall is occupied by a gigantic Buddha with a number of attendants and the two side walls also contain enormous sculpted figures. 'The enormity of their proportions is such that one can hardly appreciate the grandeur of these colossal images of the Tang dynasty unless one takes the trouble to go over to the east bank of the river I and thence view these images against the background furnished by the whole Western range.'[14] From dates inscribed on the throne of the Buddha, we know that the Feng Hsien Ssu was begun on April 1st, 672 and completed on December 30th, 675 – a period of three years and nine months. We have, of course, no idea of the number of workmen involved. The evidence indicates, however, that it was physically possible for enormous caves to be excavated in a surprisingly short period of time.[15] Presumably this involved royal patronage as well as a great concentration of men and resources. A comparable situation may not have existed in India: in fact, we know that many of the early Buddhist caves were the result of the generosity of the trader and the common man. However, the evidence from China cautions us against exaggerating the time needed to excavate caves.

In the early Buddhist caves, as at Sanchi, Bharhut, Bodh Gaya and Amaravati, the donations clearly indicate that the craftsmen must have recognized the time involved and consequently the cost of various elements. It seems likely therefore that the craftsmen were paid on a regular basis. Coomaraswamy pointed out how payment was considered especially important for ecclesiastical work, for the patron could acquire any merit only if he bore the cost. This feeling was evident when the Ruvanveli *stūpa* in Ceylon was built by Duṭṭha Gāminī (161–137 BC). The king 'took extraordinary precautions to prevent any voluntary work being done lest any of the merit should be lost to himself; he could share the merit by deliberate gift, without loss to himself, but if voluntary work were done secretly, only the doer obtained the merit.'[16] Apart from the actual payment of the craftsmen, food too would have to be provided for them. It is probable that they brought their entire families with them since work at any one site must have extended over a certain period of time. No cave complex could be commenced then without substantial grants of both food and money. Yet some of the earliest cave sites, Bhaja for example, contain no mention of such donations. Since the very existence of the caves presupposes these, we must assume that the practice of recording such gifts on the rock itself was not yet in vogue in the area of the western caves. On the other hand, it is possible that the walls and pillars of these caves were plastered and contained painted inscriptions such as may be seen in abundance in the later caves at Ajanta.

Faced with the large amount of evidence showing imitation of wooden construction, we must remember that one of the very important factors governing any artistic expression is the tradition behind the artist – the tradition of craftsmanship according to which he has been trained. This tradition was probably handed down from father to son, or from master to pupil within a guild. As Coomaraswamy has suggested, although in a different context, '. . . the trade was hereditary, and sons are brought up to it as a matter of course, and trained in the actual workshop, being given easy and monotonous work at first . . . and little by little picking up a knowledge of the craft by precept, example and practice; and so the tradition was perpetuated'.[17] It is most unlikely that, at least at this time, any theoretical experts contributed to craft education. The early architects were used to a tradition of wood-building. None of these structural monuments have survived, but fortunately an idea of their appearance may be gleaned from the bas-relief representations at Bharhut, Gaya and Sanchi. This tradition, having left no extant examples, does not intrude on our consciousness or force us to recognize it. But it is essential that we do so for 'we shall never understand the history of Indian art by taking for granted that it first came into existence when we first have tangible proof of it; we might as well try to date Indian literature by the dates of the earliest extant manuscripts'.[18]

An important factor is the mobility of the architect and his consequent exposure to new ideas. Donations from a Nasik merchant at Bharhut and from the foreman of the artisans of king Sātakarni at Sanchi, would indicate that the architects and sculptors of the western caves, along with the merchants and traders, travelled widely. We may expect the Bedsa architect, for example, to have visited Bharhut, BodhGaya and Sanchi, the important centres of stone carving in those days. Perhaps this was responsible for the innovation we find at Bedsa in the form of tall, slender columns with elaborate capitals. The Aśokan column at Sanchi may have inspired him to introduce at Bedsa a 'bell' capital with a stepped abacus supporting animal-and-rider crowning figures.

Yet another source of influence for the artist may have been reports he had heard about the art of other countries. In an earlier chapter we have shown that the rise of the Sātavāhana kingdom may have been connected with an expanding overseas trade, and that this coincides also with the first cutting of rock monasteries.[19] Traders from abroad, from Petra and from Egyptian towns, would have been found in the coastal towns of Kalyan and Sopara, at Chaul and Bharukaccha. They would have described the wonders of their country, probably exaggerating slightly as travellers abroad are inclined to do. They would have spoken of their rock-cut tombs and temples and of their pillared shrines. Artists and craftsmen must have been among those who listened to these accounts. To what extent they may have been influenced it is impossible to tell, but the stories may well have kindled their imagination. In addition to the craft tradition, and to what the artist had both seen and heard, we must further allow for the artist's own contributions, the innovations he himself made. If we consider this factor then we need not assume that the Kanheri capitals, for example, are poor copies of those at Karle: rather, their difference may be attributed to the individual taste of craftsmen.

It is doubtful whether the architects and sculptors were in any way connected with the Buddhist Order. It would seem probable that some of the craftsmen were lay followers of Buddhism, but there is no reason why they need necessarily have belonged to that faith. Some of them may have been followers of Brahmanism. Guilds of craftsmen would work readily for both Buddhist and non-Buddhist patrons. Percy Brown wrote of the 'artist-priest' in ancient India and suggested that their system of work was similar to that which prevailed until recently in Buddhist Tibet. 'When it has been decided that a certain building is to be decorated, or a piece of sculpture executed, artists are sent for from the leading religious institution, and these are retained in the monastery as part of the sacerdotal establishment until the commission is completed. . . . When the work was finished, these artists either returned to the central monastic institution, or travelled to another religious edifice which required their artistic services.'[20] While it may not be quite accurate to speak of an artist-priest in connection with the early Buddhist caves, it seems likely that these craftsmen of ancient times moved from place to place with new commissions. While forming part of a guild of artists, the architect would have been more mobile than members of the guilds of metal-workers and weavers who formed part of the village system. It is unfortunate that we do not find a reference to a guild of stone-carvers in any of the inscriptions in the early Buddhist caves. Guilds (*sreṇīs*) of bamboo-workers (*vasakaras*), brasiers (*kāsākaras*), weavers (*kolikas*) and oil-pressers (*tilapisakas*) are some of those referred to. The guild hall (*nigama-sabhā*) also finds a mention. These guilds seem to have been powerful organizations and appear to have acted also as banks, since we hear that money was vested in them and the interest arising from this was given to the Buddhist monasteries. At the same time, however, the Buddhists by no means had a monopoly over these guilds and they readily served Brahmanical or Jain organizations.

It is probable that some of the donors too were non-Buddhist. Donations to a religious establishment were always referred to as *deya dhamma*, or meritorious gift, and were believed to bring spiritual merit to the donor and his family, no matter what their personal beliefs. We know too that the Sātavāhana rulers themselves were Brahmins. The Nanaghat inscriptions confirm that they were ardent followers of the Brahmanical religion and performed sacrifices in which several thousand animals were offered up on each occasion. The later Sātavāhanas too were followers of the Brahmanical religion and the caste system, Gautamīputra Sātakarni being described as having prevented the mixing of the four castes.[21] Yet these rulers were by no means opposed to Buddhism; on the contrary, they donated entire caves to the monks and gave them grants of land and money.

Fairly substantial donations towards the construction of the western caves came from a class of people from whom such gifts are not usual. An ironmonger (*lohavāniya*) from Karadh donated a cave at Kuda, and another cave at the same site was given by a gardener (*mālākāra*). At Nasik a cave was donated by a fisherman (*dāsakas*) and at Kanheri we find a gift from a blacksmith (*kamāra*). Joint donations too are to be found: a Karle pillar was given by the traders' association (*vāniya gāma*) from Dhenukākata, and a Junnar cave by a guild of corn dealers. All this affords a striking contrast to other roughly contemporary records. The Kushāna donations, for example, are almost entirely from royalty and nobility. The Sanchi donors are slightly more varied but not to the same extent as in the western caves. In addition, the Sanchi gifts are much smaller than those in the caves, and consist mostly of crossbars and uprights of railings. In the western caves, apart from the gifts mentioned above, there are, of course, the large perpetual endowments of the rulers and the donations of *mahārathis* and *mahābhojas*, presumably high officials of some sort. The majority of endowments come, however, from the merchant class, while the next largest group (excluding royalty and high officials) are the monks and nuns themselves.

Most of the donations to any cave site were from inhabitants of the nearby town or village. At the Nasik and Kuda caves, for example, the majority of donations were from residents of Nasik and Kuda. Often, however, donations are found from residents of fairly distant towns, as may be seen from the list given below. Inhabitants of the western Deccan also travelled widely in other areas.

Cave sites	Donations from inhabitants of:
Karle	Sopara, Vejayanti, Dhenukākata
Junnar	Kalyan, Bharukaccha, Gata country (northern) *yavana*, Junnar
Bedsa	Nasik
Kanheri	Sopara, Chaul, Dhenukākata, Kalyan
Nasik	Dattamitri (northern) *yavana*, Nasik, Dasapura
Pitalkhora	Paithan, Dhenukākata
Kuda	Karadh, Kuda
Nanaghat	Sopara
Shelarvadi	Dhenukākata

Sixteen donations at Karle are from inhabitants of Dhenukākata, a town which has not yet been identified. There are in addition single Dhenukākatan donations at Kanheri, Shelarvardi and Pitalkhora. Considering the number of such donations at Karle, the town would seem to have been located somewhere nearby. D. D. Kosambi suggested that Devgadh, on the opposite curve of hills from Karle, was the ancient Dhenukākata.[22] There are a number of points in favour of such an identification, but it is by no means a certainty, and it seems doubtful whether even excavation will provide the answer. Five of the Karle donors describe themselves as *yavanas* (Greeks) from Dhenukākata, and it would appear that the town contained a Greek settlement of some sort. The fact that these *yavanas* do not describe their status or occupation as opposed to the general practice, may perhaps lead to the assumption that all *yavanas* followed some definite occupation such as trading. If, however, we accept Kosambi's reading of one of the donors' names as Milimda (as against the previous reading of Mitidasa),[23] then obviously there were exceptions to this. Milimda describes himself as a physician; although he does not specifically state that he is a *yavana*, his name (Milimda from Menander) is certainly indicative of the fact. It is probable that the *yavanas* regarded themselves as distinct from the rest of the population and considered it unnecessary to specify their profession. It is evident, however, from their often Indianized names – Dhamadhaya, Yasavadhana, Chanda – that the *yavanas* had been settled in India for quite some time. It is of interest to note that the *Mahāvamsa* tells us that this western coastal region was converted by a *yavana* Dhammarakhita. Several carvings at Pitalkhora depict a foreign style of dress and the royal physician Magila, mentioned in inscriptions at Pitalkhora, seems to have been a *yavana*. Donations at Junnar and Nasik come from Greeks from northern parts of India. It is evident that apart from the northern concentrations of *yavanas*, there was a fairly large Greek/Buddhist settlement in western India, which was gradually becoming Indianized and absorbed into the local population.

It is intriguing to speculate on how it was possible for different portions of a cave to be donated by different people. At Karle, for example, each pillar was the gift of a separate person, and the *mithuna* couples, the elephants and the *vedikā*-bands, were all individual gifts. There is no doubt that the cave is the result of a unified plan and that the various portions were by no means cut haphazardly as they were donated. It would seem that the money to start the excavation of the cave was already in the hands of the monk community. When cutting was commenced and word spread regarding the magnificent scale of the monument, large numbers of devotees must have made trips to the site to donate towards construction. It is possible too that when it was decided to excavate a *caitya*, a plan was on view and donations were invited. It is not likely that the donors decided on what they wished represented: the carving is too well organized for that and must be the result of the master craftsman's planning. Of the two explanations the first appears more plausible but it is likely that in actual practice a combination of the two situations occurred.

We find that the Buddhist monks and nuns themselves were able to donate towards the construction of the western caves, although the Buddha had sternly forbidden them to have anything to do with money. How did it come about that the monk who had to obtain his very food through seeking alms, was now able to donate towards the construction of richly decorated caves? At Kuda, entire caves were donated by nuns, and at Kanheri not only caves and cisterns but even permanent endowments were given by nuns. At Karle again, monks and nuns donated the *mithunas*, and the venerable monk Indradeva gave the elephants and the *vedikā*-bands.

Where did all this money come from? If the monks and nuns toured the countryside collecting donations, then we may assume that they would have acknowledged the fact that it was not they but an entire community that was responsible for a particular donation. It would seem that the monks were able to accumulate money from the various gifts of fields and permanent endowments that they received. The Nahapāna inscription at Karle mentions the village of Karajika as having been given for the support of the ascetics living in the Karle caves. An entire village, services and produce, would have been more than sufficient for the support of a small group of ascetics. At Nasik, fields and large permanent endowments yielding interest were given. Lay worshippers at Kanheri gave lands and perpetual endowments 'into the hands of the community', and many such gifts are recorded. We may assume that the produce of all these fields was more than enough for the simple needs of the monks: the surplus was accumulated and possibly sold to traders on their long journeys from the ports to the towns of the interior. Since the various donations imply that the monks possessed money as individuals, we may assume that money and perhaps surplus grain were distributed within the community. Kosambi suggests that the monks even lent money at interest to the passing traders. He quotes practices in the monasteries of China, which he points out, borrowed their basic organization from India. Monks deviated from the spirit of the law without deviating from the letter of the law: forbidden to touch money, they used a piece of cloth as insulation.[24] It is also possible that rich laymen, on entering the Order, donated large sums of money towards the construction of caves. This explanation may apply in certain cases, but it does not seem valid when we find gifts signed by 'the venerable monk' or 'the revered monk'. These were obviously monks who had belonged to the Order for a long time and had risen to such positions. The gifts signed by them have to be explained in some other way. Perhaps these monks had access to, or had inherited, private wealth from their families and used this money to donate images and caves.

There would seem to have been a sudden and rather rapid spread of Buddhism into western India, after which the faith entrenched itself in this area as is evident from the large number of rock-cut monasteries.[25] The *Mahāvamsa* tells us that the Aparānta, this western coastal region, was converted by Dhammarakhita, a *yavana* sent by Tissa after the Third Buddhist Council. But, apart from this, there must have been large numbers of Buddhist monks moving over from Magadha into western India. Only a movement of this nature would seem to explain the large number of rock monasteries that sprang up around the same time. A monk's primary mission was to spread the word of the Buddha. Long journeys must have been undertaken by devout monks who had given up their family and home. These journeys would naturally have been undertaken along the established trade routes in the company of merchants and traders. On these long, slow journeys the monks would have struck up acquaintance with the wealthy traders and perhaps converted some of them. Reaching the western coastal area, the monks, tired of wandering, must have wanted a place to settle down for the three months of the rainy season. Some of the merchants and traders who travelled with them would have been willing to contribute towards the building of monasteries. It was considered a meritorious act, bringing them and their families spiritual merit, and probably 'divine favour on the business enterprises at hand'. In some such way, as Sukumar Dutt proposes,[26] must these western caves have arisen.

It seems logical, however, to expect that the monks would have lived for some time in the area in wooden and brick monasteries. Only after they were well established as a community would they have had the supporters donate towards the excavation of a rock-cut monastery, which was, after all, a more ambitious undertaking than providing a wood or brick shelter. It also seems likely that one among all the rock-cut sites must have served as the prototype from which the rest took their pattern.

The reason for the location of cave sites along the main trade routes of the time is probably to be found in a combination of factors. One consideration must have been that of obtaining donations towards the construction of these rock-cut complexes. If the caves were situated on or conveniently near the trade routes, merchants and traders would be likely to visit the monasteries and make endowments. The architects and sculptors too could be more easily persuaded to work on the caves if these were conveniently located. In the early stages of such settlements such a location would be an advantage for the monks themselves as they could easily resume their wandering life once the rains were over. Soon, however, these monasteries were regarded as permanent homes, particularly after fields, villages and perpetual endowments were given to them. The cave sites were usually situated near a village or town, the inhabitants of which often made major contributions towards the construction of the rock-cut monastery.

Evidence from the large number of cave inscriptions seems to indicate that different sects predominated at various cave sites. An analysis of the records reveals Dhammotariyas at Sopara and Junnar, Bhadāyanīyas at Nasik and Kanheri, and Mahāsamghikas at Karle. Often, however, the inscriptions mention donations to *samghasa catudisasa*, or to 'the community of monks from the four points of the horizon', implying perhaps that sect distinctions were not very rigid.

We have seen in an earlier chapter that the *caityas* of western India may be regarded as a logical evolution of the Sudama and Lomasa Rishi caves of Bihar.[27] It is still somewhat intriguing that the monks should have decided to excavate caves in western India. The excavation of such monasteries was not an established practice in eastern India, and we cannot explain the western caves by suggesting that the monks brought the practice over with them. The mountain range, the western ghats, of course presented an ideal rock-face, but opportunity does not explain the actuality. Perhaps social changes – a wealthy trader class, a general increase of wealth, and the rise of great families – explain this sudden artistic activity. Such factors, described by Geoffrey Scott as 'useful satellites of architectural history'[28] must certainly have contributed towards this development, although by themselves may not be sufficient to explain it.

All this artistic activity does indeed coincide with trading activities and economic stimulation from the Mediterranean world and opens up the possibility of emulation.

There is, of course, the simple explanation that ascetics in India had always lived in caves. Many *jātaka* stories contain this idea, for example the *Indra Śāla Guhā* in which the Buddha himself lived in a cave. Added to this were the climatic advantages of such excavations which provided a shelter that remained cool during the summer months and retained the warmth during the winter. This idea, together with the precedence of the Lomasa Rishi, may well have impelled these monks to excavate such monasteries, particularly when confronted with the opportunity in the form of the ghat face, and social changes conducive to such activity. We have suggested that a single monastery was excavated first, this providing the example from which the others took their pattern. In this case the idea may even have come from one small group of monks who perhaps wanted a hall of worship as enduring as those in the Barabar hills of Bihar. The desire for permanence may well have been one of the reasons that induced them to change from wood to stone for building – not merely built-up stone, but rock hewn out of a mountainside. A Kanheri inscription certainly expresses this feeling when the donor claims the erection of a *caitya* that will endure until the end of the *kalpa* (cosmic era).[29]

7

Conclusions and Chronology

In the course of this survey of our subject we shall establish that the early Buddhist cave architecture of western India was the result of two distinct phases of activity. The first phase extended from *c.* 100 BC to *c.* 20 BC and was followed by a lull of about seventy years during which no new caves seem to have been excavated. The second phase then commenced around AD 50 and continued until AD 200, at which date cutting was apparently suspended until the later *Mahāyāna* phase. It would seem that there was no single period of continuous rock-cutting at each site, but rather that there were several phases of activity which were often the result of emulation from one site to another. The beginnings of rock architecture appear to coincide with the rise of the Sātavāhana dynasty and an expanding overseas trade. The flourishing coastal trade, both domestic and foreign, evidently brought great profits to the merchants and traders who were able to make generous donations towards the rock monasteries. Significantly, the period during which rock-cutting appears to have been suspended or was minimal (*c.* 20 BC to AD 50) coincides with the obscure period in Sātavāhana history. This strange concurrence may perhaps be interpreted to mean that the excavation of caves depended to some extent on political stability. We have seen that the dynasty split into several branch lines during this period, and we know that Sātavāhana hold over their territories was weak, since the Kshaharātas were able to take over important portions of their domains. It would thus seem a reasonable assumption that political unrest caused an ebb in general prosperity which led to an adverse effect upon the patronage of religious establishments.

The chronological scheme suggested in this chapter has been arrived at after a careful consideration and comparison of the sequences obtained by different methods in various chapters. The historical evidence, palaeographic material, and the conclusions drawn from a study of architectural and sculptural styles are combined. This evidence has been laid out on Table 11 and here we shall discuss and clarify the material, examining each site in turn. Throughout our consideration of the various sites we have suggested actual dates for the cutting of the caves. It must be emphasized that such dates are not meant to indicate a specific point in time, but are given more as an indication of the probable period during which a cave was excavated. Thus the period of *c.* 90–70 BC for the excavation of a *caitya* does not exclude the possibility that the cave may have been executed in either 100 BC or in 60 BC. We would by no means claim such precision for our dating. Of greater significance in our proposed chronology is the relative sequence, and the priority for example, of caves cut between 90–70 BC as compared with those cut between 70–50 BC. In certain instances we have definite indications that cutting was abandoned for some time and recommenced later: this may indeed have happened with other caves in which proof of such an occurrence is now lacking. It will be seen that on the whole the evidences of palaeography and history compare remarkably well with the architectural and sculptural sequences. The development of the Brāhmī script, the elaboration of the apsidal *caitya* and the progress in the sculptors' craft all go together. Occasionally, however, as with the caves at Nadsur and Kondane, the sequences suggested by architecture, sculpture and palaeography do not wholly agree with each other. Table 11 reveals that such cases are relatively rare, but in these instances we have to see how best to reconcile the material, and we must analyse the precise value that we attach to each discipline as a chronological yardstick.

In the period of the early Buddhist caves we would treat the evidence of sculpture with some caution in view of the fact that the total body of material is very small. At certain sites, indeed, an opinion has to be formed from a solitary figure or a single panel of sculpture. We have examined the trend from a shallow relief sculpture preoccupied with the depiction of surface details, to a simple and more truly sculptural style of deeper relief with an emphasis on the essential planes of the body. There also seems no reason to doubt that the stylistic change over the years involved a progression from stiff, heavy, frontal figures to relaxed and animated ones. However, a consideration of the sculptures decorating the *stūpas* at Sanchi and Bharhut indicates that occasionally two stages in the development of a style may exist together side by side during the same period. It would appear that this is particularly so in the early stages of the development of the sculptors' craft. We would like to consider a few such examples from Sanchi and Bharhut, and though this may appear to be somewhat of a digression, we shall see that it has a direct bearing on the material from the western caves.

An examination of the sculptures on the gateways of Sanchi *stūpa* I discloses some disparity in the carving. The Gajalakshmī theme on the top architrave of the south gateway reveals a simple, unsophisticated style of shallow relief in essentially two planes. The incised manner of carving suggests a completely linear treatment with little or no concern for depth, while the composition is entirely symmetrical. In contrast, the lowest architrave of the gateway displays a difference in style that becomes evident from a comparison of just the lotus stalk that appears on both architraves: the upper example reveals a flat linear treatment, while the lower, with its rounded flowing style, indicates the possibility of its existence in actuality. Again, the carving of the Vidisa panel, also on the south gateway, discloses a feeling of depth with a distinct differentiation of planes. Not only is there a conscious overlapping of figures, but some are portrayed sideways, while others are viewed from the back. The arrangement of the figures is thus more complex and sophisticated compared to those in the panel immediately above it, where we find an insistence on symmetry and a directly frontal approach. Similar divergence in style may be seen on the east gateway as well. In contrast to the sophisticated treatment of the elephant capitals, the architraves betray a simple symmetrical arrangement of their theme. A still greater contrast is presented by comparing the Kaśyapa panel with the Return to Kapilavastu. The former displays a simple approach, completely centrally aligned, devoid of overlapping figures, and a schematic representation of nature unconcerned with visual perception. The Kapilavastu panel by contrast, has a complex arrangement with a distinct three-dimensional effect. The rider at the top of the panel emerges from behind a building, and the banner he holds sweeps out and interrupts the *vedikā*-band above. Similar variations may be seen on the west and north gateways as well: some stiff, hieratically conceived figures alternate with the graceful and naturalistically rendered bracket *yakshis*.

At Bharhut too we are struck by the contrasts between the various pieces of sculpture, which fall roughly into three categories – medallions, panels and the pillar figures. The medallions reveal, as a whole, a very shallow cutting, in some cases a mere engraved style, almost incised with no attempt at overlapping of figures or at an effect of depth. The figures are clumsily depicted, the approach is directly frontal and the emphasis is on a symmetrical arrangement of figures. The panels, in general, display an advance in style, with a deeper cutting, a better organization of figures in space and less of an insistence on the frontal depiction of human figures. By contrast to both medallions and panels, the competent carving of the pillar *yakshis* and *yakshas* is indeed striking.

There are various possible reasons for these stylistic differences between pieces of sculpture belonging together to the same period. One explanation is surely that different guilds of craftsmen, whose training and apprenticeship may have varied considerably, worked together on the same monument. At Bharhut, the Kharosthi masons' marks on the gateway indicate that apart from local craftsmen, artists from the north-west too were present. In the case of the south gateway of *stūpa* I at Sanchi, the Vidisa panel was carved by craftsmen from the nearby town of Vidisa, while the top architrave (inside face) appears to have been the work of the foreman of the artisans of king Sātakarni,[1] and certainly of a different guild of craftsmen. A similar explanation may well account for differences between sculptures in the early Buddhist caves. The carving at Kondane would appear to be much in advance of that at Nadsur, yet we shall see that both probably belonged to the same phase. We must assume that the craftsmen at Nadsur were traditional in their attitude, while those at Kondane were, in a sense, looking ahead. Occasionally the craftsmen seem to have been apprenticed to more than one trade. The Vidisa panel at Sanchi was the work of ivory-carvers, and the dwarf-*yaksha* from Pitalkhora was sculpted by a goldsmith: yet both display competence in stone carving. Another explanation of the variations in style is surely to be found in the distinction between the work of a master craftsman and that of his apprentices. It is certainly possible that the medallions at Bharhut were carved by novices, while the panels and pillar figures may have been executed by the established craftsmen of repute. A similar situation must account for the differences in the carving of the *mithunas* at Karle. The two couples on either side of the main doorway are vastly superior to those facing each other at either end of the veranda. If these *mithunas* had not been *in situ* and so clearly in association, it is possible that one may have been inclined to separate them chronologically. It would appear then, that the testimony of sculpture must be treated with some caution, especially due to the restricted amount of such material from the western caves.

Architectural evidence forms a more dependable yardstick of age during this period. We are on fairly firm grounds with regard to the *caitya* form and we have seen that the development of the apsidal *caitya* allows the proposing of a distinct sequence. Variations from the apsidal plan raise difficulties, however, and *caityas* such as those at Kuda, Mahad and Karadh may not be placed with any great accuracy. The possibility of an archaic form being imitated must always be considered. It would appear that this was the case with the Budh Lena *caitya* at Junnar: both sculpture and paleography indicate an advanced date while the architectural form is early. The *vihāra* form allows the proposing of only the most basic sequence. It poses greater problems than the *caitya* as there were few distinct changes within our period, and a number of variations on the basic plan. In general, the architectural form of the caves suggests that they were simulations of structural buildings, perhaps of wood and rubble.

Palaeography constitutes a relatively reliable yardstick for the early Buddhist caves and certainly provides greater precision than has hitherto been allowed. During this period Brāhmī was still in its infancy, having been recently freed from a strict imitation of the Mauryan form. In this early stage of development we may rule out the possibility of varying forms of script existing together, such as we find in the case of the eighth-century Pallava script in south India. However, variations such as those that would result from the distinctions in style between an older and a younger scribe, must always have existed. We do not claim that palaeography provides all the answers: we see in the case of the inscriptions on the Sanchi gateways (Appendix 1) that much depends on the correct evaluation and interpretation of the evidence. Generally, however, palaeography provides us with a stable and valuable tool during this early period.

Kondivte

Architectural evidence suggests very strongly that the *caitya* at Kondivte was one of the earliest caves to be excavated in western India. Its plan indicates that it belongs to a phase somewhere between the eastern Barabar caves and the typical *caitya* of the western Deccan exemplified by Bhaja. Although rock-cutting was not an established practice in eastern India, it is evident that cutters in western India drew on the Bihar examples (as also on contemporary structural architecture) for their first *caitya*. It is unfortunate that neither sculptural nor palaeographic evidence can come to our aid in helping to place the cave more exactly. The right wall of the rectangular chamber contains later images of the Buddha, but there are no early carvings in the cave. The single inscription above the lattice window, to the right of the doorway leading into the circular chamber, belongs to Series III, or approximately to AD 100, and does not appear to belong to the period of excavation. Only an eye-copy of this worn and fragmentary inscription has been published.[2] On the overwhelming strength of the architectural evidence we would place the Kondivte *caitya* (and probably a couple of *vihāras* at the site, one of which contains a row of stepped merlons), at around 100 BC, or slightly earlier.

Nadsur

Purely on the basis of architectural form we would suggest that the simple apsidal aisle-less *caitya* at Nadsur belongs to a phase between the Kondivte *caitya* and the regular western *caitya* at Bhaja. We have seen that the sculptures in *vihāras* VII and XV at Nadsur display affinities with the reliefs on Sanchi *stūpa* II and with the Bharhut medallions, and thus with the Bhaja *vihāra* reliefs in general. Palaeographic evidence indicates, however, that the inscription to be found in *vihāra* VII belongs to Series I (b), or to *c.* 70–50 BC. The record in the adjoining *caitya* VIII consists of a few straggling letters and may possibly belong to the same phase. It is evident that there is some conflict between the architectural, sculptural and palaeographic evidence. We have earlier discussed in some detail the value we would attach to each discipline, and have indicated that in our opinion palaeography is the more reliable. We would suggest then, that the Nadsur caves were probably excavated towards the upper limits of the dates suggested by palaeography – around 70 BC. Although the typical *caitya* form had been established at Bhaja, and perhaps imitated by this time at Ajanta *caitya* X, Pitalkhora III and Kondane, it would appear that the rock-cutters at Nadsur nevertheless followed the simpler pattern.

Bhaja

The typical western *caitya*, which was to be copied at other sites and later elaborated upon, makes its first appearance at Bhaja. The Kondivte *caitya*, and possibly some of the small Pitalkhora examples, seem to have constituted the earliest attempts in western India to hew monasteries from the living rock. With the Bhaja *caitya*, however, the complete plan was achieved: its success may be gauged from the number of rock-cut monasteries, apparently modelled on Bhaja, that arose soon after.

The simple apsidal plan of the Bhaja *caitya*, divided into nave and side aisles, its wooden frontage, slanting octagonal columns, and decorative motifs including stepped merlons and brackets, indicate the early date of the cave. The rows of tiny pinholes on the fronton of the *caitya* arch imply further wooden additions of some nature and would seem to attest its priority to the *caityas* at Kondane, Pitalkhora III and Ajanta X where this feature is absent. The rudimentary curve of the *caitya* arch is also indicative of an early date for Bhaja. This is also corroborated by sculptural evidence. The reliefs in *vihāra* XIX at Bhaja appear to be somewhat in advance of the carvings on *stūpa* II at Sanchi and roughly contemporary with the Bharhut sculptures. The carving centres around the schematically conceived frontal human figure, a shallow relief and an emphasis on surface details.

Palaeographic evidence indicates that the monastery at Bhaja was occupied over a period of some 250 years. Inscriptions on the wooden beams spanning the vault of the *caitya*, and a record in one of the *vihāras* belongs to Series I (a), or to *c.* 90–70 BC. Inscriptions belonging to Series I (b), or to *c.* 70–50 BC are to be found on the row of rock-cut *stūpas* and in another *vihāra*. A much later record, belonging to Series IV, or roughly between AD 110–150, reports the gift of a cistern and shows that the community was flourishing at that date.

It would appear that excavation of the *caitya*, of the sculptured *vihāra* XIX and of a few other *vihāras*, took place around 90 or 80 BC. Work appears to have been recommenced some ten or twenty years later, perhaps with the growth of the community of monks, when the row of *stūpas* and presumably some further *vihāras* were excavated. As the number of caves at Bhaja are few and as a period of twenty to forty years to excavate them seems excessive, we may assume that work at the site was not continuous over that period of time. Two cisterns were added at a much later date between AD 110–150. Subsequent Mahāyāna occupation of the site is indicated by paintings of the Buddha and bodhisattvas on the pillars of the *caitya*.

Kondane

Architecturally, the Kondane *caitya* is exactly similar to that at Bhaja, the only distinction being the absence of pinholes on the fronton of the *caitya* arch, and the more definite and stronger curve of the arch itself. Palaeographic evidence agrees with the architectural in assigning the *caitya* to a phase probably following soon after Bhaja. The single inscription on the façade of the Kondane *caitya* belongs to Series I (a), or to *c*. 90–70 BC. The sculptural decoration, however, supplies partly contradictory evidence. The panels of dancing men and women depict animated, graceful figures that reveal the artist's mastery over his craft, and the emphasis on the essential planes of the body suggests a phase as advanced as the Sanchi gateways. On the other hand, the fragmentary head lower down on the *caitya* façade reveals a style still preoccupied with surface decoration. On the basis of the *yaksha* head alone we would have few doubts about assigning the *caitya* to an early phase, but the handling of the dancing figures is highly accomplished. However, the strength of the palaeographic and architectural material, combined with the somewhat conflicting evidence of sculpture, indicates that the *caitya* belongs to an early date and we must resort to an explanation in the form of the very rapid advance in the sculptors' craft during this early phase. We have earlier seen the contemporaneity of varying styles of sculpture on the Bharhut and Sanchi I *stūpas*. We may further point to the contrast between the carvings on Sanchi *stūpa* II and the Bharhut pillar figures: these sculptures are apparently separated by a period of ten years at the most and yet the development from one to the other is significant. We would suggest that the Kondane *caitya* belongs towards the lower limits of the date indicated by palaeography – to *c*. 70 BC. We have no way of determining whether work at the site was continuous, or whether it may have extended over a period of years as seems likely at Bhaja. There is no evidence of Mahāyāna occupation of Kondane.

Pitalkhora

On architectural grounds it appears likely that the newly discovered caves on the opposite side of the ravine from the known group were among the earliest to be excavated at Pitalkhora. Some of them may, in fact, belong to a phase prior to Bhaja and soon after the Kondivte *caitya*. Caves XII and X are simple apsidal pillarless *caityas*, but the situation is somewhat complicated by the stone façade of cave X, which points to a slightly later date. Cave XI contains three *stūpas* which would appear to belong to the same category as the row of *stūpas* at Bhaja. Cave XIII is a tiny but fully developed *caitya* complete with nave and side aisles. What appears to be rather enigmatic is that three *caityas* are excavated side by side. Because of their diminutive size one wonders if they were not intended as private chapels for the chief monks of that particular community. Alternatively they could have been excavated in the early days of settlement at Pitalkhora when there were fewer monks at the site. When the community was later firmly established and became larger, the rock-face opposite was chosen and the main *caitya* III was cut.

Architectural evidence indicates that *caitya* III belongs to the same general period as the Bhaja *caitya*. The inscriptions on the pillars within the cave confirm this as they belong to Series I (a), or to *c*. 90–70 BC. The most impressive sculptures associated with the *caitya* are the over life-size guardian *yaksha* and the dwarf-*yaksha* figure. Both are more advanced than the carvings at Bhaja but are among the earlier images at the site, showing affinities with some of the accomplished sculptures at Bharhut. The inscription on the hand of the dwarf-*yaksha* belongs to Series I (a) and would support the sculptural evidence which suggests that this figure is among the earlier pieces carved at Pitalkhora. The human amulet worn by the figure is certainly an elaboration of the inverted *triratnas* on the necklets of the *yakshas* and *yakshis* at Bharhut.

The adjoining *vihāra IV* appears to be of slightly later date as inscriptions in the cave belong to Series I (c) and would indicate that work at the site was going on as late as *c*. 50 or 40 BC. The elephant plinth in front of the *vihāra*, with the sculptured doorway flanked by guardians and a Gajalakṣmī panel above, belongs to a phase somewhat in advance of Bharhut and is more akin to the carvings at BodhGaya. This would seem to be in accord with the palaeographic material. The sculptural material illustrates the various stages in the transition from the flattened stiff style reminiscent of Bharhut to the free easy movement of the human body evident at BodhGaya and to a fuller extent on the Sanchi gateways. Sculptures representing the more advanced style are invariably carved on detached pieces of stone. These were apparently set up against the rock-face, at a date later than the actual cutting of the caves, to cover the badly worn surfaces of the poor quality rock at Pitalkhora.

We may assume that rock-cutting at the site was not continuous over a lengthy period of thirty years and more. The decorated façade of *caitya* III and *vihāra* IV, now largely fallen away, extended up to a considerable height, and must in its day have been more impressive than even Karle. There is also a considerable amount of sculpture, but there is no necessary connection between this quantity and the number of years of cutting. It would appear that *caitya* III with some sculptural decoration, and a couple of *vihāras* were excavated around 80 or 70 BC. Cutting was then recommenced some ten or twenty years later when *vihāra* IV and much of the sculptural decoration at the site were carved. The cutting of detached pieces of sculpture continued for some further time. Occupation of the site in Mahāyāna days is proved by paintings of the Buddha and bodhisattvas on the pillars of *caitya* III. This later artistic activity seems to have been confined to painting as there are no Mahāyāna sculptures at the site.

Ajanta

Most cave sites consist of a single *caitya* with a number of *vihāras* to house the monks, but at Ajanta we find two sizeable *caityas* (unlike the tiny ones at Pitalkhora) immediately adjoining each other. Examining their position on the rock-face we find that *caitya* IX is lower down and nearer the stream. It is also the smaller of the two, being in fact half the size of *caitya* X. One would perhaps be inclined to assume that *caitya* IX was excavated first to serve the needs of a small community of monks, the larger cave being added with the growth of the settlement. This, however, is not so. On architectural grounds *caitya* X belongs to the same phase as the *caityas* at Bhaja, Kondane and Pitalkhora, while *caitya* IX with its stone façade belongs to a later stage of development. Palaeographic evidence indicates that the inscription on the facade of *caitya* X, as also the two new inscriptions, one engraved and the other painted, discovered within the cave, belong to Series I (a), or to *c.* 90–70 BC. The tiny *vihāra* XXX probably belongs to this same phase. A much weathered inscription in *vihāra* XII and the painted record No. 14 in *caitya* X belong to Series I (b), or to *c.* 70–50 BC. It is possible that *caitya* IX was excavated around this date or slightly later. The introduction of the entirely rock-cut façade seems to have taken place about this time at either Nasik or Ajanta IX. If Nasik was the first to make this innovation, and this seems likely, it is probable that *caitya* IX at

Ajanta was built in emulation, at a site where there was already one large *caitya*.

We have seen that the paintings in both *caityas* X and IX display stylistic affinities with the sculptures at BodhGaya and with the advanced carvings at Kondane and Pitalkhora. While the rock inscription uncovered beneath a layer of mud plaster in cave X would seem to imply the later addition of the murals, the newly discovered painted record belonging to the same palaeographic phase, suggests that the concept of the painted embellishment of the walls of *caitya* X arose very soon after the completion of its excavation. The painted inscription No. 14 in cave X belongs palaeographically to Series I (b), or to *c.* 70–50 BC, and is quite definitely associated with the scene depicting the king and his retinue. Palaeographic evidence may be interpreted then as being in accord with the stylistic indications of the murals. The *Chaddanta jātaka* scenes in *caitya* X, with their free and easy conception of the theme and the softly rounded contours of the figures, appear to be of slightly later date, and the counterpart of the advanced Sanchi gateway sculptures.

Activity at Ajanta appears to have commenced around 80 or 70 BC with the excavation of *caitya* X and of *vihāra* XXX. Soon after the completion of the cutting of *caitya* X the conception of the painted embellishment of its walls arose. Some ten to twenty years later, between *c.* 70–50 BC, *caitya* IX and *vihāra* XII were cut, and most of the paintings in both *caityas* were completed. At a slightly later date, perhaps between *c.* 50–25 BC, the *Chaddanta jātaka* scenes appear to have been painted in *caitya* X. When the site was occupied in Mahāyāna days an extensive set of caves was cut on either side of the early group. Figures of the Buddha were carved beside the façade of *caitya* IX and paintings depicting the Buddha and bodhisattvas were added to the murals in *caityas* X and IX.

Aurangabad

Architectural evidence would assign *caitya* IV at Aurangabad, with its flat side aisle ceilings and plain pillars, to the same phase as *caitya* IX at Ajanta. The entire frontage of the cave has fallen away and there is no figural sculpture within. Palaeography cannot come to our aid either, as no inscriptions now remain in the cave. We are left then with architectural evidence alone, and on the grounds of the similarity with Ajanta IX we suggest that this *caitya* was executed around 70–50 BC. We may assume with some confidence that there must have been some early *vihāras* at Aurangabad. At present, however, the remaining caves of this group, and indeed of other groups at Aurangabad, appear to belong to Mahāyāna times.

Nasik

Rock-cutting at Nasik extended over a period of several centuries. The earliest excavation appears to be *vihāra* XIX which contains an inscription assigned palaeographically to Series I (a), or to *c*. 90–70 BC. The record also mentions that it was engraved in the reign of the Sātavāhana king Kanha, the second ruler of the dynasty. The adjoining *caitya*, with its stone frontage, belongs, together with Ajanta IX, to a phase later than the *caityas* at Bhaja, Kondane, Pitalkhora III and Ajanta X, which have wooden façades. The pillars inside the Nasik *caitya* have a base consisting of a *ghaṭa* standing on a stepped platform, and those along the left aisle have a rudimentary capital. We have seen that the sculpture appears to be roughly contemporary with some of the advanced carvings at Pitalkhora, and reveals a workmanship somewhat earlier than that of the Sanchi gateways. The inscriptions on the façade of the *caitya* belong to Series I (b), or to *c*. 70–50 BC. This date applies to its commencement only, but indicates that the stone façade was an early innovation. An inscription on two of the interior pillars belongs to Series I (d) and suggests that the *caitya* was not completed until around 25 BC. This tiny cave could not have taken some twenty-five years and more to complete, and we must assume that work was not continuous. Architectural evidence confirms this as the inconsistency of the capitals of the interior pillars indicate two clear phases of construction. The *caitya* may be considered to be approximately contemporary with *caitya* IX at Ajanta, although its prolonged excavation indicates its later completion.

After this phase of construction there followed a considerable period of time during which rock-cutting ceased at Nasik. Then, towards the end of the first century AD, cutting began again in earnest. *Vihāra* X, with its bas-relief *stūpa* against the back wall, was probably one of the first caves to be excavated. The veranda pillars belong to the third phase in the development of the 'bell' capital – to a phase later than Karle. The cave, known also as the Nahapāna *vihāra*, contains a number of inscriptions of that ruler, one of which mentions the year 42 of his reign, or AD 96 according to our chronology. By this date the *vihāra* was complete. *Vihāra* III seems to have been commenced soon after and to have been modelled on *vihāra* X. The capitals of the veranda pillars belong to the final phase in the development of the 'bell' capital. We have seen that the cave was the result of two periods of cutting. An inscription of Gautamīputra Sātakarni in the year 14 of his reign suggests that the original cave had been completed by the year AD 100, while a record of Pulumāvi indicates that the cave was later enlarged to reach its present form.

The veranda pillars and the 'bell' capitals of *vihāras* V, VIII, XX and of cave XVII are similar to those of *vihāra* X and were perhaps cut around AD 100. Caves XVII and XX contain inscriptions that throw light on their construction. The record above the doorway of cave XVII tells us that it was excavated as a *caitya* by Indragni-mitra, a *yavana* from the north. The shrine beyond the hall had just been commenced and would have been flat-roofed and somewhat similar in plan to the Kuda *caityas*. The inscription belongs palaeo-graphically to Series IV and would suggest that the cave was cut after AD 110. We may thus conclude that the rectangular, flat-roofed *caitya* at Nasik appears first after AD 110. The inscription in *vihāra* XX is dated in the seventh year of Yajñaśrī, or AD 159, and states that the cave was under construction for many years and was finally com-pleted by the wife of the commander-in-chief. Caves II and IX both contain inscriptions belonging palaeographically to Series IV, or roughly between AD 110–150. Cave II is among those converted to later Mahāyāna use.

Excavation at Nasik extended over both phases of early rock-cutting in western India. The tiny *vihāra* XIX, which contains an inscription engraved in the reign of Kanha Sātavāhana, was ex-cavated some time between *c.* 90–70 BC. The adjoining *caitya* was commenced around 70–50 BC, but was apparently abandoned for a time and completed around 25 BC. After a lull of about a century, cutting was resumed and there was a period of intense activity. *Vihāra* X, probably the first cave to be excavated, was completed in AD 96. The original *vihāra* III had been cut by around AD 100, and was enlarged to reach its present form by AD 129. Between AD 100–150, *vihāras* II, V, VIII, IX, and the incomplete *caitya* XVII were executed. *Vihāra* XX, which must have been started soon after AD 100, was completed only in AD 159. Occupation of the site during the days of Mahāyāna Buddhism is indicated by a number of new caves containing sculptures of the Buddha and bodhisattvas. Several earlier caves were also converted to Mahāyāna usage.

60, 61   The façade of the unfinished Amba/Ambika *caitya* in the Manmodi hills at Junnar. The modern restoration of the two central columns has omitted the stepped abacus of the capitals (*cf.* engaged columns). *Above*, detail of *caitya* window.

62, 63 *Left*, the interior columns of
caitya VI in the Lenyadri hills at Junnar.
Below, the *stūpa* at the far end of the nave.

64 Façade of Lenyadri *caitya* VI. The *caitya* arch
is a 'blind' one, but the traditional shape of the
arch is retained.

65　The veranda of the Gaṇeśa Lena *vihāra* in the Lenyadri hills. Note its similarity to Nasik *vihāra* X and III (*cf.* Plates 47, 48).

66 The geometric painted decoration on the ceiling of *caitya* XLVIII at Shivneri.

67 The *stūpa* within the flat-roofed rectangular *caitya* XLVIII on the Shivneri hills at Junnar. As in other *caityas* of this plan, the *stūpa* has its *chatra* engraved directly on the low ceiling above.

68   The hall of Kuda *caitya* VI, with *mithuna* couples on the rear wall and the animal-and-herdsmen frieze beside and below them. The sculptures on the side walls are later additions.

69   Animal-and-herdsmen frieze beside *mithuna* panels in Kuda *caitya* VI.

70, 71   The *mithuna* couples in Kuda *caitya* VI.

72 The veranda pillars of *caitya* IX at Kuda.

73 The façade of *caitya* VI at Kuda. The projection in front of the veranda was originally held up at either end by elephants: today, only the one, at the left end, remains.

74 The isolated *vihāra* at Ambivale.

75, 76 The Kanheri *caitya*. *Above*, the façade; *left*, the interior with an imposing *stūpa* at the far end of the nave. Note the inconsistency in the treatment of the pillars. The cave was the result of two phases of construction and the original plan for the sculpting of the pillars was not adhered to when it was completed.

77 Details of the block of relief sculpture that crowns the capital of two of the columns within the Kanheri *caitya*.

78, 79 The *mithunas* in the veranda of the Kanheri *caitya*.

80, 81 Coins of Gomitra (*left and centre*), a native ruler of Mathura, depicting the tree-in-railing motif. Note the dotted square marked round it. *Right*, the reverse of a coin of Apollodotus depicting the tripod-lebes contained within a dotted square. Note the close resemblance of the tree-in-railing on Gomitra's coins to the tripod-lebes.

82 Bronze toy female elephant, South-east Deccan, third century AD. The piece is 7 inches high and was hollow cast.

83 Bronze figure of an elephant and four riders, found in a trader's stock in the course of excavations at the site of Brahmapuri. This highly accomplished example of Sātavāhana metal casting is only $2\frac{1}{2}$ inches long and 2 inches high.

84 Detail of an elephant head from a bronze hanging lamp. Also part of the trader's stock from Brahmapuri.

85 Ivory figure of a *yakshi* found at Ter. The figurine has a hole bored through its head reaching to the level of the navel. Remains of a protrusion of some sort may be seen to the right of the *yakshi*'s head.

86 Ivory *yakshi* discovered in the ruins of Pompeii. This figurine also has a hole bored through the head, reaching down to the level of the loins. There is a protrusion to the left of her head and the general pose is similar to that of the Ter *yakshi*. It seems likely that the Pompeii ivory is of Sātavāhana workmanship.

87, 88 Gajalakshmī medallion (*left*) and centaur medallion (*right*) from the railing of *stūpa* II at Sanchi. Note the insistence on the frontal presentation of the upper portion of the bodies of both the centaur and the female rider, although the figures are undoubtedly intended to be in 'profile'.

89 Gajalakshmī medallion from the railing of the Bharhut *stūpa*.

90 Guardian from the north gateway of *stūpa* I at Sanchi.

Bedsa

The Bedsa *caitya*, with its apsidal plan elaborated through the addition of a veranda wider than the interior of the cave itself, belongs architecturally to a more advanced date than the *caityas* so far considered. Sculptural evidence confirms this as the carving of the animal-and-rider figures crowning the capitals of the veranda columns suggests close affinities with the sculptures on the gateways of Sanchi *stūpa* I. Palaeographic evidence indicates that the three inscriptions in the Bedsa caves, one of which is above the doorway of a cell in the *caitya* veranda, belongs to Series I (c), or to *c.* 50–30 BC. Thus, architectural, sculptural and palaeographic evidence agree in assigning the caves at Bedsa to around this date. Mahāyāna occupation of the site is evident from reports of paintings of the Buddha and bodhisattvas on the walls of the *caitya*: these were apparently covered with a layer of whitewash and are no longer in existence.

Karle

Architectural evidence indicates for the Karle *caitya* a date somewhat in advance of Bedsa. The *caitya* has here been further elaborated by the addition of an outer screen with free-standing columns beyond this. We have seen that the sculpture is of a highly advanced character and comprises some of the finest examples of the sculptors' craft from the western caves. Earlier we pointed to the differences in the quality of the carving of the *mithuna* couples and suggested that these variations were probably the result of the distinctions between the work of a master craftsman and his pupils. Palaeographically, a date roughly between AD 50–70 is probable for the inscriptions recording the donation of various portions of the *caitya*. The cave was certainly completed before the engraving of the Nahapāna inscription which records the grant of a village to the monks at Karle. If Nahapāna had anything to do with the construction or even the completion of the *caitya*, this would surely have been mentioned. Some scholars have identified the Ushavadāta mentioned on a pillar within the *caitya*, with the son-in-law of Nahapāna, who was also known by that name, and have hence placed the *caitya* at a somewhat later date.[3] However, the son-in-law of Nahapāna always described himself as Ushavadāta, son of Dinika and son-in-law of the king Satrap Kshaharāta Nahapāna; while the pillar record merely mentions Ushavadāta from Dhenukākata. It therefore seems unlikely that the two refer to the same person. In addition, the script of the two records is different, the pillar inscription being palaeo-graphically earlier.

The construction of the Karle *caitya* may then be placed around AD 50–70, depending on the number of years considered necessary to complete its excavation. We have indicated that a period of ten to fifteen years appears quite adequate to us. Inscriptions of Nahapāna, Gautamīputra Sātakarni and of Pulumāvi are to be found in the veranda of the *caitya*, recounting the grants of villages and their produce to the monk community at Karle. The two-storeyed *vihāra* belongs to a later date than the *caitya* and contains an inscrip-tion reporting its dedication in the twenty-fourth year of Pulumāvi, or AD 134. Evidence of later Mahāyāna occupation at Karle is abundant. In the *caitya* veranda itself, all available spaces on the side walls, and above and below the *mithunas* are filled in with panels of the Buddha and his attendants. In some places, even the *vedikā*-band has been cut away to make room for such panels. Several small excavations with Buddha figures sculpted within them belong to this later phase.

Kuda

Architectural evidence gives us few clues as to the date of the rectangular, flat-roofed *caityas* at Kuda. The pillars of *caitya* IX have a 'bell' capital of the second phase and this would suggest that the cave is later than Bedsa and is perhaps contemporary with the Karle *caitya*. Sculptural evidence indicates that the *mithunas* in *caitya* VI with their shallower relief but free and easy style, belong to a later date than those at Karle. Fortunately, however, the evidence of palaeography is more illuminating. The caves at Kuda apparently belong to two phases of construction. The inscriptions in caves VIII–XIV and in caves XVIII–XXIV belong to Series III, or approxi-mately to AD 90–110. The *caityas* at Kuda are all flat-roofed, rec-tangular structures. We have already seen that this plan first appears at Nasik after AD 110, but at Kuda we find an earlier beginning for this innovation. The inscriptions in caves I–VII and caves XV–XVII appear to belong towards the end of Series IV, or towards AD 138–150. *Caitya* VI, with its elephant supports outside the veranda and the *mithuna* couples within, belongs to this advanced phase. The extraordinary flourishes of script to be seen at Kuda appear to have been a local variation. Mahāyāna occupation of the site is indicated by panels depicting the Buddha and bodhisattvas sculpted on the side walls of *caitya* VI, as well as on the façade beside the elephant supports.

Junnar

The seven sets of caves around Junnar, including the caves at the head of the Nanaghat pass, appear to range over a wide period of time.[4] We shall examine each group in turn, considering them in their probable order of excavation. Nowhere at Junnar, in either sculpture or painting, is there any evidence of Mahāyāna occupation.

Nanaghat

The inscribed cave at the head of the Nanaghat pass contains no traces of architectual embellishment, and neither the floor nor the lower portion of the side walls appear to have been finished. The rear wall of the cave once had engraved against it full-length relief portraits of the early members of the Sātavāhana royal family. It is indeed unfortunate that these figures are so greatly damaged as to be almost non-existent: only the feet of three of the figures may still be discerned. However, the identifying labels placed directly above them leave no doubt of their having existed once and indicate that the portraits represented Simuka, the founder of the dynasty, Sātakarni and his queen Nayanikā, a general, and three princes. The side walls of the cave are covered with the inscriptions of queen Nayanikā, recording the generosity of the royal family at the performance of Brahmanical sacrifice. Palaeography and historical data provide undeniable evidence of the excavation of the cave around 70–60 BC. An entire series of cisterns exists beside the inscribed cave. A small cave and cistern may be seen on the rock-face opposite, but the cave is so roughly hewn that it could easily be taken for a natural one. It seems possible to trace the existence of a few other excavations along the same scarp. The Nanaghat caves seem to have been used for some secular purpose, probably as a rest-house by the traders and merchants making the steep and lengthy ascent of the pass, before proceeding via Junnar to the market towns of the interior. Two more records, belonging palaeographically to Series IV, testify to the continued importance of the pass for at least another couple of centuries.

Tulja Lena

Architectural evidence has shown that the pillared, circular *caitya* at Tulja belongs to an early stage in the development of the *caitya* form.

The presence of pillars to mark a circumambulatory path suggests a date somewhat in advance of the Guntupalli *caitya*, and indicates that it may be a variant form belonging to the same phase as Bhaja. The half-arched ceiling of the circumambulatory passage, the plain octagonal columns with a gentle rake towards the upper end, and the brackets among the *vihāras* all indicate an early date. Traces of painting may be seen on the *caitya* pillars and one fragment, depicting a standing woman, seems to indicate contemporaneity with the *Chaddanta jātaka* paintings in *caitya* X at Ajanta. It is unfortunate that no inscriptions remain at the site. We may assume, however, with some confidence that the Tulja caves were cut in the first phase of such activity in western India, some time between *c.* 100 BC and *c.* 25 BC. More probably, the caves were executed after Nanaghat (after *c.* 70–60 BC), with the paintings added at a slightly later date.

Budh Lena (*Manmodi Hill*)

Architecturally the Budh Lena *caitya* with its simple apsidal plan without a veranda, but with a stone frontage, belongs to an early phase. It should be regarded as being prior to the Bedsa *caitya* and contemporary with Ajanta IX and Nasik. The assured treatment of the sculptural decoration indicates, however, a date much in advance of the Sanchi gateways and Bedsa. The seven sculptured petals contained within the 'blind' arch on the façade portray an unusual Gajalakshmī theme, and the figures bear affinities with the *mithunas* on the Karle *caitya*. The inscription on the façade of the *caitya* appears to belong to Series II, and is thus contemporary with the Karle records. The Budh Lena *caitya* seems to have been the first apsidal *caitya* in the Junnar region and it would appear that the early *caitya* form was imitated. The 'blind' arch seems to be a regional variation of uncertain chronological significance. We could accept the palaeographical and sculptural evidence in assigning the *caitya* to a phase contemporary with the Karle *caitya* – to around AD 50–70. As the *caitya* remained unfinished while the *vihāras* were completed, we must assume that the latter were cut before the *caitya*.

Lenyadri

Caitya VI at Lenyadri is an apsidal cave with arched side aisle ceilings and a narrow pillared veranda in front. The bell-shaped inverted *ghaṭa* on the pillars belong to the third phase in the development of the 'bell' capital and suggest that the *caitya* belongs to a phase later than Karle. The inscription recording the donation of the cave belongs to Series III and confirms this dating. The 'blind' arch of the *caitya*, to be found also on the Budh Lena and Bhima Shankar *caityas* at Junnar but nowhere else in western India, appears to have been a regional variation. Two inscriptions reporting the gift of cisterns also belong to this phase. The adjoining Gaṇeśa Lena *vihāra* is excavated on a plan similar to *vihāras* X and III at Nasik. It displays greater affinities with Nasik X in having a bell-shaped *ghaṭa* of the third phase, similar also to that of Lenyadri *caitya* VI. Architectural evidence gives us little hint as to the date of the rectangular flat-roofed *caitya* XV. Palaeography, however, indicates that the *caitya* was excavated sometime between AD 110–150, as the inscription reporting the donation of the cave belongs to Series IV. An inscription on one of the *vihāras* also belongs to this phase.

Excavation at Lenyadri appears to have commenced around AD 90–100 when *caitya* VI, Gaṇeśa Lena *vihāra* VII, two cisterns and presumably other *vihāras* were cut. Soon after, probably between AD 110–150, *caitya* XV and some further *vihāras* and cisterns were excavated.

Amba/Ambika (Manmodi Hill)

The interior of the Amba/Ambika *caitya* is left unfinished, apparently due to a large natural fault in the rock towards the back of the cave. It was however intended to be apsidal-ended with a vaulted ceiling. The veranda pillars have a rounded inverted *ghaṭa* belonging to the final phase of the 'bell' capital, and much in advance of Karle. The *caitya* contains ten inscriptions engraved on the back wall of the veranda, all of which belong to Series IV and assign the cutting of the cave to around AD 110–150. The inscriptions on the *vihāras* of this group appear to belong to Series III (with one exception, which belongs to Series IV). Rock-cutting at the site apparently commenced around AD 100 with the *caitya* and one *vihāra* being cut at a slightly later date.

Bhima Shankar (Manmodi Hill)

The unfinished Bhima Shankar *caitya* has a veranda with pillars belonging to the same phase as those of the Amba/Ambika. The interior, however, is quite differently treated and is a long rectangular chamber with a flat roof. A deep well at the far end apparently led to the abandonment of the project. A fragmentary inscription on the rock-face just outside the cave belongs to Series IV and suggests that this *caitya* belongs with the Amba/Ambika to a date between

AD 110–150. Excavation at the site appears to have started at an earlier date as an inscription above a cistern to the far east of the *caitya* was engraved by Ayama, minister of Nahapāna, in the year 46 or AD 100. The *caitya* was apparently cut at a somewhat later stage.

Shivneri

The pillars in the flat-roofed rectangular *caitya* XLVIII have a capital with a rounded inverted *ghaṭa* that belongs to the final phase of the 'bell' capital. This would suggest that the cave belonged to an advanced date. No sculptural embellishment is to be found in this group of caves, and the painted decoration appears to be confined to Plate 66 geometric designs on the ceiling of *caitya* XLVIII and the adjoining *vihāra*. Sections of this are fairly well preserved but offer few clues as to the date of the caves. The inscription recording the donation of *caitya* XLVIII belongs palaeographically to Series IV, which implies that the cave was executed between AD 110–150. All other records in the Shivneri group belong to this same palaeographic period, and we may thus assume that excavation at the site began at a relatively advanced date.

Ambivale

At Ambivale we find a single *vihāra* with a cistern nearby. The situation seems ideal with a river winding below and mountains in the distance, and the rock does not appear to have any obvious flaws in it: yet there is just this one cave. Architectural evidence suggests that this *vihāra*, with veranda pillars displaying a rounded inverted *ghaṭa* belongs to a late stage of development. Palaeographic evidence is somewhat uncertain though it would in general agree with a late date. Records C, D and E belong undoubtedly to Series IV, or to AD 110–150. Records A and B appear to belong to an earlier phase. None of the inscriptions seem to form a complete record and they do not appear to be in Pali. We would be inclined to consider the cave as belonging to the period AD 110–150, although it is possible that it was commenced earlier, being left incomplete for a period of time.

Mahad

The apsidal *caitya* is not to be seen at Mahad, its place having been taken by the rectangular flat-roofed *caitya*. We have seen at Nasik (cave XVII), Kuda and Shivneri at Junnar that this type of cave appears at a relatively advanced date – around AD 100 or later. An inscription on the wall of *caitya* VIII at Mahad belongs to Series III and assigns the cutting of the cave to around AD 100. An inscription outside *vihāra* XXVII belongs to Series IV. It would appear to us that the period between AD 90–150 would probably cover the cutting of the caves at Mahad.

Karadh

The majority of the *caityas* at Karadh are of the rectangular flat-roofed variety, and we have seen that this plan appears first around AD 100. Only one, rather defaced, inscription remains in the caves at Karadh and this seems to belong palaeographically to Series III. *Caitya* V at Karadh is an unusual cave: apsidal but without aisles, it has a stone façade and a low roof with the *chatra* of the *stūpa* engraved on the ceiling. This latter feature is usually associated only with the rectangular *caityas*, and the cave would seem to be a variation of this rectangular variety. We would on the whole be inclined to assign the caves at Karadh to between AD 90–150.

Shelarvadi

The single rectangular flat-roofed *caitya* at Shelarvadi contains a donatory inscription belonging to Series IV, which assigns the cave to the period AD 110–150. One of the *vihāras* contains pilasters with bell-shaped inverted *ghaṭas* of the third phase of the 'bell' capital. An inscription in this *vihāra* also belongs to Series IV, and the evidence suggests that the caves at Shelarvadi were all excavated during this advanced phase.

Kanheri

Architectural and sculptural evidence indicates that the Kanheri *caitya* was excavated some time after Karle. Exactly how long after we would have no way of knowing[5] except for the palaeographic evidence that assigns the *caitya* to the reign of Yajñaśrī Sātakarni. It was thus excavated some time between AD 152–181. The inconsistent sculpting of the interior pillars reveals, however, that the cave was executed in two stages quite apart from the later Mahāyāna additions. It also appears that the façade was left incomplete as even the fronton of the *caitya* arch was not marked. Excavation at Kanheri started at a relatively late date and the earliest records belong palaeographically to Series III. The majority of Kanheri excavations belong to the general period of AD 90–181, though a large number of these caves were later converted to Mahāyāna use. Inscriptions of the ninth, tenth and eleventh centuries indicate that the site was probably occupied longer than any other in the area.

Saurashtra

The caves at Sana and Talaja appear to belong to the second phase of architectural activity in western India which commenced around AD 50. The *caityas* at these two sites are akin to those at Karadh and Mahad, and seem to belong to an advanced stage in the development of the *caitya* form. On present evidence these *caityas* are probably to be assigned to the period AD 90–150. However, the absence of the typical apsidal western *caitya* and of the quadrangular *vihāra* suggests that the Saurashtra caves are apart from the main development of cave architecture in the Deccan. There are no inscriptions at either Sana or Talaja to give us any definite indication of the date of the caves. An inscription on a block of stone, belonging to the grandson of Jayadāman (probably Rudrasimha, the son of Rudradāman) was found among the caves at Junagadh, and a fragmentary record also of a later date was recovered among the caves at Siddhsar. We have no indications, inscriptional, architectural or sculptural, of any cave architecture in Saurashtra prior to AD 100.

Concluding Remarks

The early Buddhist caves of western India, palaeographically, sculpturally as well as architecturally, may be regarded as part of the general artistic activity of India during the two centuries preceding and following the birth of Christ. Our chronological scheme suggests that the tradition of excavating monasteries in the Deccan commenced around 100 BC, approximately contemporary with the carving of the railings of the *stūpas* at Bharhut and Sanchi, and some twenty years prior to the construction of a small *stūpa* at Amaravati. This artistic activity arose in the western Deccan with the establishment of the Sātavāhana dynasty; in the Bharhut and Sanchi area, towards the end of the reign of the Śungas; and in the Amaravati region, under an unknown local dynasty. Early rock architecture includes the sites of Kondivte, Nadsur, Bhaja, Tulja, Pitalkhora, Kondane, Ajanta, Nasik, and Bedsa, and comes to an end around 25 BC. Work on the gateways of *stūpa* I at Sanchi was also completed around this same date. During this first phase it seems best to treat all this activity as part of a single early Indian artistic tradition.

The second phase of activity commences around the middle of the first century AD, and, apart from extensive additions at Nasik and Junnar, brings several new sites into focus – notably Karle, Kuda, Mahad, Karadh, Shelarvadi and Kanheri. During this phase it becomes possible to distinguish regional styles of sculpture, as between the western caves and Amaravati, and similar regional variations may be seen in the field of palaeography also. However, roughly parallel developments are to be seen throughout these regions and it is only after AD 150, towards the end of the period of the early Buddhist caves, that such regional styles become more important and may be distinguished sharply.

Sanchi Gateway Inscriptions

It has generally been agreed on the evidence of sculptural style that the south gateway of *stūpa* I at Sanchi was the first to be erected. The fact that the Aśokan pillar stands near that gateway and that the steps leading to the upper circumambulatory path are also located at the south entrance has been taken as additional confirmation of this view. Palaeographic evidence, we have seen, assigns the north gateway records to Series B (*c.* 80–60 BC), while allocating those on the south, west and east gateways to Series C (*c.* 50–25 BC). As this appears to contradict the generally accepted view, we shall examine in detail the location of inscriptions on each of the gateways and consider the possibility of their having been added at a later date. We shall also discuss the contents of these records to see if this gives any clue to the prior erection of one or the other.

North Gateway
There are six inscriptions on the north gateway of which the first four belong palaeographically to Series B.

1 The gift of a monk Dhamagiri is engraved on the narrow platform below the elephant at the centre top of the gateway (inner face).
2 The gift of Balamita is on the leg of the winged lion on the top architrave, left end (outer face).
3 The gift of Asamita is on the leg of the elephant to the extreme right above the lowest architrave (outer face).
4 The gift of the Vedisikas is on the leg of the elephant, second from the left, above the lowest architrave (outer face).

These inscriptions report the donation of specific portions of the gateway and their location indicates that they were engraved during the actual phase of construction. The fifth record is a fragmentary imprecation inscribed on the threshold of the gateway (left side, outer face). It belongs quite definitely to Series C and may be grouped with the records on the other three gateways. The sixth record, also apparently part of an imprecation, is engraved on the right threshold (outer face). It is in a very damaged condition and the couple of letters that remain do not allow us to assign it to a specific palaeographic position. These two inscriptions, both imprecatory, are located on portions of the gateway normally left unoccupied: for confirmation we have only to glance at the inner face of the gateway. This feature, considered together with the fact that similar imprecatory records are to be found on the other gateways, makes it likely that the imprecations were inscribed on all the gateways shortly after they had all been erected.

South Gateway

There are four inscriptions on the south gateway, one of which is imprecatory. The location of these is of interest in view of the claim that this gateway was the first to be erected. We have seen that palaeographic evidence points to its later date: if indeed this was the first, then perhaps the inscriptions are later additions.

1 The donation of the foreman of the artisans of Śri Sātakarni is engraved on a relief *stūpa* in the centre of the top architrave (inner face).

2 The gift of Balamitra, pupil of the preacher Aya Cuda is on a relief *stūpa* in the centre of the middle architrave (outer face).

3 The gift of the ivory-workers of Vidisa is inscribed above the lowest panel on the left pillar, facing east.

4 A fragmentary imprecation may be seen on the threshold of the gateway.

The donative records are closely associated with particular pieces of sculpture and certainly appear to belong to the period of construction. It does not appear possible to consider them to be later additions.

West Gateway

1 The gift of Balamitra, pupil of Aya Cuda, is inscribed above the first panel on the right pillar (outer face). A comparison with record 2 on the south gateway leads to the inevitable conclusion that the two refer to donations by the same person. It is apparent that the south and west gateways belong to the same period of construction.

2 The gift of a pillar by the Kurarīya Nāgapīya, the banker of

Acavada and his son Sagha, is engraved just below the capital on the left pillar (outer face).

3 An imprecation is engraved on the threshold of the gateway.

East Gateway

1 The gift of a pillar by Nāgapīya of Kurara, the banker of Acavada, is inscribed above the third panel of the left pillar. A comparison of this record with the second inscription on the west gateway reveals that both refer to donations by the same person. The east and west gateways hence belong to the same phase of construction.

2 The gift of Jīva may be seen on the platform below the crowning *triratna*.

3 An imprecation is engraved on the threshold of the gateway.

Conclusions

1 The north gateway records (apart from the imprecations) belong to Series B, while those on the south, west and east belong to Series C. This fact, while *apparently* indicating the prior construction of the north gateway, certainly implies that the south was not the first to be constructed, but belongs together with the west and east gateways.

2 All the donative records belong to the period of construction and were probably engraved soon after the sculpture was completed. The imprecations appear to have been inscribed on the thresholds of the gateways after all four had been erected.

3 The south and west gateway inscriptions reveal gifts by the same person, and a similar situation exists with regard to the west and east gateways. It is apparent that the south, west and east gateways belong to the same phase of construction. Here again, it does not seem possible to maintain the priority of the south.

Despite these points, it does not appear correct to state that the north gateway was the first to be erected. It is impossible to ignore the evidence of sculptural style which indicates quite definitely that the sculptures on all four gateways belong to one general period. We cannot, however, deny the validity of the palaeographic evidence. One solution suggests itself to us. The monk allocated the duty of writing up the donations of the north gateway may have been a revered and aged monk, who would quite naturally have used the form of writing current in the days of his youth although this was no longer in vogue. Further research may suggest alternative solutions.

Karle Radiocarbon Dates

In a recent publication D. D. Kosambi unquestioningly accepted the radiocarbon date of 290 ± 150 BC announced for a wooden pin from the Karle *caitya*, and referred to the *caitya* as being 'dated by radiocarbon to a pre-Aśokan epoch'.[1] Two further readings have since been made from portions of the wooden ribbing of the ceiling of the *caitya*, and the dates of 230 ± 95 BC and 125 ± 100 BC have been announced.[2] We find it impossible to accept these dates in view of what is known of the architecture, palaeography and history of the period: most scholars, we feel confident, would agree with us here.

The rock architecture of Aśokan times is exemplified by the Sudama and Lomasa Rishis *caityas* in the Barabar hills near Bodh-Gaya. We have seen that these caves, each consisting of a small empty circular chamber and an adjoining rectangular hall, represent the early stages in the evolution of the plan of the typical *caitya*. Contrasting with this we have the tremendous degree of sophistication, the great technical advance and the imaginative architectural and sculptural planning evident in the Karle *caitya*. An Aśokan or a pre-Aśokan date for Karle cannot be seriously considered on architectural grounds. Palaeography too rules out this possibility. The script of the Karle records is highly advanced when compared to Aśokan Brāhmī and, as we have seen, a period of about three centuries separates them.

The impossibility of accepting a radiocarbon date such as 290 ± 150 BC becomes even more apparent when we consider the historical adjustments to be made if we take the true age to be even 290 minus $150 = 140$ BC. (We find it quite impossible to consider a pre-Aśokan date.) The Nahapāna inscription at Karle, donating a village to the monks of Valūraka (Karle) without any mention of sect, implies that the monks had only recently settled at the site and that there had been insufficient time for any one sect to predominate. This in turn implies that the *caitya* had been completed only recently, and would incline us to place Nahapāna soon after 140 BC, say at 120 BC. In view of the Nahapāna/Gautamīputra synchronism discussed in detail in Chapter I, the last date of Gautamīputra would then be 110 BC. This would mean that the Sātavāhana dynasty itself ended around 20 BC (120 minus 28, Pulumāvi; minus 14, Śivaśrī and Śivaskanda; minus 29, Yajñaśrī; minus 20, others). If we take the radiocarbon age to be 125 minus 100 BC = 25 BC, then the dynasty would have ended around AD 75. The impossibility of such dates for the end of the dynasty is obvious. The *Periplus* and Ptolemy's *Geography*, works belonging to the first and second centuries of the Christian era, clearly mention Sātavāhana and Kshaharāta rulers. There is also the undisputed reference to a Sātavāhana king in the Girnar inscription of Rudradāman which belongs to the year AD 150. It would seem that on historical grounds too we must reject the validity of the Karle radiocarbon dates as applied to the cutting of the *caitya*.

It is a widely accepted fact that the use of the Carbon-14 method of dating in the field of historical archaeology is rather limited. The factor of the standard deviation which is almost negligible when considering dates for the Prehistoric, greatly reduces the value of the method in historic times. In the case of a radiocarbon age such as 500±100, the true age lies fairly probably (two cases out of three) between 600 and 400, probably (nineteen cases out of twenty) between 700 and 300, and highly probably (997 cases out of 1000) between 800 and 200. Harold Barker tells us that 'for ordinary purposes one can say that there is a reasonable certainty that the true result lies within the limits of two standard deviations from the experimental value'.[3] In the case of the Karle dates, two standard deviations leaves us with the periods of 590 BC to AD 10 (for 290± 150 BC), 420 BC to 40 BC (for 230±95 BC), and 325 BC to AD 75 (for 125±100 BC). It is apparent then 'that the carbon-14 dating method is at its best in fixing the broad outlines of a chronology rather than the fine detail'.[4]

Early Amaravati Inscriptions

A recent and significant surface find from Amaravati consists of a fragmentary inscription on a sandstone slab that bears some trace of an original polish. D. C. Sircar suggests that the piece was cut from an Aśokan pillar, and points out that the language clearly resembles that of the Girnar version of Aśoka's edicts.[1] The script certainly reveals early features that may well be Aśokan.

The next group of inscriptions at Amaravati, best described as post-Aśokan, may be divided into two phases. Phase A comprises a large group of records, some fifty in number, engraved on pillars, cross-bars and coping fragments. It includes R. P. Chanda's inscription No. 1 and Nos. 3–20,[2] and some twenty-five or more records at the Amaravati museum and on the site itself. Some of this latter group have been noticed in the *Annual Report on Indian Epigraphy* for 1959/60,[3] but the list given there does not appear to be complete. This group also includes the sculptured and inscribed piece, a cross-bar, reproduced by Phillipe Stern and Mireille Bénisti in their work on Amaravati.[4] These inscriptions of Phase A exhibit letter-forms earlier than those of Nanaghat. There is no attempt at the equalization of the verticals of any of the letters, and the forms of *ga* and *ta* still reveal a tendency towards angularity. Very early forms of *bha* are to be found side by side with some later ones; and similarly, angular flat-based forms of *ma* may be found with the earlier variety. Palaeographic evidence indicates that these records were probably engraved during the period *c.* 80–60 BC.

Phase B of the post-Aśokan group includes the records on the carved pillar published by A. Ghosh;[5] Chanda No. 2; and Chanda 37, 38 and 43. The important sculptured pillar depicts several scenes from the life of the Buddha, cut in shallow relief, with labelling inscriptions clearly associated with the carving. Chanda No. 2 was erroneously attributed to Amaravati and Douglas Barrett points out that it is engraved instead on a fragment from Jaggayyapeta.[6]

Table 8

Chanda 37, 38, 43 are all to be found on a single slab, carved on both sides with a very shallow relief sculpture, now in the Madras Museum.[7] These inscriptions have a later form of *ta*, but reveal a *pa* in which the verticals have not yet been completely equalized. We would hesitate to assign a definite date to these records of post-Aśokan Phase B, but they probably belong somewhere within the general period of *c.* 60–25 BC. It is likely that the *Neranjara Gamanam* inscription on the much damaged sculptured pillar reproduced by P. R. Srinivasan,[8] also belongs to Phase B. The record consists of so few letters that it is difficult to be more categorical regarding its palaeographic position.

It would appear that a small *stūpa* of some type existed at Amaravati at a very early date. This was probably surrounded by a plain railing to which the inscribed fragments belong, with a few sculptured pillars located perhaps at the entrance. Sivaramamurti suggested that the group of fragments published by Chanda could possibly belong to the *harmikā*, but the many more pieces of a similar type recovered recently suggests that several of them were part of the railing of a small early *stūpa*. This *stūpa* would appear to belong to a date soon after the Bharhut and Sanchi II *stūpas*, and the references in the inscriptions to a general and a princess indicate that it arose under some local dynasty. The bulk of the sculptures and inscriptions from Amaravati belong together to a date some hundred years later. It has been suggested that the Amaravati region was a remote and backward area at this time and was some fifty years or more behind the Deccan in scriptual and presumably also sculptural development.[9] Such an explanation would bring the earliest inscriptions forward and would certainly lessen the time-lag involved. Present evidence can neither prove nor disprove such a view. When extended to the Orissa region, however, the theory appears more vulnerable: the Hathigumpha inscription of Khāravela very specifically mentions a Sātakarni ruling in the west whom Khāravela disregarded. Orissa would not appear to have been isolated or cut off from developments in the Deccan. We prefer then to acknowledge the existence of this appreciable time-lag between the small early *stūpa* at Amaravati and the main monument with its abundant sculptural decoration.[10]

Tables

Table 1   Early Indian Palaeography

	AŚOKAN		BESNAGAR	GHOSUNDI	BHARHUT	SANCHI		BHARHUT	GAYA
	Standard -Uposak	Variants			Railings	*Stūpa* I Railings	*Stūpa* II Railings	Gateway	
a									
ā									
i									
u									
e									
o									
ka									
kha									
ga									
gha									
ca									
cha									
ja									
jha									
ña									
ṭa									
ṭha									
ḍa									
ḍha									
ṇa									
ta									
tha									
da									
dha									
na									
pa									
pha									
ba									
bha									
ma									
ya									
ra									
la									
va									
śa									
ṣa									
sa									
ha									

able 2 Early Indian Palaeography

	SANCHI	BHILSA	SANCHI	SANCHI	ŚOḌĀSA	AYODHYA	PABHOSA	KUSHĀNA	
	N. Gateway		E., S., W. Gateways	*Stupa* III				Kanishka	Huvishka

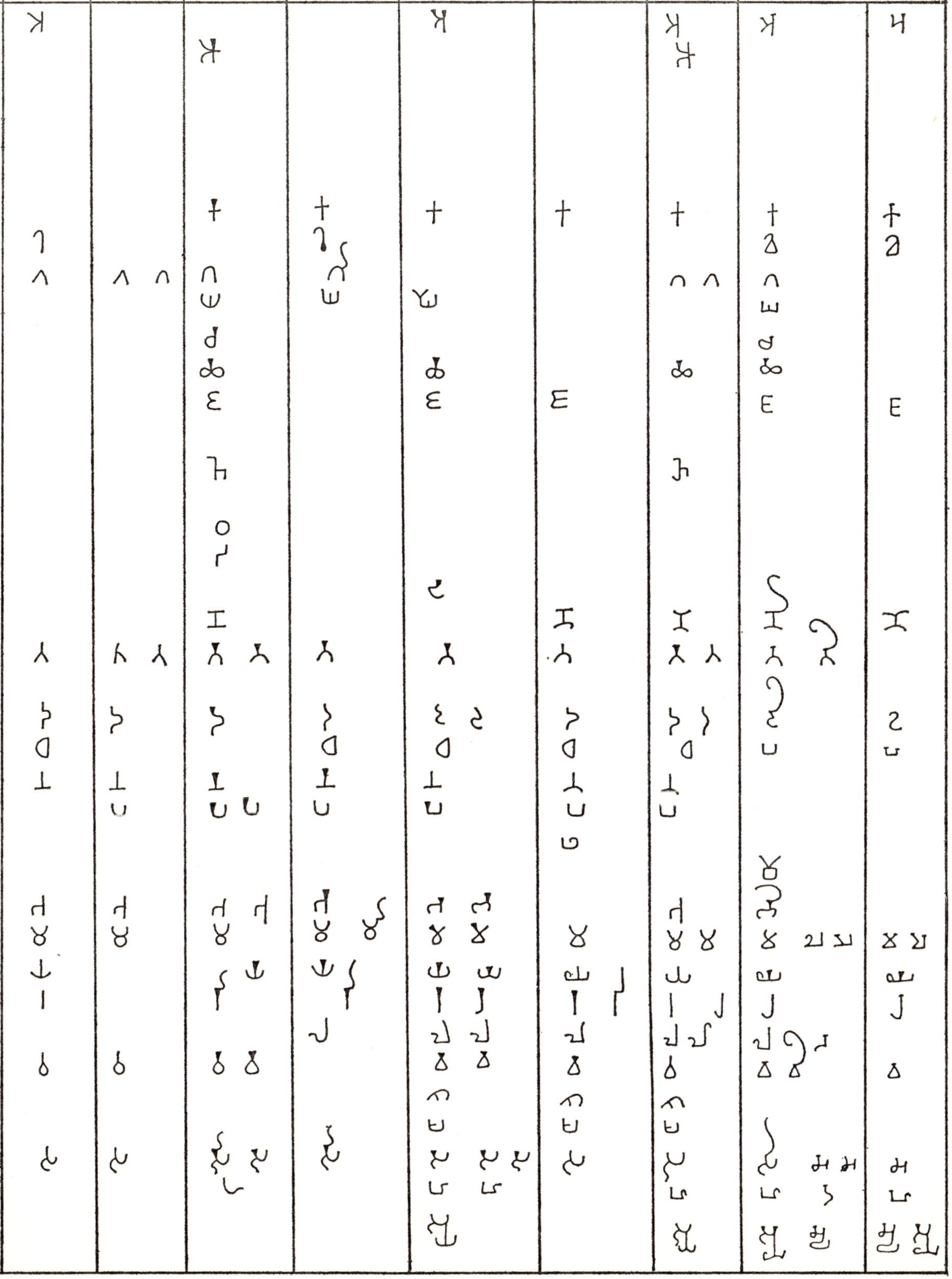

a
ha
a
ha
a
ha
a
ha
a
a
ha
a
ha
a
a
ha
a.
ha
a
a
ha
a
ha
na
a
a
a
a
a
a
a
ha
ya

Table 3 Coin Legends : Mathura and Ayodhya

	MATHURA: EARLY RULERS								
	Gomitra	Brahmamitra	Dradhamitra	Sūryamitra	Vishnumitra	Purushadatta	Utamadatta.	Rāmadatta	Kān...
ka									
kha									
ga	不								
gha									
ca									
cha									
ja									
jha									
na								ৼ	⊦
ta									
tha									
da									
dha			৬						
ña									
ṭa	⋋	ᕁ	⋋	ᕁ	ᕁ	⋋	⋋ ᕁ	⋋	
ṭha									
ḍa			੭			੭	੭	⅄	
ḍha									
ṇa	⊥								
pa						५			
pha									
ba		ᑫ							
bha									
ma	४	४	४	४ ४	४		४	४	
ya	↓			↓					
ra	∣					∣		∣	
la									
va					ꝺ				
śa									
ṣa					ᗸ	ᗺ			⟨glyph⟩
sa	ᘰ	ᘰ ৼ	ᘰ	⋋ ᘰ	ᗺ	ᗺ	ᘰ	ᘰ	⊦
ha									

tta	Balabhūti	Maharaja?	KSHATRAPAS				AYODHYA: EARLY RULERS			
			Śivadatta	Hagāmasha Hagāna	Rājuvula	Śoḍāsa	Mūladeva	Vāyudeva	Visakhadeva	Dhanadeva

Table 4 Inscriptions from the Early Buddhist Caves

	NASIK no. 1	BHAJA no. 1	BHAJA wood	KONDANE	PITALKHORA nos. 1 & 2	AJANTA no. 1	NANAGHAT	BHAJA nos. 2–6	NASIK no. 2	AJANTA no. 2	AJANTA no. 14	NADSUR	PITALKHORA nos. 3–7	BEDSA	NASIK no. 4
a															
ā															
i															
u															
e															
o															
ka															
kha															
ga															
gha															
ca															
cha															
ja															
jha															
ña															
ṭa															
ṭha															
ḍa															
ḍha															
ṇa															
ta															
tha															
da															
dha															
na															
pa															
pha															
ba															
bha															
ma															
ya															
ra															
la															
va															
śa															
ṣa															
sa															
ha															

Table 5   Inscriptions from Karle, Nasik, Junnar, Amaravati

	KARLE. nos. 1–3	JUNNAR no. 30	no. 7	NAHAPĀNA KARLE	NAHAPĀNA NASIK	NAHAPĀNA JUNNAR	GAUTAMĪPUTRA SĀTAKARNI Karle	GAUTAMĪPUTRA SĀTAKARNI Nasik	AMARAVATI Pulumāvi	AMARAVATI Śivamaka Sada
a										
ā										
i										
u										
e										
o										
ka										
kha										
ga										
gha										
ca										
cha										
ja										
jha										
ña										
ṭa										
ṭha										
ḍa										
ḍha										
ṇa										
ta										
tha										
da										
dha										
na										
pa										
pha										
ba										
bha										
ma										
ya										
ra										
la										
va										
śa										
ṣa										
sa										
ha										

Table 6 Inscriptions from the Early Buddhist Caves

	PULUMĀVI		JUNNAR		KUDA		SHELARVADI	BHAJA
	Nasik	Karle	no. 4	nos. 9–19	in Caves I–VII, XV	in Caves VIII–		no. 7
a								
ā								
i								
u								
e								
o								
ka								
kha								
ga								
gha								
ca								
cha								
ja								
jha								
ña								
ṭa								
ṭha								
ḍa								
ḍha								
ṇa								
ta								
tha								
da								
dha								
na								
pa								
pha								
ba								
bha								
ma								
ya								
ra								
la								
va								
śa								
ṣa								
sa								
ha								

Table 7 Inscriptions of the Western Satraps and the later Satavahanas

	ANDHAU	GIRNAR Rudradāman	Vāsishtīputra Siri Sātakarni	YAJÑAŚRĪ	Ābhīra Īśvarasena	Mādharīputra	MYAKADONI
a							
ā							
i							
u							
e							
o							
ka							
kha							
ga							
gha							
ca							
cha							
ja							
jha							
ña							
ṭa							
ṭha							
ḍa							
ḍha							
ṇa							
ta							
tha							
da							
dha							
na							
pa							
pha							
ba							
bha							
ma							
ya							
ra							
la							
va							
śa							
ṣa							
sa							
ha							

Table 8 Inscriptions from Amaravati and Hathigumpha

	Aśokan			Post-Aśokan		
					AMARAVATI	
	MYSORE EDICTS	AMARAVATI	CHANDA 1, 3–20	(An. Rep. Ind. Ep. 1959–60) CROSS-BARS & PILLARS *P h a s e 'A'*	OTHER FRAGMENTS (at Site)	(A.I. 20/21) GHOSH PILLAR *P*
a						
ā						
i						
u						
e						
o						
ka						
kha						
ga						
gha						
ca						
cha						
ja						
jha						
ña						
ṭa						
ṭha						
ḍa						
ḍha						
ṇa						
ta						
tha						
da						
dha						
na						
pa						
pha						
ba						
bha						
ma						
ya						
ra						
la						
va						
śa						
ṣa						
sa						
ha						

CHANDA 2 s e 'B'	CHANDA 37, 39, 43	PRE-NAHAPĀNA	Early Phase NAHAPĀNA and GAVTAMĪPUTRA	PULUMĀVI	HATHIGUMPHA

Table 9 Location of Inscriptions

[Unless otherwise stated, all references are from A.S.W.I. IV]

	INSCRIPTIONS	LOCATION	CONTENTS
SERIES I (a)	NASIK 1 (Pl. LI)	Vihāra XIX (p.98)	Records excavation in reign of Kanha Satavahana (p.98)
	BHAJA 1 (Pl.XLIV)	Vihāra XVII (p.82)	Gift of cell (p.82)
	BHAJA WOOD (Lalit Kala 6 Pl.X)	Wooden beams spanning vault of caitya (Lalit Kala 6 p.31)	Fragmentary (Lalit Kala 6 p.31)
	PITALKHORA 1 & 2 (Pl.XLIV)	Pillars within caitya III (p.83)	Gift of pillars (p.83)
	PITALKHORA A (A.I.15 Pl.LII D)	Right hand of dwarf-yaksha figure (A.I.15 p.82)	Records its making by a goldsmith (A.I.15 p.82)
	KONDANE (Pl.XLIV)	Facade of caitya, beside damaged sculptured head (p.83)	Made by Balaka, pupil of Kanha (p.83)
	AJANTA1 (Pl.LVI)	Facade of caitya X, to right of main arch (I.C.T. p.67)	Donation of cave facade (I.C.T. p.67)
	AJANTA NEW ROCK RECORD } Ars Orientalis 7 Pl.1	Caitya X, beneath mud plaster in left aisle, just below first to third ribs (Ars Orientalis 7, p.147 f.)	Donation of wall by Kanhaka (Ars Orientalis 7, p.148)
	AJANTA NEW PAINTED RECORD }	Caitya X, on third rafter of left aisle (Ars Orientalis 7, p.148)	Gift for the ascetics, by Dhamadera (Ars Orientalis 7, p.149)
SERIES I (b)	NANAGHAT 1 & 2 (A.S.W.I.V Pl.LI)	Side walls of cave (A.S.W.I.V p.59)	Records generosity of Sātavāhanas at performance of Brahmanical sacrifices (A.S.W.I.V pp.60–64)
	NANAGHAT 3-8 (A.S.W.I.V Pl.LI)	Back wall of cave, above now non-existent 'portraits' (A.S.W.I.V p.59)	Names of members of royal family (A.S.W.I.V p.64)
	NASIK 2 & 3 (Pl.LI)	Facade of caitya (p.40)	Donatory. No. 2—Gift of Nasik inhabitants (p.98 f.)
	BHAJA 2–5 (Pl.XLIV)	On series of rock-cut stupās to right of caitya (p.82 f.)	Dedicatory (p.82 f.)
	BHAJA 6 (Pl.XLIV)	Cave VI, over cell doorway (p.83)	Donatory (p.83)
	NADSUR (A.S.W.I.XII Pl.VI)	Vihāra VII & caitya VIII (A.S.W.I.XII..p.6 f.)	Fragmentary/Donatory (A.S.W.I.XII p.6 f.)
	AJANTA (Pl.LVI)	Vihāra XII, beside cell doorway (I.C.T. p.68)	Donatory (I.C.T. p.68)
	AJANTA14 (I.C.T. Pl.facing p.84)	Painted record in caitya X. On left wall opposite 3rd pillar (I.C.T. p.84)	Fragmentary (I.C.T. p.84)
SERIES I (c.)	BEDSA 1 (Pl.XLVII)	Beside doorway of cell in caitya veranda (p.23)	Donatory (p.89)
	BEDSA 2 (Pl.XLVII)	Behind small rock-cut stupa (p.89)	Donatory (p.89)
	BEDSA 3 (Pl.XLVII)	Above cistern (p.90)	Gift of Mahaderi (princess), Maharathiui, daughter of Mahabhoja (p.90)
	PITALKHORA 3-7 (Pl.XLIV)	Vihāra IV, adjoining caitya III (p.84)	Gifts of royal physician and family (p.84)
SERIES I (d)	NASIK 4 (Pl.LI)	Along lengthwise section of 2 pillars within caitya (p.40)	Completed by grand-daughter of Maha Hakusiri, wife of royal minister (p.99)
SERIES II	KARLE 1 (Pl.XLVII)	Left end of caitya veranda (p.23)	Rock-mansion completed by Seth Bhūtapāla (p.90)
	KARLE 2 (Pl.XLVII)	Lion-pillar (p.90)	Gift of Maharathi Agnimitra (p.90)
	KARLE 3 (Pl.XLVII)	Right wall of veranda, below feet of elephants (p.23)	Gift of elephants & vedika band by monk Indradera (p.90)
	JUNNAR 7 (I.C.T. Pl.facing p.43)	Facade of Budh Lena caitya, engraved within sculptured half-lotus (I.C.T. p.43)	Gift of facade by Yavana Chandra (I.C.T. p.43)
SERIES III	KARLE19—NAHAPĀNA—(Pl.LI)	Karle caitya—on band to right of entrance, on level with springing of caitya window (p.24)	Grant of village by Ushavadata (p.101)
	NASIK5—NAHAPĀNA—(Pl.LII)	Across veranda wall of vihāra X (p.41)	Construction of cave by Ushavadāta (p.99 f.)
	NASIK6-9—NAHAPĀNA—(Pl.(LII & LIII)	Vihāra X (p.41 f.)	Gifts from Ushavadāta & his family, No.7 mentions yr.42 (p.101 ff.)

Series	Inscription	Location	Content
			& postscript of yr.24 (p.104 ff.)
SERIES III	KARLE 21—GAUTAMĪPUTRA SĀTAKARNI—(Pl.LIV)	Right of caitya doorway—awkward placing—interrupted by beam ends (p.24)	Grant of village—yr.14 (p.112f.)
	KUDA 14-22,28-31 (I.C.T. Pl.facing p.12,16,27)	Caves VIII-XIV & XVIII-XXIV (I.C.T. p.13-16 & 19-21)	Donatory (I.C.T. pp.13-16 & 19-21)
	MAHAD 1 (PL.XLVI)	Caitya VIII (p.18)	Gift of prince (p.88)
	JUNNAR 8 & 21 (I.C.T. Pl.facing p.43,49)	Amba/Ambika vihāras (I.C.T. p.44,50)	Donatory (I.C.T. p.44,50)
SERIES IV	KARLE 20—PULUMĀVI—(Pl.LIV)	Band to left of caitya doorway, on level with springing of caitya window (p.107)	Grant of village by Maharathi—7th yr. of Pulumāvi (p.107f.)
	NASIK 14 & 15—PULUMĀVI—(Pl.LII)	Back wall of veranda of vihāra III (p.40f.)	Balaśri's eulogy—19th yr. of Pulumāvi + postscript in 22nd yr. (p.109ff.)
	KARLE 22—PULUMĀVI—(Pl.LIV)	Vihāra II (p.25)	Gift of cave—24th yr. of Pulumāvi (p.113f.)
	NASIK 13—PULUMĀVI—(Pl.LIV)	Cave II (p.40)	Fragmentary—6th yr. of Pulumāvi (p.107)
	NASIK 12—PULUMĀVI—(Pl.LIV)	Recess beyond cave XXV (p.42)	Fragmentary—2nd yr. of Pulumāvi (p.107)
	AMARAVATI—PULUMĀVI—(A.S.S.I. Pl.LVI1)	Fragmentary slab (A.S.S.I. p.100)	Donation of dharmachakra at West gateway (A.S.S.I. p.100)
	AMARAVATI—ŚIVAMAKA SADA (A.S.S.I. Pl.LVI2)	On sculptured slab (A.S.S.I. p.61 & Pl.XXVII.1)	Fragmentary (A.S.S.I. p.61)
	KANHERI 11—VĀSISHTĪPUTRA SIRI SĀTAKARNI (A.S.W.I.V Pl.LI)	Above cistern, a short distance from caitya (A.S.W.I.V p.78)	Fragmentary—Queen of Vāsishṭīputrā, daughter of mahakshatrapa Ru... descended from the Kārddamaka kings (A.S.W.I.V p.78)
	JUNNAR 1-6 (I.C.T. Pl.facing p.42 & 43)	No 4—Shivneri caitya right of entrance. Others—Shivneri vihāras (I.C.T. pp.41-43)	Donatory (I.C.T. pp.41-43)
	JUNNAR 9-19 (I.C.T. Pl.facing p.44,47,49)	Veranda of Amba/Ambika caitya. Some engraved on fronton of arch itself (I.C.T. pp.44-49)	Donatory (I.C.T. pp.44-49)
	JUNNAR 29 & 26 (I.C.T. Pl.facing p.53 & 51)	No.29—Veranda of Lenyadri caitya XV. No.26—a vihāra (I.C.T. p.52f.)	Donatory (I.C.T. p.52f.)
	NANAGHAT 9 (A.S.W.I.V Pl.LI)	Above cistern (A.S.W.I.V p.64)	Donation by inhabitant of Sopara (A.S.W.I.V p.64)
	KUDA 1-13,23-27 (I.C.T. Pl.facing p.4,9,12,16,19)	Caves I-VII, XV-XVII (I.C.T. p.4-13,17-19)	Donatory (I.C.T. pp.4-13,17-19)
	SHELARVADI (Ep.Ind.XXVIII Pl.14)	Left of inner entrance to cave (Ep.Ind.XXVIII p.76f.)	Donation as caitya (Ep.Ind.XXVIII p.76f.)
	BHAJA 7 (Pl.XLIV)	Above cisterns (p.83)	Gift of Maharathi (p.83)
	NASIK 19 (Pl.LV)	Cave XVII (p.38)	Gifts a caitya. by Daltamitri yavana (p.114f.)
	NASIK 24 (Pl.LV)	Cave VIII (p.41)	Donatory (p.116)
	NASIK 21 (Pl.LV)	Cave XI (p.42)	Donatory (p.115)
	NASIK 17 & 18 (Pl.LV)	Cave XXVII (p.42)	Gifts of writer of Saka, & family (p.114)
	NASIK 22 & 23 (Pl.LV)	Cave IX (p.41)	Gifts of fisherman & his family (p.115)
	NASIK 20 (Pl.LV)	Ruined vihāra (p.42)	Donatory (p.115)
	MAHAD 2 (PL.XLVI)	Vihāra XXVII, outside veranda (p.19)	Fragmentary (p.88f.)
SERIES V	KANHERI 4 & 5—YAJÑAŚRĪ SĀTAKARNI (A.S.W.I.V Pl.LI)	Left and right gateposts of caitya (A.S.W.I.V p.75f.)	Fragmentary. Mentions completion of caitya & record several other benefactions (A.S.W.I.V p.75ff.)
	KANHERI 15—YAJÑAŚRĪ SĀTAKARNI (A.S.W.I.V Pl.LV)	Outside veranda of cave LXXXI (A.S.W.I.V p.79)	Donatory—16th yr. of Yajñaśri (A.S.W.I.V p.79f.)
	NASIK 16—YAJÑAŚRĪ SĀTAKARNI (Pl.LV)	Cave XX (p.39)	Completion of cave by wife of Commander-in-Chief, after being under construction for several years—7th yr. of Yajñaśri (A.S.W.I.V p.114)
	MYAKADONI—PULUMĀVI [II] (Ep.Ind.XIV Pl.II)	Engraved on natural boulder (Ep.Ind.XIV p.153)	Reservoir—8th yr. of Pulumāvi (Ep.Ind.XIV p.153ff.)
	NASIK 10—ĀBHĪRA ĪSVARASENA (Pl.LIII)	Outside vihāra X (p.42)	Endowments to monks—9th yr. of Ābhīra Īsvarasena (p.103f.)
	KANHERI 14—MĀDHARĪPUTRA ŚAKASENA (A.S.W.I.V Pl.LI)	Outside veranda of cave XXXVI (A.S.W.I.V p.79)	Donatory—8th yr. of Mādharīputra (A.S.W.I.V p.79)

Table 10 Caitya : Architectural Development

v.=variation / n.a.=not ascertainable / unf.=unfinished	APSIDAL PLAN — Plan				APSIDAL PLAN — Facade				OTHER PLAN	CEILING		
	without aisles	with aisles	without veranda	with veranda	original wooden facade	entire stone facade	with *caitya* window	'blind' *caitya* window	without *caitya* window	arched side aisles	flat side aisles	vaulted roof above *stūpa*
KONDIVTE	XV		X		n.a.	n.a.	n.a.	n.a.				X
NADSUR	X		X		n.a.	n.a.	n.a.	n.a.				X
PITALKHORA XII	X		X		n.a.	n.a.	n.a.	n.a.				X
PITALHKORA X	X		X			X	Xv.					X
BHAJA		X	X		X		X			X	..	X
KONDANE		X	X		X		X			X		X
PITALKHORA XIII		X	X		n.a.	n.a.	n.a.	n.a.		X		X
PITALKHORA III		X	X		X ·		X			X		X
AJANTA X		X	X	..	X		X			X		X
TULJA LENA	Xv.	X			n.a.	n.a.	n.a.	n.a.	X	X		Xv.
BUDH LENA	X	X				X		X		X		X
AJANTA IX		X	X			X	X				X	X
AURANGABAD IV		X	X		n.a.	n.a.	n.a.	n.a.			X	X
NASIK		X	X			X	X			X		X
BEDSA		X		X		X	X			X		X
LENYADRI VI		X		X		X		X		X		X
KARLE		X		X		X	X				X	X
AMBA/AMBIKA	unf.			X		X	X			unf.	unf.	unf.
BHIMA SHANKAR				X		X		X	X	unf.	unf.	
SHIVNERI XLVIII						X		X	X			
KUDA VI				X		X		X	X			
KUDA IX				X		X		X	X			
LENYADRI XV						X		X	X			
SHELARVADI						X		X	X			
MAHAD VIII						X		X	X			
KARADH XI, XIV						X		X	X			
KARADH V	X			X		X	Xv.					Xv.
KANHERI		X		X		X	X				X	X

PILLARS (Octagonal)   STŪPA   USE OF WOOD

slanting inwards towards top	pillar	pillar	pillar	pillar	pillar	proportion of drum to aṇḍa (dome)	proportion of drum to aṇḍa (tall)	single drum + aṇḍa	single drum + aṇḍa + vedikā band	double drum + aṇḍa	double drum + aṇḍa + vedikā bands	wooden ribs in side aisles	stone ribs in side aisles	wooden ribs in nave	stone ribs in nave
						x			x						
						x		x							
							x		x						x
							x		x						
x						x		x				x	x		
x						x			x			x	x		
x						n.a	n.a.	n.a.	n.a.	n.a.	n.a.		x		x
x						x		x				x	x		
x						x				x		x	x		
x						x		x							
unf.						x		x							
x							x	x						x	
							x	x							x
		x					x		x			x	x		
			x				x				x	x	x		
				x			x		x					x	x
		x	x			x					x			x	
					x	unf.	unf.	unf.	unf.	unf.	unf.	unf.	unf.	unf.	unf.
					x	unf.	unf.	unf.	unf.	unf.	unf.	unf.	unf.	unf.	unf.
				x		x			x						
				x		x			x						
		x					x	xv.							
							x		x						
						n.a.	n.a.	n.a.	n.a.	n.a.	n.a.				
						n.a.	n.a.	n.a.	n.a.	n.a.	n.a.				
						x			x						
			x			x		x							
					x	x				x				x	

Pillar sub-labels: "lion pillar interior", "veranda"

Table II   Comparative Chronology

DATES	HISTORY [Chapter I]	PALAEOGRAPHY [Chapter II]	PALAEOGRAPHY [Chapter III]	ARCHITECTURE [Chapter IV]	SCULPTURE [Chapter V]
120 BC	SIMUKA				
110 BC					
100 BC	KANHA	BHARHUT RAILINGS; SANCHI I RAILINGS		KONDIVTE *CAITYA*; NADSUR *CAITYA*; PITALKHORA XII, X (?)	NADSUR *VIHĀRA* XV; BHAJA *VIHĀRA* XIX
90 BC		SANCHI II RAILINGS	BHAJA 1 & WOOD; KONDANE.	BHAJA *CAITYA*; KONDANE *CAITYA*; PITALKHORA III & XIII; AJANTA X	PITALKHORA (some pieces)
80 BC		BHARHUT GATEWAY	PITALKHORA 1 & 2 & A; AJANTA 1; NASIK 1	TULJA LENA	
70 BC	SĀTAKARNI I	GAYA	BHAJA 2–6		
60 BC		SANCHI NORTH GATEWAY	AJANTA 2 & 14; NASIK 2 & 3; NANAGHAT	AJANTA IX; AURANGABAD IV; NASIK *CAITYA*; BUDH LENA	PITALKHORA (some pieces); AJANTA X & IX paintings
50 BC			NADSUR		NASIK *CAITYA*; KONDANE; AJANTA X (some paintings)
40 BC		SANCHI I GATEWAYS— EAST, SOUTH, WEST	PITALKHORA 3–7; BEDSA	BEDSA *CAITYA*	
30 BC		SANCHI III			
20 BC			NASIK 4		
10 BC					
0					
10 AD					
20 AD					

50 AD			EARLY KARLE (e.g., 1–3)	KARLE *CAITYA*	BUDH LENA
60 AD			JUNNAR 7 (Budh Lena)	LENYADRI VI	KARLE
70 AD	NAHAPĀNA				
80 AD					
90 AD				KUDA IX	
100 AD			NAHAPĀNA inscriptions at Nasik, Karle, Junnar JUNNAR 27, 28, 30	NASIK *VIHĀRA* X NASIK XVII	
	GAUTAMĪPUTRA SĀTAKARNI		GAUTAMĪPUTRA records at Karle, Nasik KUDA 14–22, 28–31. MAHAD 1 JUNNAR 8, 21	NASIK *VIHĀRA* III	
110 AD					
120 AD			PULUMĀVI inscriptions at Karle, Nasik, Amaravati KANHERI record of VĀSISHTĪPUTRA	KUDA VI	KUDA VI
	PULUMĀVI	ANDHAU INSCRIPTIONS	AMARAVATI record of ŚIVAMAKA SADA	AMBA/AMBIKA *CAITYA*	
130 AD			NANAGHAT 9 JUNNAR 29, 1–6, 9–19, 26 BHAJA 7	BHIMA SHANKAR *CAITYA* SHIVNERI *CAITYA*	
140 AD	VĀSISHTĪPUTRA SIRI SĀTAKARNI		MAHAD 2 KUDA 1–13, 23–27 SHELARVADI		
150 AD	ŚIVASKANDA SĀTAKARNI	GIRNAR INSCRIPTION—RUDRADĀMAN	NASIK 17–24 AMBIVALE		
160 AD			KANHERI records of YAJÑAŚRĪ	KANHERI *CAITYA*	KANHERI
	YAJÑAŚRI SĀTAKARNI		NASIK record of YAJÑAŚRĪ		
170 AD			KANHERI—MĀDHARĪPUTRA ŚAKASENA NASIK—ĀBHĪRA ĪŚVARASENA		
180 AD					
190 AD	DECLINE		NYAKADONI—PULUMĀVI II		
200 AD					

Notes on the Text

Abbreviations

ABORI	*Annals of the Bhandarkar Oriental Research Institute*
AI	*Ancient India*
ARASI	*Annual Report of the Archaeological Survey of India*
ASSI	Burgess, J. 'The Buddhist Stupas of Amaravati and Jaggayyapeta' (London, 1887)
ASWI IV	Burgess, J. 'Report on the Buddhist Cave Temples and their Inscriptions' (London, 1833)
ASWI V	Burgess, J. 'Report on the Elura Cave Temples and the Brahmanical and Jain caves in western India' (London, 1883)
ASWI XII	Cousens, H. 'An Account of the caves at Nadsur and Karsambla' (Bombay, 1891)
Ep. Ind.	*Epigraphia Indica*
ICT	Burgess, J. and Indraji, Bhagvanlal. *Inscriptions from the Cave-Temples of Western India* (Bombay, 1881)
JBBRAS	*Journal of the Bombay Branch of the Royal Asiatic Society*
JBORS	*Journal of the Bihar and Orissa Research Society*
JNSI	*Journal of the Numismatic Society of India*
JRAS	*Journal of the Royal Asiatic Society*
Luders' List	Luders, H. 'A List of Brahmi Inscriptions', Appendix to *Epigraphia Indica*, X, 1909/10
MASI	*Memoirs of the Archaeological Survey of India*
PIHC	*Proceedings of the Indian History Congress*
Upasak	Upasak, C. S. *The History and Palaeography of the Mauryan Brahmi Script* (Varanasi, 1960)

Notes to Chapter 1

1 Advocates of an early establishment of the dynasty include G. Venket Rao, 'The Pre-Satavahana and Satavahana Periods', chapter II in G. Yazdani (ed.), *The Early History of the Deccan* (Oxford, 1960), 90 and K. Gopalachari, 'The Satavahana Empire', chapter X in N. Sastri (ed.), *A Comprehensive History of India* (Calcutta, 1957), Vol. II, 295 (note).

2 Followers of this dating include D. C. Sircar, 'The Satavahanas and the Chedis', chapter XIII in R. C. Majumdar (ed.), *The Age of Imperial Unity* (Bombay, 1960), 195; H. C. Raychaudhari, *Political History of Ancient India* (Calcutta, 1932), 278; D. Barrett, *Sculptures from Amaravati in the British Museum* (London, 1954), 14; W. Spink, 'On the Development of Early Buddhist Art in India', *Art Bulletin*, XL, 1958, 100.

3 G. Venket Rao, 86.

4 Complete dynastic lists may be found in E. J. Rapson, *Catalogue of the Coins of the Andhra Dynasty* (London, 1908), lxvi-lxvii.

5 See chapters II and III, especially chapter III.

6 R. G. Bhandarkar, *The Early History of the Dekhan* (Bombay, 1895), 30.

7 See D. Barrett, *op. cit.*, 12–16, for a brief statement of the various theories.

8 M. Rama Rao, *Satavahana Coins in the Andhra Pradesh Government Museum* (Hyderabad, 1961).

9 M. Rama Rao lists 74 copper and lead coins of Gautamīputra Sātakarni from Kondapur and Pedabankur, some rectangular, others round, yet others oval, with clearly inscribed legend *Rājno Gotamīputasa Siri Sātakanasa* on several of the coins. See also M. Rama Rao, 'Did Pulumavi Conquer Andhradesa?', *PIHC* 1953, 35–8; and M. Rama Rao, 'Gautamiputra Satakarni and Andhradesa', *PIHC* 1949, 49–53. Information received from the Archaeological Survey of India, Madras, indicates that a coin mould of Pulumāvi was found in recent excavations at Nagarjunakonda. However, no coins from this mould were discovered.

10 See pp. 30–31.

11 W. Schoff (ed.), *The Periplus of the Erythraean Sea* (New York, 1912), paragraphs 51, 52, have been read as giving an indication of this later situation. When the Kshaharātas obtained control over Nasik, Karle and Junnar and hence over the heads of the passes, the Sātavāhanas were unable to send their goods out from Paithan and Ter through the normal routes. One solution must have been to divert goods via the smaller passes beyond the Bhor ghat through the port of Chaul. The *Periplus* tells us of the other rather devious route through Broach. This appears to have been a Kshaharāta port and by forcing Sātavāhana trade through it the Kshaharātas could presumably collect heavy taxes.

12 Quoted in G. F. Hourani, *Arab Seafaring in the Indian Ocean in Ancient and Early Medieval Times* (Princeton, 1951), 21.

13 Hourani, 24.

14 In placing the discovery of Hippalus around 90 BC, we are largely following W. W. Tarn, *The Greeks in Bactria and India* (Cambridge, 1951), 367ff. From the Arretine ware found at Arikamedu, Sir R. E. M. Wheeler concludes in *Rome Beyond the Imperial Frontiers* (Harmondsworth, 1955), 156–7, that the discovery of Hippalus may be assumed 'to have been in full and undisguised use at the end of the reign of Augustus', and that it may well have been a trade secret of the Arab middlemen long before it became familiar to Rome and Alexandria.

15 See chapter 3 p. 47

16 See chapter 2 pp. 42–43

17 See chapter 2 pp. 38–41

18 H. D. Sankalia, *From History to Pre-History at Nevasa* (Poona, 1960), 162.

19 *idem.*

20 *ibid.*, Fig. 84.

21 S. Kusumgar, D. Lal, R. P. Sarna, 'Tata Institute Radiocarbon Date List I', *Radiocarbon*, 5, 1963, 278.

Indo-Roman, Period V: 1755 ± 105 $=$ AD 195; Early Historic, Period IV: $1675 \pm 96 =$ AD 275; Early Historic Period IV: $1860 \pm 100 =$ AD 90.

22 A. S. Altekar, 'The Coinage of the Deccan', part XI in G. Yazdani (ed.), *The Early History of the Deccan* (Oxford, 1960), 792.

23 D. C. Sircar, 'The Satavahanas and the Chedis', 200.

24 V. V. Mirashi, 'Date of Nahapana', *Journal of Indian History*, 1965, 111–18, brings up several interesting points. Among them are the following: (1) If Nahapāna ruled for 46 years it is surely surprising that no records earlier than the year 41 have been found. We would point out that the early Jain chronicles also give Nahapāna a long reign of 40 or 42 years; (2) Mirashi analyses the terminology of inscriptions to see how the mention of a regnal year differed from that of an era date. Of the three records of Nahapana two are 'not distinctive', but one he considers indicative of an era date. Surely the weight of the other two preclude any certainty on the matter; (3) There is no proof that 'Nahapana was evidently subordinate to some imperial power'. Our knowledge of this period is very limited and available evidence does not justify the conclusion that the Kshaharātas were appointed by the Kadphises kings.

25 G. Venket Rao, 100–101.

26 There are various readings of the name of this ruler. D. Barrett in 'Correspondence', *Lalit Kala*, 6, 1959, 76f., informs us that the reading in the British Museum Ms. 19,391 is definitely Manbanou.

27 D. Barrett, *Lalit Kala*, 6, refers to J. A. B. Palmer, '*Periplus Maris*

Erythraei: The Indian Evidence as to the Date', *Classical Quarterly*, XLI, 1947, 136–40.

28 See, for example, P. K. Hitti, *History of the Arabs* (London, 1961), chapter VI.

29 G. Venket Rao, 103.

30 Jacqueline Pirenne, *Le Royaume Sud-Arabe de Qatabân et sa datation* (Louvain, 1961), chapter V in particular.

31 P. R. Coleman-Norton, 'Pliny', in *Encyclopaedia Americana* (1963, ed.), vol. 22, 249.

32 W. Schoff (ed.) *Periplus*, paragraphs 43–6.

33 Reverend H. R. Scott, 'The Nasik (Jogalthembi) Hoard of Nahapana's Coins', *JBBRAS* XXII, 1908 223–44.

34 G. Venket Rao, 95.

35 Gautamīputra's Nasik inscription mentions the donation of a field 'hitherto enjoyed by Ushavadāta', and indicates that it is likely that Nahapāna's last year, 46, coincides with Gautamīputra's first year, 14. E. Senart, 'Inscriptions in the caves at Nasik', *Ep. Ind.* VIII, 1904–5, reads Gautamīputra's first year as 18. This would involve a minor adjustment of four years in our proposed chronology.

36 In our analysis of the history of the later Sātavāhanas we must acknowledge our debt to the editorial article 'The Date of the Karle Chaitya', *Lalit Kala*, 3/4, 1956/57, 11–26. For detailed argument on Andhau inscriptions, see 16–17.

37 Śivaskanda is probably to be identified with king Śivamaka Sada

mentioned in an inscription at Amaravati (Luders' List, No. 1279).

38 If the year of Gautamīputra Sātakarni's Nasik inscription is 18 rather than 14, our dates for Nahapāna would be AD 58–104. Dates for Nahapāna similar to ours are given by A. S. Altekar, 'Date of Nahapana', *PIHC* 1950, 35–42: AD 55–105; K. Gopalachari, *Early History of the Andhra Country* (Madras, 1941): last date for Nahapāna of AD 99 or 100; *Lalit Kala*, 3/4: AD 55–101 or AD 59–105.

39 Bhagvanlal Indraji, 'Antiquarian Remains at Sopara and Padana', *JBBRAS* XV, 1883, 313–14.

40 K. Gopalachari, 'The Satavahana Empire', chapter X in N. Sastri (ed.), *A Comprehensive History of India* (Calcutta, 1957), vol. II, 322 (note).

41 H. C. Ghose, 'The Chronology of the Kshatrapas and Andhras', *Indian Historical Quarterly*, VI, 1930, 747–56, states that the 16th year of Yajñaśrī + y = AD 153. Yajñaśrī's Nasik inscription proves that Aparānta was in his possession in his 16th year, while Rudradāman claims the area as part of his domains in the Girnar epigraph: Yajñaśrī's 16th year must therefore lie before the year of Rudradāman's inscription. The territorial basis for this equation is no doubt quite valid. The explanation lies, however, in the fact that the 16th year of Yajñaśrī falls well after AD 150 (Ghose's post-dating of the Girnar epigraph has no supporters) – in AD 168 according to our chronology. Rudradāman himself was no longer ruling at this date and the area was certainly part of Yajñaśrī's domains.

42 K. Gopalachari, 'The Stavahana Empire', 323.

43 A. S. Altekar, 'Some Rare and Unique Coins in the Prince of Wales Museum', *JNSI* XI, 1949, 44–63.

44 A. S. Altekar, 'The Coinage of the Deccan', part XI in G. Yazdani (ed.), *Early History of the Deccan* (Oxford, 1960), 793.

45 Vijaya Sātakarni inscription: H. Sarkar, 'Nagarjunakonda Prakrit Inscription of Gautamiputra Vijaya Satakarni, Year 6', *Ep. Ind.* XXXVI, 1966, 273–4; Candraśrī inscription: Luders' List, No. 1341; Pulumāvi record: V. S. Sukhthankar, 'A New Andhra inscription of Siri-Pulumavi', *Ep. Ind.* XIV, 1917/18, 153–5.

46 D. C. Sircar, 'Silver Coin of Vasishtiputra Satakarni', *Ep. Ind.* XXXV, 1962, 247–52, reads, as Telegu;
obverse: *Rāno Vasishtiputasa Siri Sātakanisa*
reverse: *Arahanasha Vahittimakanasha Tiru Hatakanisha.*
R. Nagaswamy, 'A Bilingual Coin of a Satavahana', *Seminar on Inscriptions, 1966, Speeches and Papers* (Madras, 1968), 200–202, reads the reverse as *Aracansa Vacitti Makansa Tiru Catakanisa*, clearly Tamil.

47 V. V. Mirashi, 'A new Hoard of Satavahana Coins from Tarhala (Akola District)', *JNSI* II, 1940, 83–94.

48 V. V. Mirashi, 'A Coin of Kausikiputra Satakarni', *JNSI* VIII, 1946, 116–18.

49 These routes and passes are discussed in K. de B. Codrington, 'Ancient Sites near Ellora, Deccan', *Indian Antiquary*, LIX, 1930, 10–13 and map. See also J. A. B. Palmer, 'Periplus Maris Erythraei: The Indian Evidence as to the Date', *Classical Quarterly*, XLI, 1947, 136–40 and map.

50 Reverend J. E. Abbott, 'Recently discovered Buddhist Caves at Nadsur and Nenavli in the Bhor State', *Indian Antiquary*, XX, 1891, 121.

51 D. D. Kosambi, 'Dhenukakata', *Journal of the Asiatic Society of Bombay*, 30, 1955, 51–2.

Notes to Chapter 2

1 G. Buhler, 'Indian Palaeography', Appendix to *Indian Antiquary*, XXXII, 1904.

2 R. P. Chanda, 'Dates of the Votive Inscriptions on the Stupas at Sanchi', *MASI* I, 1919.

3 A. H. Dani, *Indian Palaeography* (Oxford, 1963).

4 We cannot agree with Dani's premise that the thickening of the tops of the letters, which is the result of the use of the reed pen, makes its first appearance in the script of the Mathura Kshatrapas in the first half of the first century A D. We shall demonstrate that (1) such thickening is already evident in the coins of the earliest Kshatrapas who date back to *c.* 50 B C; (2) it is also seen on the coins of the Mathura local rulers and may hence be dated back to *c.* 100 B C. This important disagreement accounts for a number of differences between Dani's chronology and ours.

5 W. M. Spink, *Rock-Cut Monuments of the Andhra Period: Their Style and Chronology*. Unpublished Ph.D. thesis (Harvard, 1954), 94. See also Spink, 'Ajanta's Chronology: The Problem of Cave Eleven', *Ars Orientalis*, VII, 1968, 155–68.

6 Dani, 35. See also Upasak, 29. It must be pointed out that when Buhler wrote his work the Yerragudi, Maski

and other southern edicts were unknown. It is a study of these, among other factors, that led to a breakdown of the idea of regional scripts in Aśokan times.

7 See, for example, A. K. Narain, *The Indo-Greeks* (Oxford, 1957), 181. Also W. W. Tarn, *The Greeks in Bactria and India*, 313–14.

8 Dani, 62–5.

9 A gift of prince Vadhapāla, son of king Dhanabhūtī, is to be found on the railing, while that of his father is on the gateway. Cunningham's eye-copy (A. Cunningham, *Stupa of Bharhut* (London, 1879), Plate LVI, No. 54) does, in fact, reveal a slightly earlier script in the Vadhapāla inscription. Presumably the change in script from railing to gateway is one that took place within a decade, or is to be explained by variations in style between different scribes.

10 Sir John Marshall and A. Foucher, *Monuments of Sanchi* (Calcutta, *c.* 1935/36), *cf.* inscriptions Nos 562 and 664, and Nos 310 and 671.

11 Dani, 57–9.

12 Two other fragmentary inscriptions also record the erection of gateways. One of these also commences with the words *Suganam Raje*. See Cunningham *op. cit.*, Plate LIII. Also Luders' List, Nos 687, 688 and 689.

13 Professor Jagannath, 'Post-Mauryan Dynasties', chapter IV in N. Sastri (ed.) *A Comprehensive History of India* (Calcutta, 1957), Vol. II, 94–102.

14 Dani, 64.

15 *ibid.*, 52.

16 W. M. Spink, in an Appendix to *Rock-Cut Monuments*, puts forward

the theory that Śoḍāsa should not be dated earlier than AD 50, and supports his statement by the following argument based on the date of the Moga copperplate of the year 78. (1) The year 78 is to be dated from Maues' accession, which he places at 95 BC. The date of the copperplate is thus 17 BC. (2) At that date Patika was the untitled son of mahākshatrapa Liaka Kusulaka. (3) In the Mathura lion capital, when Patika appears as mahākshatrapa, Śoḍāsa is only kshatrapa. (4) In the *Amohini* tablet, Śoḍāsa is mahākshatrapa. These various changes in status could not have taken place in a period of 31 years (17 BC to AD 15): hence Śoḍāsa is to be placed after AD 50. In reply (1) We would like to quote A. L. Basham ('A New Study of the Saka-Kushana Period', *Bulletin of the School of Oriental and African Studies*, XV, 1953, 85) on the dangers of basing a chronology on titular considerations. 'It should be noted that in the Sui Vihar inscription dated in the year 11, Kanishka is given the titles *maharaja rajatiraja devaputra*, while in the Manikiala inscription of the year 18 he is a mere *maharaja*. This is not taken to imply that the latter is earlier than the former, but merely that the styles and titles of the king were not rigidly fixed'. (2) The dating of the Moga copperplate from 95 BC is entirely arbitrary. The date of Maues' accession is by no means certain. (3) W. W. Tarn, *op. cit.* (Appendix 16, 'The Era of the Moga Copperplate from Taxila', 494–502), attributes the copperplate to an era of 155 BC and hence as dating to *c.* 77 BC. Tarn tells us that Rapson, Marshall and Konow all attribute the plate to an era of *c.* 150 BC and hence as dating to 72 BC. A. K. Narain (*The Indo-Greeks*, 143) would not make this

rather fine distinction and accepts an era beginning about the middle of the second century BC. This widely accepted dating allows ample time for the changes in status described by Spink. (4) Finally, it is just plausible for these changes to have taken place even in the 31 years provided by Spink's dating.

17 See, for example, W. W. Tarn, 325.

18. P. L. Gupta, 'A Further Note on the Identity of the Kings Satavahana and Sati', *JNSI* XVI, 1954, 86–9, points out that coins bearing the name of the ruler without any title are definitely earlier than those in which titles appear.

19 This statement is made after a personal examination of the coins in the British Museum.

20 The records of the minister of a Gomitra, perhaps the same as our first Mathura ruler, have been found inscribed on fragments of bricks and brickbats at Mathura (H. Luders, *Mathura Inscriptions* (Gottingen, 1961), 158ff. Plate facing 304). The forms of the letters suggest a date at least as early as the Besnagar inscription.

21 See D. W. MacDowall and N. G. Wilson, 'Apollodoti Reges Indorum', *Numismatic Chronicle*, XX, 1960, 221–8.

22 Professor Jagannath, *op. cit.*, 108.

23 J. Rapson, 'Notes on Indian Coins and Seals', *JRAS* 1905, 812.

24 Buhler, 'Indian Palaeography', describes this practice from personal experience. He tells us that the mason received a copy of the document (an eulogy of the donor) of exactly the size of the stone on which it was to be engraved. Under the supervision of a

Pandit, the letters were first drawn on the stone and only then incised.

25 The only actual evidence of ink script from ancient India is provided by a record on the inner lid of a steatite casket from Andher, now in the British Museum. The inscription is rather faint and does not appear to reveal the use of the reed pen.

26 Sir E. M. Thompson, *An Introduction to Greek and Latin Palaeography* (Oxford, 1912), 39; 'The Egyptians employed the reed, frayed at the end in the fashion of a paint-brush; and the Greeks in Egypt no doubt imitated that method in the earliest times, adopting the pen-shaped reed perhaps in the third century B.C.'

27 Dani has not considered the contents of this or any other inscription.

28 Krishnadeva, 'The Temples of Khajuraho in Central India', *AI* 15, 1959, 54.

29 K. P. Jayaswal, 'Hathigumpha Inscription of Kharavela', *JBORS* XIII, 1927, 221–46.

30 B. M. Barua, 'The Hathigumpha Inscription of Kharavela', *Indian Historical Quarterly*, XIV, 1938, 465. See also A. K. Narain, 40–45, for a good discussion of this point. G. Venket Rao is one of the few scholars who still accepts this reading.

31 B. M. Barua, 'Kharavela as King and Builder', *Journal of the Indian Society of Oriental Art*, XV, 1947, 54.

32 K. P. Jayaswal, 'Hathigumpha Inscription of the Emperor Kharavela', *JBORS* III, 1917, 425–72. Accepted reading: '. . . in the second year, disregarding Satakarni [Khāravela] dispatches a large army of horse, elephant

foot and chariot to the western quarter . . .'

33 Dani, Plate VI, *cf.* 4 and 9. He assigns both groups to 'early 1st century A.D.'

Notes to Chapter 3

1 Luders' List No. 799 (Bharhut: gift from Nasik merchant); Nos 705, 763, 809 (Bharhut: gift from traders from Karhad); No. 346 (Sanchi: gift from foreman of the artisans of king Sātakarni).

2 These records are somewhat intriguing: raised high above the eyes of the worshippers they were obviously not engraved for the purpose of proclaiming the name of the donor or of the craftsmen concerned. The two radiocarbon dates published for Bhaja (D. P. Agrawal and S. Kusumgar, 'Tata Institute Radiocarbon Date List IV', *Radiocarbon*, 8, 1966, 445) are obviously from samples of wooden ribbing that were part of the modern renovations to the *caitya*. The dates yielded are AD 1600 and AD 1875.

3 See M. K. Dhavalikar, 'New Inscriptions from Ajanta', *Ars Orientalis*, VII, 147–54 and Plate I especially.

4 The Budh Lena *caitya* has engraved within the *caitya* arch an inscription donating its façade, but the interior remains incomplete. The Amba/Ambika *caitya* has some ten inscriptions on the veranda wall and on the fronton of the arch itself, but here again, excavation of the interior has been abandoned.

5 See chapter 1, p. 19.

6 R. P. Chanda, 'Dates of the Votive Inscriptions on the Stupas at Sanchi', *MASI* 1, 1919, and N. G. Majumdar

in Sir John Marshall and A. Foucher, *Monuments of Sanchi*, arrive at a similar date for the Nanaghat records. G. Venket Rao makes the following statement, 'Chanda's argument runs directly against that of Dr. Buhler who had given the Nanaghat record the date 200–150 B.C. on palaeographical grounds . . . We agree with Dr. Buhler regarding the date of the record', 88f. The author, a protagonist of the extended Sātavāhana chronology, is ignoring the progress made in Indian palaeography since Buhler. When that scholar dated the Nanaghat record to 150 BC, the valuable Besnagar inscription was unknown, the only comparative material being the Aśokan edicts. Without the Besnagar record to guide him, it is not surprising that Buhler assigned the Nanaghat inscriptions to an early date. But to ignore Chanda, who discusses the importance of the Besnagar record, in favour of Buhler, is incomprehensible.

7　See chapter 1, p. 19.

8　The *selaghara* has so far been taken to indicate the Karle *caitya* as a whole. D. D. Kosambi, 'Dhenukakata', *Journal of the Asiatic Society of Bombay*, 30, 1955, 63, is of the opinion that the phrase refers to the five-storeyed relief mansion in the veranda, and this interpretation certainly appears more acceptable.

9　H. Barker and J. Mackay, 'British Museum Natural Radiocarbon Measurements III', *British Museum Quarterly*, XXVII, 1963/64, 55.

10　D. P. Agrawal and S. Kusumgar, 'Tata Institute Radiocarbon Date List IV', *Radiocarbon*, 8, 1966, 448–9.

11　D. D. Kosambi, *The Culture and Civilisation of Ancient India in Historical Outline* (London, 1965), 183 and 140.

12　The exact location of this record is of some interest. The Nahapāna record is engraved along the plain band of moulding to the right of the main arch, on the level of the top of the doorway, while the Pulumāvi record is on the corresponding band on the left. The inscription of the year 14 attributed to Gautamīputra has been inserted in a very awkward place, along a protruding moulding to the right of the main doorway, with beam ends interrupting it, and has been continued below, just above the *mithunas*. Its position might lead one to conclude that when it was engraved the two plain bands were already occupied, and this would lead to the further conclusion that the inscription must then belong to Pulumāvi. This does not, however, seem to be the case on palaeographic grounds. The fact that the script is even earlier than records of Gautamīputra at Nasik would seem to indicate that the record definitely belongs to Gautamīputra. The contents of the inscription, re-donating the village given by Nahapāna, are also suggestive of this. Nevertheless, its positioning remains intriguing.

Notes to Chapter 4

1　Hermann Goetz, *India; Five Thousand Years of Indian Art* (London, 1960), 55. Goetz presumably has in mind the caves at Ramgarh and Silahara in central India. An inscription in the Silahara cave describes it as *ārāmam-pavate*, or pleasure house on the hills (Bhandarker, 'Silahara Cave Inscriptions', *Ep. Ind.* XXII, 30–36). One of the Ramgarh caves may have been an amphitheatre and another contains an inscription indicating it was a pleasure den (Bloch, 'Caves and Inscriptions in Ramgarh Hill', *ARASI* 1903/04, 123–31). We fail to understand how Goetz could possibly have grouped these caves with the western India cave monasteries. The two groups have *nothing* in common.

2 The absence of an Aśokan record on the Lomasa Rishi cave has led to many conjectures about the later date of the excavation, but its plan is so similar in every respect to that of the Sudama with its Aśokan inscription, that there is no doubt that they belong together (*Fig. 2*). Theories have also been put forward regarding the later date of the façade alone. For example, A. Banerji-Sastri ('The Lomas Rishi Cave Façade', *JBORS* XII, 1926, 309–11) suggested that Khāravela was responsible for the cutting of the façade. If this was indeed the case, it is difficult to explain why such a façade should have been added to an unfinished, partly hewn cave, when the complete, fully polished, Sudama cave stood just nearby. It would certainly seem that façade and interior belong together.

3 R. A. Jairazbhoy, *Foreign Influence in Ancient India* (Bombay, 1963), 126. Admittedly the plan of the basilica resolved itself, as in the *caitya*, into a central nave separated by columns from the side aisles. But the entire conception of these parts was different in a basilica. Where an apse existed, there was always a distinct break between nave and apse, and a double-storeyed basilica was quite common. In addition, the earliest extant basilica, Pompeii, dates from 100 BC. The earliest apsidal example, at Praeneste, belongs to 80 BC, and here there is no division into nave and aisles. It is only in the first century AD that basilicas

became almost universal in Roman towns. Thus we see that a consideration of plan and of purpose (the basilica housed a tribunal) reveals sufficient differences to make the derivation of one from the other highly doubtful, while a consideration of dates completely denies the possibility.

4 J. Burgess and J. Fergusson, *The Cave Temples of India* (London, 1880), 175–6.

5 G. Yazdani, *Early History of the Deccan* (Oxford, 1960), 725; Percy Brown, *Indian Architecture* (Bombay, 1959), Vol. I, 26.

6 W. M. Spink, 'On the Development of Early Buddhist Art in India', *Art Bulletin*, XL, 1958, 103.

7 Percy Brown, *op. cit.*, chapters V and VI.

8 W. Willetts, 'Excavation at Pitalkhora', *Oriental Art*, VII, 1961, 63.

9 S. K. Saraswati in R. C. Majumdar (ed.) *Age of Imperial Unity* (Bombay, 1951), 499, 'The progress was slow and steady, and may be recognised in the gradual emancipation from wooden conventions'.

10 E. Panofsky, *Meaning in the Visual Arts* (New York, 1955), 9.

11 Phillipe Stern and Mireille Bénisti, *Évolution Du Style Indien D'Amaravati* (Paris, 1961), use the word concomitance to designate the simultaneous presence of diverse motifs at certain stages of development.

12 A. Cunningham, *Bhilsa Topes* (London, 1854), 178.

13 Viewed in a broader perspective, of course, such additions as the cult figure of the Buddha in the later

Ajanta *caityas* clearly represent an evolutionary stage. But within our period, no clearcut criteria of this sort present themselves.

14 This is an example of what Panofsky terms an organic situation in which we seem to be assuming what we have set out to prove. However, Guntupalli shares features with the caves of the Barabar group (*cf.* Plates 1 and 3), while no serious argument can be adduced to place Karle before the first century of the Christian era.

15 D. Barrett, *Sculptures from Amaravati in the British Museum*, 45, 'That a progression from simple to more elaborate represents a chronological sequence is a dangerous principle, except where there is a large body of material, and that from the same locality'.

16 Stuart Piggott, 'The Earliest Buddhist Shrines', *Antiquity*, XVII, 1943, 1–10, describes a circular shrine with a central *stūpa* surrounded by a ring of wooden pillars, that existed at Bairat as early as the Mauryan period. The Bharhut relief of the *Sudhamma Sabhā* depicts a domed, pillared circular *caitya*, and also suggests the early date of this plan. Both examples also provide evidence of the one-time existence of structural *caityas* on which the rock-cut examples must have been based.

17 See A. K. Coomaraswamy, *La Sculpture De Bharhut* (Paris, 1956), Plate IV, Fig. 13.

18 W. Willetts, *op. cit.*, 63, tells us that flat side aisle roofs may be seen at Ajanta IX, Nasik, Bedsa and Karle. Checking our field notes against Burgess and Fergusson, *Cave Temples*, we find that at both Nasik and Bedsa the side aisle ceilings are *not* flat, but half-arched.

19 The possible significance of the appearance of the tie-rod at Sanchi emerged in the course of discussions with Professor J. Leroy Davidson at the University of California, Los Angeles. Even at Sanchi we have one instance where the arch is depicted without the tie-rod – on the topmost panel of the left pillar of the south gateway. It is apparent that this was a very recently introduced feature.

20 We use the term *āmalaka* to identify the flat, fluted, cushion-like member found on pillars in the western caves between the 'bell' and the stepped abacus, and usually enclosed within a frame or between two slabs of stone.

21 Compare, for example, the Gupta lion pillar at Sanchi, which undoubtedly imitates the Aśokan example, reproducing its archaic features but, as at Karle, not quite succeeding in this.

22 Pillars represented on the reliefs at Bharhut, BodhGaya and Sanchi occasionally reveal two styles of capitals side by side.

23 M. N. Deshpande, 'The Caves: Their Historical Perspective', in A. Ghosh (ed.) *Ajanta Murals* (Delhi, 1967), 4, considers the Nasik *caitya* to be later than Ajanta IX because of the more detailed sculptural decoration of the façade.

24 Burgess, *Cave Temples* . . . , informs us that the pillars slant inwards. This is not obvious, however, as it is at Bhaja or Ajanta IX.

25 *ASWI IV, cf.* inscriptions Nos 13, 14 (104–7) with Nos 18, 19 (108–12).

26 N. Sastri, 'The Later Satava-hanas and Sakas', *JRAS* 1926, 665.

27 K. Gopalachari, *Early History of the Andhra Country* (Madras, 1941), 65f. See also R. D. Banerji, 'Naha-pana and the Saka Era', *JRAS* 1925, 3.

Notes to Chapter 5

1 See note 1 to chapter 3. Among the donations at Junnar are two from *yavanas* from the Gata country, con-sidered to be somewhere in the north (Luders' List, Nos 1154, 1182). It may be noted that D. D. Kosambi, 'Dhen-ukakata', *Journal of the Asiatic Society of Bombay*, 30, 1955, 66f., considers the word *gata* to indicate departed or dead, and hence to indicate a posthumous gift.

2 R. G. Gyani, 'Identification of the So-called Surya and Indra Figures in Cave No. 10 of the Bhaja group', *Prince of Wales Museum Bulletin*, I, 1950–51, 15–21, maintains that they depict incidents from the story of Māndhātā. E. H. Johnston, 'Two Buddhist Scenes at Bhaja', *Journal of the Indian Society of Oriental Art*, VII, 1939, 1–7, suggests that they represent stories from the *Samyuttanikaya*.

3 S. K. Saraswati in R. C. Majumdar (ed.), *Age of Imperial Unity*, 503 (note 4).

4 *ASWI IV*, 5.

5 *ASWI XII*.

6 W. Willetts, 'Excavation at Pitalk-hora', *Oriental Art*, VII, 1961, 65.

7 M. N. Deshpande, 'A Plea for a Deccan School of Satavahana Sculp-ture', *Seminar on Indian Art History 1962*, Lalit Kala Akademi (New Delhi, n.d.), 17.

8 M. N. Deshpande, 'The Rock-Cut Caves of Pitalkhora in the Deccan', *AI* 15, 1959, 86.

9 Odette Viennot, 'Le makara dans la décoration des monuments de l'Inde ancienne', *Arts Asiatiques*, V, 1958, 288.

10 M. N. Deshpande, 'The Rock-Cut Caves . . .', 70.

11 Deshpande, 'A Plea for a Deccan School . . .', 22, seems to consider the Nasik *yaksha* as representative of a stage in advance of Kondane. If his statement is meant to include the panels of dancing figures at Kondane, we must disagree with him. We would, however, fully endorse his statement that Nasik (and Kondane too) marks a stage towards the climax of Karle.

12 Phillipe Stern, 'Les Ivoires et Os decouverts à Begram. Leur place dans L'Évolution de L'Art de L'Inde', in J. Hackin, *Nouvelles recherches archéo-logiques à Begram* (Paris, 1954), 44, considers the Kondane sculptures to be slightly later than Sanchi *stūpa* I.

13 V. Mishra, 'A Unique Painting in Tulja Caves at Padali (Junnar)', *Journal of Indian History*, XXXVIII, 1960, 189–90.

14 Phillipe Stern, *op. cit.*, 44, con-siders the Budh Lena carvings to belong together with Kondane to a phase slightly later than the Sanchi gateways.

15 V. Smith, *A History of Fine Art in India and Ceylon*, and (rev. and en-larged by K. Khandalwala, Bombay, 1961), caption to Plate 27A.

16 Niharranjan Ray, 'Art', chapter XX, in R. C. Majumdar (ed.), *Age of Imperial Unity*, 516.

17 Percy Brown, *op. cit.*, 25.

18 See D. Barrett, *Ter* (Bombay, 1960), 8 and Plates 8, 9.

19 See D. Barrett, *Sculptures from Amaravati . . .*, Plate XXXVIII.

20 See K. Khandalwala, 'Brahmapuri', *Lalit Kala*, 7, 1960, Plate XII, Figs 1, 2.

21 *ibid.* 63.

22 *ibid.* Plate XVIII.

23 *ibid.* Plate XIX.

24 *ibid.* 72.

25 D. Barrett, *Ter*, 9.

26 Moti Chandra, 'An Ivory Figure from Ter', *Lalit Kala*, 8, 1960, 8.

27 M. N. Deshpande, 'Some Observations on the Ivory Figure from Ter', *Lalit Kala*, 10, 1961, 55f.

28 E. H. Gombrich, *Art and Illusion* (London, 1962), 78.

29 The *fleur de lis* armlet may be seen on a dwarf-*yaksha* on the south gateway, lowest architrave, outer face; also possibly on the *yaksha* figure on the top of the north gateway (H. Zimmer, *The Art of Indian Asia* (New York, 1955), Vol. II, Plate 12).

30 J. Hackin, *op. cit.*, Figs 241, 242. Its occurrence at Begram was brought to my attention by Professor J. Leroy Davidson.

31 D. D. Kosambi, 'Dhenukakata', 57, states that the sphinx is 'unknown elsewhere in Indian iconography'. In support of a foreign derivation he further remarks, 'Indian iconography generally favours a human body with an animal head'. This is certainly true of later sculpture, but during the period we are concerned with, the reverse

appears to be the case. The sphinx, in particular, is to be seen also on a pilaster on the back wall of *vihāra* IV at Pitalkhora, and crowning a pillar in *vehāra* X at Nasik (facing inwards). We have already noted the representations of centaurs at Sanchi *stūpa* II (see Plate 87) and at BodhGaya.

Notes to Chapter 6

1 A. K. Coomaraswamy, 'The Philosophy of Ancient Asiatic Art', in Mulk Raj Anand, *The Hindu View of Art* (Bombay, 1957).

2 See Luders' List No. 773 (Bharhut); No. 154 (Sonari *stūpa* I); No. 1250 (Amaravati). The Bharhut *navakarmika* is also a preacher (*bhānaka*).

3 Luders' List No. 346; inscription on the inner face of the top architrave of the south gateway.

4 *ASWI V*, Inscription No. 4, on the right gatepost of the *caitya*. It also mentions *kaḍhicakas* and *mahākaṭakas*.

5 B. M. Barua and K. G. Sinha, *Barhut Inscriptions* (Calcutta, 1929), No. 92.

6 Bloch, 'Caves and Inscriptions in Ramgarh Hill', *ARASI* 1903/04, 123–31.

7 T. Fyfe, *Hellenistic Architecture; An Introductory Study* (Cambridge, 1936), 105.

8 Hermann Goetz, *India; Five Thousand Years of Indian Art* (London, 1960), 55, suggests that 'rows of vertical holes [were driven] into the bottom of parallel tunnels, then wooden bolts were inserted and soaked with water, thus detaching huge stone blocks. This process was repeated until the general excavation of the cave was about

finished, after which the finishing off and the sculptures were done with a chisel.' There is no evidence for such a practice in the area of the western caves. At Mamallapuram, near Madras, there is a much later unfinished cave, the front of which has been blocked out in squares, and which may be interpreted as evidence of such a practice. Goetz's explanation, however, ignores the fact that the unfinished Buddhist caves clearly reveal that their general excavation went hand in hand with the finishing and sculptures.

9 Editorial article, 'Date of the Karle Chaitya', *Lalit Kala*, 3/4, 23.

10 W. M. Spink, 'On the Development of Early Buddhist Art in India', *Art Bulletin*, XL, 99.

11 See chapter 4, pp. 95–96.

12 D. D. Kosambi, *Introduction to the Study of Indian History* (Bombay, 1956), 251.

13 D. Barrett, 'Correspondence', *Lalit Kala*, 6, 77, suggests a period of ten years.

14 Seiichi Mizuno and Tosio Nagahiro, *A Study of the Buddhist Cave-Temples at Lung-Men, Ho-nan* (Tokyo, 1941), 7.

15 Further evidence is available from Yun-Kang, where we find a series of very large caves all containing enormous sculptured figures. Mizuno arrives at the conclusion that 'about six years were required for excavating caves V and VI, and eight years for caves VII and VIII and caves IX and X respectively' – S. Mizuno and T. Nagahiro, *Yun-Kang*; *The Buddhist Cave-Temples of the Fifth Century A.D. in North China* (Kyoto, 1951–6), Vol. XVI, 17.

16 A. K. Coomaraswamy, *Medieval Sinhalese Art* (New York, 1956), 57.

17 *ibid.* 64.

18 A. K. Coomaraswamy, 'Origin of the Lotus (So-Called Bell) Capital', *Indian Historical Quarterly*, VI, 1930, 375.

19 See chapter 1, pp. 17–18.

20 Percy Brown, *Indian Painting* (Calcutta, n.d.), 9.

21 Balaśrī's eulogy at Nasik: *ASWI IV*, No. 18, 108ff.

22 D. D. Kosambi, 'Dhenukakata', 59–60.

23 *ibid.* 65 and inscription no. 20.

24 *ibid.* 52ff.

25 H. D. Sanaklia 'Discovery of a Most Important Stone Inscription of Jainism', *Dharmayug* ([Hindi weekly] 16–12–1968, 22f.) suggests that an inscription found in a small *vihāra* near Karle, which starts with the words *Namo Arahatānām*, is evidence of the spread of Jainism to western India at an early date. While the term *Arhat* is most often applied to a Jain saint, it must be pointed out that a number of early, specifically Buddhist records also refer to *arhats* (e.g. Luders' List No. 1280: *Arhat* Buddharakhita at Amaravati). From such instances it is apparent that at this early stage the term *Arhat* had not yet acquired an exclusively Jain connotation.

26 Sukumar Dutt, *Buddhist Monks and Monasteries of India* (London, 1962), 138f.

27 See chapter 4, pp. 71–73.

28 Geoffrey Scott, *The Architecture of Humanism* (London, 1961), 25f.

29 *ASWI, V*, Inscription No. 4, 75.

Notes to Chapter 7

1 It seems reasonable to assume that the foreman of the artisans, appointed to a Sātavāhana ruler, would not have commissioned the work to another group of craftsmen, but would either have carved the architrave himself, or seen to it that his artists were responsible for the work.

2 E. W. West, 'Copies of Inscriptions from the Buddhist Cave-temples of Kanheri &c., in the Island of Salsette, with a Plan of the Kanheri Caves', *JBBRAS* VI, 1862, 56.

3 E. Senart, 'The Inscriptions in the Caves at Karle', *Ep. Ind.* VII, 1902/3, 56.

4 See also V. Dehejia, 'Early Buddhist Caves at Junnar', *Artibus Asiae*, XXXI, 2/3, 1969, 147–66.

5 Editorial article, 'Date of the Karle Chaitya', *Lalit Kala*, 3/4, 26, 'We would normally expect such changes and deterioration [in sculpture and architecture] to be separated from the completion of Karle by about half a century'.

Notes to Appendix 2

1 D. D. Kosambi, *The Culture and Civilisation of Ancient India in Historical Outline* (London, 1965), 183. Radiocarbon date of 290 ± 150 BC: H. Barker and J. Mackay, 'British Museum Natural Radiocarbon Measurements III', *British Museum Quarterly*, XXVII, 1963/64, 55.

2 D. P. Agrawal and S. Kusumgar, 'Tata Institute Radiocarbon Date List IV', *Radiocarbon*, 8, 1966, 448f.

3 Harold Barker, 'Radiocarbon Dating: Its Scope and Limitations', *Antiquity*, XXXII, 1958, 259.

4 *ibid.* 263.

Notes to Appendix 3

1 D. C. Sircar, 'Fragmentary Pillar Inscription from Amaravati', *Ep. Ind.* XXXV, 1962, 40–43.

2 R. P. Chanda, 'Some Unpublished Amaravati Inscriptions', *Ep. Ind.* XV, 1919/20, 258–75.

3 47–50.

4 Phillipe Stern and Mireille Bénisti, *Évolution du Style Indien D'Amaravati* (Paris, 1961), Pl. IIb.

5 A. Ghosh and H. Sarkar, 'Beginnings of Sculptural Art in South-East India: A Stele from Amaravati', *A.I.* 20/21, 1964 & 65, 168–77.

6 D. Barrett, 'The Early Phase at Amaravati', *British Museum Quarterly*, XXXII, 1967, 45.

7 C. Sivaramamurti, *Amaravati Sculptures in the Madras Government Museum* (Madras, 1942), Plate XIV, 2, 3.

8 P. R. Srinivasan, 'Recently discovered Early Inscriptions from Amaravati and Their Significance', *Lalit Kala*, 10, 1961, Plate XXXVII, Fig 2.

9 A. H. Dani, *Indian Palaeography*, 72.

10 For a more detailed discussion of the subject, see V. Dehejia, 'Early Activity at Amaravati', *Archives of Asian Art*, XXIII, 1969–70, 41–54.

Glossary

āmalaka	Flat, fluted, cushion-like member, usually enclosed within a frame, that formed part of the capitals of pillars
anḍa	The hemispherical dome of the *stūpa*
asura	Demon
bodhi tree	The tree under which the Buddha obtained enlightenment
bodhisattva	A Mahāyāna Buddhist divinity, at the stage just prior to the attainment of Buddhahood
caitya	Buddhist chapel
chatra	Ceremonial umbrella above the Buddhist *stūpa*
drum	Circular base of the *stūpa*
fleur de lis	A type of armlet with three 'petals'
Gajalakshmī	A popular theme in Indian art, representing the goddess Lakshmī standing on a lotus, and elephants on either side with waterpots in their upraised trunks
ghaṭa	Water-pot; and from this, the member of the base and capitals of pillars shaped thus
harmikā	The parapet-like structure at the top of the *stūpa*, from within which the shaft of the ceremonial umbrella rises
Hīnayāna	Early form of Buddhism representing the doctrine as propounded by the Buddha himself, before the Founder was deified. The accompanying phase of art never depicts the Buddha in human form, but always indicates his presence by an emblem
jātaka	Stories of the former lives of the Buddha
kshatrapa	Satrap; king
linga	Phalliform emblem of the Hindu god Śiva
Mahāyāna	Later form of Buddhism in which several changes had been introduced into the doctrine, and the Buddha himself had been deified. In sculpture and painting the Buddha was now depicted in human form
makara	Mythical creature with the head of an elephant and body of a crocodile
merlon	Decorative motif resembling the embattled parapet between two embrasures
mithuna	Loving couple
nāga	Serpent; also a semi-divine being

stūpa	Originally a funerary mound containing relics of Buddhism. In the early Buddhist caves, this hemispherical structure was the object of worship – a symbol of the Buddha
triratna	A Buddhist trident emblem, representing the three jewels: the Buddha, the Law, the Order
vedikā	Railing; usually one surrounding a religious monument
vihāra	Residential hall for monks; monastery
yaksha	Semi-divine being, male
yakshi	Semi-divine being, female
yashṭi	Pole or shaft supporting the ceremonial umbrella above the *stūpa*
yavana	A Greek; a foreigner

Bibliography

General Bibliography

ABBOTT, REV. J. E. 'Recently discovered Caves at Nadsur and Nenavli in the Bhor State, Bombay Presidency', *Indian Antiquary*, XX (1891).

ALLAN, J. *Catalogue of the Coins of Ancient India*, London, 1936.

ALTEKAR, A. S. 'Date of Nahapana', *Proceedings of the Indian History Congress*, (1950).

— 'When did the Satavahana Dynasty begin to rule?' *Proceedings of the Indian History Congress*, (1952).

— 'Economic Condition of Western India during 200 B.C. to 500 A.D.', *Proceedings of the Indian History Congress*, (1951).

— 'Some Rare and Unique Coins in the Prince of Wales Museum, Bombay', *Journal of the Numismatic Society of India*, XI (1949).

— 'The Coinage of the Deccan', Part XI in YAZDANI, G. ed. *Early History of the Deccan*, Oxford, 1960.

ARAVAMUTHAN, T. G. *Portrait Sculpture in South India*, London, 1931.

BAKHLE, V. S. 'The Capital of Nahapana', *Indian Antiquary*, LX (1926).

— 'Satavahanas and the Contemporary Kshatrapas', *Journal of the Asiatic Society of Bombay*, III (1928) and IV (1928).

BANERJI, R. D. 'Nahapana and the Saka Era', *Journal of the Royal Asiatic Society* (1917 and 1925).

BANERJI–SASTRI, A. 'The Lomas Rishi Cave Façade', *Journal of the Bihar and Orissa Research Society*, XII (1926).

BARKER, H. 'Radiocarbon Dating: Its Scope and Limitations', *Antiquity*, XXXII (1958).

BARRETT, DOUGLAS. *Sculptures from Amaravati in the British Museum*, London, 1954.

— *A Guide to the Karla Caves*, Bombay, 1957

— *A Guide to the Buddhist Caves of Aurangabad*, Bombay, 1957.

— *Ter*, Bombay, 1960.

— 'An Early Indian Toy', *Oriental Art*, IV (1958).

— 'The Early Phase at Amaravati', *British Museum Quarterly*, XXXII (1967).

— 'Correspondence', *Lalit Kala*, 6 (1959).

BARUA, B. M. *Barhut*, Calcutta, 1934–7.
— *Gaya and Buddha-Gaya*, 2 vols., Calcutta, 1931–4.
— 'Kharavela as King and Builder', *Journal of the Indian Society of Oriental Art*, XV (1947).
BASHAM, A. L. (ed.) *Papers on the Date of Kaniska*, Leiden, 1968.
BHANDARKAR, R. G. *Early History of the Dekhan*, Bombay, 1895.
BROWN, PERCY. *Indian Architecture; Buddhist and Hindu*, Bombay, 1959.
— *Indian Painting*, Calcutta, n.d.
BURGESS, J. 'Memorandum on the Buddhist Caves at Junnar', *Archaeological Survey of Western India*, I, Bombay, 1874.
— 'Report on the Antiquities of Kathiawad and Kachh', *Archaeological Survey of Western India*, II, London, 1876.
— 'Report on the Buddhist Cave Temples and their Inscriptions', *Archaeological Survey of Western India*, IV, London, 1883.
— 'Report on the Elura Cave Temples and the Brahmanical and Jain Caves in Western India', *Archaeological Survey of Western India*, V, London, 1883.
— 'Notes on the Bauddha Rock-Temples of Ajanta', *Archaeological Survey of Western India*, IX, Bombay, 1879.
— 'The Buddhist Stupas of Amaravati and Jaggayyapeta', *Archaeological Survey of Southern India*, I, London, 1887.
— 'Notes on the Amaravati Stupa', *Archaeological Survey of Southern India*, III, Madras, 1882.
BURGESS, J. and FERGUSSON, J. *The Cave Temples of India*, London, 1880.
BURGESS, J. and INDRAJI, BHAGVANLAL. *Inscriptions from the Cave-Temples of Western India*, Bombay, 1881.
CHANDA, R. P. 'The Beginnings of Art in Eastern India', *Memoirs of the Archaeological Survey of India*, 30 (1927).
— 'Archaeology and Vaisnava Tradition', *Memoirs of the Archaeological Survey of India*, 5 (1920).
— 'Date of Kharavela', *Indian Antiquary*, XLVIII (1919).
CHARLESWORTH, M. P. 'Some Notes on the Periplus Maris Erythraei', *Classical Quarterly*, XXII (1928).
— 'Roman Trade with India: A Re-Survey', in COLEMAN–NORTON, P. R. ed., *Studies in Roman Economic and Social History in Honour of Allan Chester Johnson*, Princeton, 1951.
CODRINGTON, K. DE B. *Ancient India*, London, 1926.
— 'Ancient Sites Near Ellora, Deccan', *Indian Antiquary*, LIX (1930).
COOMARASWAMY, A. K. *La Sculpture de Bharhut*, Paris, 1956.
— *La Sculpture de BodhGaya*, Paris, 1935.
— *History of Indian and Indonesian Art*, London, 1927.
— *The Indian Craftsman*, London, 1909.
— *Medieval Sinhalese Art*, New York, 1956.
— 'Origin of the Lotus (So-Called Bell) Capital', *Indian Historical Quarterly*, VI (1930).
COUSENS, H. 'An Account of the Caves at Nadsur and Karsambla', *Archaeological Survey of Western India*, XII, Bombay, 1891.
CUNNINGHAM, SIR A. *The Bhilsa Topes*, London, 1854.

CUNNINGHAM, SIR A. *The Stupa of Bharhut*, London, 1879.
— *Mahabodhi*, London, 1892.
DEHEJIA, VIDYA. 'Early Buddhist Caves at Junnar', *Artibus Asiae*, XXXI (1969), Nos 2/3.
— 'Early Activity at Amaravati', *Archives of Asian Art*, XXIII (1969-70).
DEO, S. B. 'New Coins of King Satavahana', *Journal of the Numismatic Society of India*, XXII (1960).
DESHPANDE, M. N. 'The Rock-Cut Caves of Pitalkhora in the Deccan', *Ancient India*, 15 (1959).
— 'Some Observations on the Ivory Figure from Ter', *Lalit Kala*, 10 (1961).
— 'A Plea for a Deccan School of Satavahana Sculpture', *Seminar on Indian Art History 1962*, Lalit Kala Akademi, New Delhi, n.d.
DIKSHIT, M. G. 'Fresh Light on the Pitalkhora Caves', *Journal of the Bombay Historical Society*, VI (1941).
— *The Origin and Development of the Buddhist Settlements of Western India*, Unpublished Ph.D. thesis, Bombay University, 1942.
DUTT, S. *Buddhist Monks and Monasteries of India*, London, 1962.
FERGUSSON, J. *Tree and Serpent Worship*, London, 1873.
— *Illustrations of the Rock-Cut Temples of India*, London, 1845.
— *History of Indian and Eastern Architecture*, 2 vols, London, 1910.
GARDNER, P. *The Coins of the Greek and Scythic Kings of Bactria and India*, London 1886.
GHOSE, H. C. 'The Chronology of the Western Kshatrapas and the Andhras', *Indian Historical Quarterly*, VI and VII (1930 and 1931).
GHOSH, A. (ed.) *Ajanta Murals*, Delhi, 1967.
GHOSH, A. and SARKAR, H. 'Beginnings of Sculptural Art in South-East India: A Stele from Amaravati', *Ancient India*, 20/21 (1964 & 65).
GOMBRICH, E. H. *Art and Illusion*, London, 1962.
— *Meditations on a Hobby Horse*, London, 1963.
GOPALACHARI, K. *Early History of the Andhra Country*, Madras, 1941.
— 'The Satavahana Empire', chapter X in SASTRI, N. (ed.), *A Comprehensive History of India*, Vol. II, Calcutta, 1957.
GUPTA, P. L. 'A Further Note on the Identity of the Kings Satavahana and Sati', *Journal of the Numismatic Society of India*, XVI (1954).
GUPTE, R. S. and MAHAJAN, B. D. *Ajanta, Ellora and Aurangabad*, Bombay, 1962.
GYANI, R. G. 'Identification of the So-called Surya and Indra Figures in Cave No. 10 of the Bhaja Group', *Prince of Wales Museum Bulletin*, I (1950-51).
HOURANI, G. F. *Arab Seafaring in the Indian Ocean in Ancient and Early Medieval Times*, Princeton, 1951.
JAGANNATH, PROF. 'Post-Mauryan Dynasties', chapter IV in SASTRI, N. (ed.), *A Comprehensive History of India*, Vol. II, Calcutta, 1957.
JOGLEKAR, S. A. 'Satavahana and Satakarni', *Annals of the Bhandarkar Oriental Research Institute*, XXVIII (1946).
JOHNSTON, E. H. 'Two Buddhist Scenes at Bhaja', *Journal of the Indian Society of Oriental Art*, VII (1939).
— 'Two Notes on Ptolemy's Geography of India', *Journal of the Royal Asiatic Society* (1941).

KATARE, S. L. 'Simuka, Satakarni, Satavahana', *Indian Historical Quarterly*, XXVIII (1952).

KENNEDY, J. 'Eastern Kings Contemporary with the Periplus', *Journal of the Royal Asiatic Society*, (1918).

KHANDALWALA, K. 'Brahmapuri', *Lalit Kala*, 7 (1960), revised and enlarged in SMITH, V. *A History of Fine art in India and Ceylon*, Bombay, 1961.

KHANDALWALA, K. and MOTI CHANDRA. 'Date of the Karle Chaitya', *Lalit Kala*, 3/4 (1956/57).

KOSAMBI, D. D. *An Introduction to the Study of Indian History*, Bombay, 1956.

— *The Culture and Civilisation of Ancient India in Historical Outline*, London, 1965.

— 'Dhenukakata', *Journal of the Asiatic Society of Bombay*, 30 (1955).

— 'The Basis of Ancient Indian History', *Journal of the American Oriental Society*, 75 (1955).

LONGHURST, A. H. 'The Buddhist Monuments at Guntupalle, Kistna District', *Annual Report of the Archaeological Survey, Southern Circle*, (1916–17).

MACDOWALL, D. W. and WILSON, N. G. 'Apollodoti Reges Indorum', *Numismatic Chronicle*, XX (1960).

MAJUMDAR, R. C. *The Classical Accounts of India*, Calcutta, 1960.

— (ed.) *The Age of Imperial Unity*, Bombay, 1951.

— 'The Date of the Periplus of the Erythraean Sea', *Indian Historical Quarterly*, XXXVIII (1962).

MALHOTRA, S. L. 'Commercial Rivalry in the India Ocean in Ancient Times', *Journal of the Asiatic Society of Bombay*, 33 (1958).

MARSHALL, SIR J., FOUCHER, A. and MAJUMDAR, N. G. *Monuments of Sanchi*, 3 vols, Calcutta, *c.* 1935/36.

MIRASHI, V. V. 'The Date of Nahapana', *Journal of Indian History*, XLIII (1965).

— 'A Ship-Type Coin of Yajna Satakarni', *Journal of the Numismatic Society of India*, III (1941).

— 'A New Hoard of Satavahana Coins from Tarhala (Akola district)', *Journal of the Numismatic Society of India*, II (1940).

— 'A Coin of Kausikiputra Satakarni,' *Journal of the Numismatic Society of India*, VIII (1946).

MISHRA, V. 'A Unique Painting in Tulja Caves at Padali (Junnar)', *Journal of Indian History*, XXXVIII (1960).

MOTI CHANDRA. 'An Ivory Figure from Ter', *Lalit Kala*, 8 (1960).

MUKHERJEE, B. N. 'Satavahana Coinage', *Indian Historical Quarterly*, XXXIV (1958).

— *The Lower Indus Country*; *c. A.D.* 1–150, Unpublished Ph.D. thesis, London University, 1963.

NARAIN, A. K. *The Indo Greeks*, Oxford, 1957.

— 'Numismatic Evidence and Historical Writing', *Journal of the Numismatic Society of India*, XVIII (1956).

PALMER, J. A. B. '*Periplus Maris Erythraei*: The Indian Evidence as to the Date', *Classical Quarterly*, XLI (1947).

— 'The identification of Ptolemy's Dounga', *Journal of the Royal Asiatic Society*, (1946).

PANOFSKY, E. *Meaning in the Visual Arts*, New York, 1955.

PIRENNE, JACQUELINE. *Le Royaume Sud-Arabe de Qatabân et sa datation*, Louvain, 1961.

RAMARAO, M. *Satavahana Coins in the Andhra Pradesh Government Museum*, Hyderabad, 1961.

— 'Did Pulumavi conquer Andhradesa?' *Proceedings of the Indian History Congress*, (1953).

— 'Gautamiputra Satakarni and Andradesa', *Proceedings of the Indian History Congress*, (1949).

— 'The Satavahana Rival of Rudradaman', *Proceedings of the Indian History Congress*, (1951).

RAPSON, E. J. *Catalogue of the Coins of the Andhra Dynasty*, London, 1908.

RAY, N. 'Art', chapter XX in MAJUMDAR, R. C. (ed.), *Age of Imperial Unity*, Bombay, 1951.

RAYCHAUDHARI, H. *Political History of Ancient India*, Calcutta, 1923.

ROWLAND, B. *The Art and Architecture of India*, Harmondsworth, 1959.

— 'Buddhist Primitive Schools', in *Encyclopaedia of World Art*, Vol. II, 1960.

SARASWATI, S. K. *A Survey of Indian Sculpture*, Calcutta, 1957.

'Architecture', in chapter XX in MAJUMDAR, R. C. (ed.), *Age of Imperial Unity*, Bombay, 1951.

SASTRI, N. (ed.) Vol. II 'Mauryas and Satavahanas', of *A Comprehensive History of India*, Calcutta, 1957.

— 'The Later Satavahanas and the Sakas', *Journal of the Royal Asiatic Society*, (1926).

SCHOFF, W. H. (ed.) *The Periplus of the Erythraean Sea*, New York, 1912.

— 'The Date of the Periplus', *Journal of the Royal Asiatic Society* (1917).

SCOTT, H. R. 'The Nasik (Jogalthembi) Hoard of Nahapana's Coins', *Journal of the Bombay Branch of the Royal Asiatic Society*, XXII (1908).

SIRCAR, D. C. *Select Inscriptions bearing on Indian History and Civilisation*, Calcutta, 1942.

— 'Silver Coin of Vasishtiputra Satakarni', *Epigraphia Indica*, XXXV (1962).

— 'The Saka Satraps of Western India', and 'The Satavahanas and the Chedis', chapters XII and XIII in MAJUMDAR, R. C. (ed.) *Age of Imperial Unity*, Bombay, 1951.

SIVARAMAMURTI, C. *Amaravati Sculptures in the Madras Government Museum*, Madras, 1942.

SMITH, V. *A History of Fine Art in India and Ceylon*, Revised and enlarged by KHANDALWALA, K., Bombay, 1961.

SOHONI, S. V. 'Notes on Satavahana Bust Coinage', *Journal of the Numismatic Society of India*, XVIII (1956).

SPINK, W. M. 'On the Development of Early Buddhist Art in India', *Art Bulletin* XL (1958).

— *Rock-Cut Monuments of the Andhra Period: Their Style and Chronology*, Unpublished Ph.D. thesis, Harvard University, 1954.

SRINIVASAN, P. R. 'Recently discovered Early Inscriptions from Amaravati and their Significance', *Lalit Kala*, 10 (1961).

STERN, P. 'Les Ivoires et Os decouverts à Begram; Leur Place dans L'Evolution de L'Art de L'Inde,' in HACKIN, J. *Nouvelles recherches archéologiques à Begram*, Paris, 1954.

STERN, P. and BÉNISTI, M. *Évolution du Style Indien D'Amaravati*, Paris, 1961.

SUKHTHANKAR, V. S. 'On the Home of the So-called Andhra Kings'. *Annals of the Bhandarkar Oriental Research Institute*, I (1918).

TARN, W. W. *The Greeks in Bactria and India*, Cambridge, 1951.

TRIVEDI, H. V. 'A Unique Portrait Coin of Vasishtiputra Pulumavi', *Journal of the Numismatic Society of India*, XIV (1952).

VENKET RAO, G. 'The Pre-Satavahana and Satavahana Periods', chapter II, in YAZDANI, G. (ed.), *Early History of the Deccan*, Oxford, 1960.

— 'Vindication of the Matsya Purana List of the Andhra Kings', *Proceedings of the Indian History Congress* (1950).

VIENNOT, ODETTE. 'Le makara dans la décoration des monuments de L'Inde Ancienne', *Arts Asiatiques*, V (1958).

WAUCHOPE, R. S. *Buddhist Cave Temples of India*, Calcultta, 1933.

WHEELER, SIR R. E. M. *Rome Beyond the Imperial Frontiers*, Harmondsworth, 1955.

WHITEHEAD, R. B. 'Indo-Greek Coins', Vol. I of *Catalogue of the Coins in the Punjab Museum, Lahore*, Oxford, 1914.

WILLETTS, W. 'Excavation at Pitalkhora', *Oriental Art*, VII (1961).

YAZDANI, G. (ed.) *Early History of the Deccan*, Oxford, 1960, *Ajanta*, 4 vols. of text and 4 vols. of Plates, London, 1930–55.

ZIMMER H. *The Art of Indian Asia*, 2 vols., Completed and edited by CAMPBELL, J., New York, 1955.

Bibliography of Inscriptions and Palaeography

BANERJI, R. D. 'The Andhau Inscriptions of the Time of Rudradaman', *Epigraphia Indica*, XVI (1921/22).

— 'The Palaeography of the Hathigumpha and the Nanaghat Inscriptions', *Memoirs of the Archaeological Survey of Bengal*, XI (1931).

BARUA, B. M. 'The Hathigumpha Inscription of Kharavela', *Indian Historical Quarterly*, XIV (1938).

BARUA, B. M. and SINHA, K. G. *Barhut Inscriptions*, Calcutta, 1929.

BHANDARKAR, D. R. 'Silahara Cave Inscriptions', *Epigraphia Indica*, XXII (1933/34).

— 'Mauryan Brahmi Inscription of Mahasthan,' *Epigraphia Indica*, XXI (1931/32).

BLOCH, T. 'Caves and Inscriptions in Ramgarh Hill', *Annual Report of the Archaeological Survey of India*, (1903/4).

BUHLER, J. G. 'Indian Palaeography', Appendix to *Indian Antiquary*, XXXIII (1904).

— 'The Banawasi Inscription of Haritiputa Satakamni', *Indian Antiquary*, XIV (1885).

— 'A New Inscription of the Andhra King Yajnasri Gautamiputra', *Epigraphia Indica*, I (1892).

— 'Jaina Inscriptions from Mathura', *Epigraphia Indica*, II (1894).

— 'Indian Inscription to be read from below', *Vienna Oriental Journal*, V (1891).

BUHLER, J. G. 'The Barabar and Nagarjuni Cave Inscriptions of Asoka and Dasaratha', *Indian Antiquary*, XX (1891).
— 'Asokan Rock Edicts', *Epigraphia Indica*, II (1894).
— 'The Bhattiprolu Inscriptions', *Epigraphia Indica*, II (1894).
BURGESS, J. 'Report on the Buddhist Cave Temples and their Inscriptions', *Archaeological Survey of Western India*, IV, London, 1883.
— 'Report on the Elura Cave Temples and the Brahmanical and Jain Caves in Western India', *Archaeological Survey of Western India*, V, London, 1883.
— 'The Buddhist Stupas of Amaravati and Jaggayyapeta', *Archaeological Survey of Southern India*, I, London, 1887.
BURGESS, J. and INDRAJI, BHAGVANLAL. *Inscriptions from the Cave-Temples of Western India*, Bombay, 1881.
CHAKRAVARTI, S. N. 'Ninth Rock Edict of the Maurya King Asoka at Sopara, Bombay State', *Lalit Kala*, 3/4 (1956/7).
CHANDA, R. P. 'Archaeology and Vaisnava Tradition', *Memoirs of the Archaeological Survey of India*, 5 (1920).
— 'Dates of the Votive Inscriptions on the Stupas at Sanchi', *Memoirs of the Archaeological Survey of India*, 1 (1919).
— 'Some Unpublished Amaravati Inscriptions', *Epigraphia Indica*, XV (1919/20).
COUSENS, H. 'An Account of the Caves at Nadsur and Karsambla', *Archaeological Survey of Western India*, XII, Bombay, 1891.
CUNNINGHAM, A. *Mahabodhi*, London, 1892.
DANI, A. H. *Indian Palaeography*, Oxford, 1963.
DASGUPTA, C. C. 'Shelarvadi Cave Inscription', *Epigraphia Indica*, XXVIII (1949/50).
DESHPANDE, M. N. 'Important Epigraphical Records from the Chaitya Cave, Bhaja', *Lalit Kala*, 6 (1959).
— 'The Rock-Cut Caves of Pitalkhora in the Deccan', *Ancient India*, 15 (1959).
DHAVALIKAR, M. K. 'New Inscriptions from Ajanta', *Ars Orientalis*, VII (1968).
DIKSHIT, M. G. 'Ambivale Cave Inscriptions', *Annals of the Bhandarkar Oriental Research Institute*, XXII (1941).
FUHRER, A. 'Pabhosa Inscriptions', *Epigraphia Indica*, II (1894).
GHOSH, A. and SARKAR, H. 'Beginnings of Sculptural Art in South-East India: A Stele from Amaravati', *Ancient India*, 20/21 (1964 & 5).
HULTZSCH, E. 'Inscriptions of Asoka,' *Corpus Inscriptionum Indicarum*, I (1925).
— 'The Sunga Inscription of the Bharhut Stupa', *Indian Antiquary*, XIV (1885).
INDRAJI, BHAGVANLAL. 'Nasik Inscriptions', chapter XIV in *Bombay Gazetteer*, Vol. XVI, 1883.
— 'On Ancient Nagari Numeration; from an Inscription at Naneghat', *Journal of the Bombay Branch of the Royal Asiatic Society*, XII (1850).
JAYASWAL, K. P. 'Hathigumpha Inscription of the Emperor Kharavela', *Journal of the Bihar and Orissa Research Society*, III (1917).
— 'Hathigumpha Inscription of Kharavela', *Journal of the Bihar and Orissa Research Society*, XIII (1927).
— 'An Inscription of the Sunga Dynasty', *Journal of the Bihar and Orissa Research Society*, X (1924).
— 'The Ghosundi Stone Inscription', *Epigraphia Indica*, XVI (1921/22).

JAYASWAL, K. P. 'The Text of the Sohgaura Plate', *Epigraphia Indica*, XXII (1933/34).

JAYASWAL, K. P. and BANERJI, R. D. 'The Hathigumpha Inscription of Kharavela', *Epigraphia Indica*, XX (1929/30).

JOSHI, M. C. and PANDE, B. M. 'A Newly Discovered Inscription of Asoka at Bahapur, Delhi', *Journal of the Royal Asiatic Society* (1967).

KIELHORN, F. 'Jungadh Rock Inscription of Rudradaman; the Year 72', *Epigraphia Indica*, VIII (1905/6).

KOSAMBI, D. D. 'Dhenukakata', *Journal of the Asiatic Society of Bombay*, 30 (1955).

LUDERS, H. 'A List of Brahmi Inscriptions', Appendix to *Epigraphia Indica*, X (1909/10).

— *Mathura Inscriptions*, Gottingen, 1961.

— (ed.) 'Barhut Inscriptions', *Corpus Inscriptionum Indicarum*, II (1963).

MARSHALL, SIR J., FOUCHER, A. and MAJUMDAR, N. G. *Monuments of Sanchi*, Calcutta, c. 1935/36.

OJHA, GAURISHANKAR. *Bhāratīya Prāchīna Lipimālā*, Ajmer, 1918.

PANDEY, RAJ BALI. *Indian Palaeography*, Banaras, 1952.

PEPPE, W. C. 'The Piprahwa Stupa, containing Relics of Buddha', *Journal of the Royal Asiatic Society* (1898).

SAHNI, D. R. 'Sunga Inscription from Ayodhya', *Epigraphia Indica*, XX (1929/30).

— 'Mathura Pedestal Inscription of the Kushana Year 14', *Epigraphia Indica*, XIX (1927/8).

— 'Seven Inscriptions from Mathura', *Epigraphia Indica*, XIX (1927/8).

SARKAR, H. 'Nagarjunakonda Prakrit Inscription of Gautamiputra Vijaya Satakarni, Year 6', *Epigraphia Indica*, XXXVI (1966).

SASTRI, N. and GOPALACHARI, K. 'Epigraphic Notes', *Epigraphia Indica*, XXIV (1937/8).

SENART, E. 'The Inscriptions in the Caves at Karle', *Epigraphia Indica*, VII (1902/3).

— 'The Inscriptions in the Caves at Nasik', *Epigraphia Indica*, VIII (1905/6).

SIRCAR, D. C. *Select Inscriptions bearing on Indian History and Civilisation*, Calcutta, 1942.

— 'Fragmentary Pillar Inscription from Amaravati', *Epigraphia Indica*, XXXV (1962).

SRINIVASAN, P. R. 'Recently discovered Early Inscriptions from Amaravati and their Significance', *Lalit Kala*, 10 (1961).

SUKHTHANKAR, V. S. 'A New Andhra Inscription of Siri-Pulumavi', *Epigraphia Indica*, XIV (1917/18).

THOMPSON, E. M. *An Introduction to Greek and Latin Palaeography*, Oxford 1912.

UPASAK, C. S. *The History and Palaeography of the Mauryan Brahmi Script*, Varanasi, 1960.

VATS, M. S. 'Unpublished Votive Inscriptions in the Chaitya Cave at Karle', *Epigraphia Indica*, XVIII, (1925/6).

VOGEL, J. PH. 'The Garuda Pillar of Besnagar', *Annual Report of the Archaeological Survey of India* (1909/10).

Vogel, J. Ph. 'Epigraphical Discoveries at Sarnath', *Epigraphia Indica*, VIII (1905/6).

— 'Explorations at Mathura', *Annual Report of the Archaeological Survey of India* (1911/12).

West, E. W. 'Copies of Inscriptions from the Buddhist Cave-temples of Kanheri &c., in the Island of Salsette, with a Plan of the Kanheri Caves', *Journal of the Bombay Branch of the Royal Asiatic Society*, VI (1862).

Sources of Illustrations

Grateful acknowledgement is made to the following institutions and persons who have provided photographs and the permission to reproduce them: The Archaeological Survey of India, Government of India, 5, 9-14, 17, 18, 20, 21, 25-32, 34, 37-40, 42-50, 65, 68, 75, 77-79, 85, 87-90; The Kolhapur Museum, 83, 84; Ray Gardner, 80, 81; Douglas Barrett, 82; The Naples Museum, 86. All other photographs were taken by the author, who also drew up the figures and Tables; and the map is by Shalom Schotten after the author's draft.

List of Illustrations

Figures

Tables

Index